K.b. 788

STUDIES IN WELSH HISTORY

Editors

RALPH A. GRIFFITHS   KENNETH O. MORGAN
GLANMOR WILLIAMS

———————

9

LEADERS AND TEACHERS

ADULT EDUCATION AND THE CHALLENGE OF
LABOUR IN SOUTH WALES, 1906–1940

LEADERS AND TEACHERS

ADULT EDUCATION AND THE CHALLENGE OF
LABOUR IN SOUTH WALES, 1906–1940

by

RICHARD LEWIS

Published on behalf of the
History and Law Committee
of the Board of Celtic Studies

CARDIFF
UNIVERSITY OF WALES PRESS
1993

British Library Cataloguing-in-Publication Data

A catalogue record for this book is available from the British Library.

ISBN 0-7083-1219-5

Jacket design by Cloud Nine, Cardiff
Typeset by Alden Multimedia, Northampton
Printed in Great Britain by Hartnolls Ltd., Bodmin

EDITORS' FOREWORD

Since the Second World War, Welsh history has attracted considerable scholarly attention and enjoyed a vigorous popularity. Not only have the approaches, both traditional and new, to the study of history in general been successfully applied to Wales's past, but the number of scholars engaged in this enterprise has multiplied during these years. These advances have been especially marked in the University of Wales.

In order to make more widely available the conclusions of recent research, much of it of limited accessibility in postgraduate dissertations and theses, in 1977 the History and Law Committee of the Board of Celtic Studies inaugurated this new series of monographs, *Studies in Welsh History*. It was anticipated that many of the volumes would originate in research conducted in the University of Wales or under the auspices of the Board of Celtic Studies. But the series does not exclude significant contributions made by researchers in other universities and elsewhere. Its primary aim is to serve historical scholarship and to encourage the study of Welsh history. Each volume so far published has fulfilled that aim in ample measure, and it is a pleasure to welcome the most recent addition to the list.

CONTENTS

EDITORS' FOREWORD   V

ACKNOWLEDGEMENTS   ix

LIST OF ABBREVIATIONS   xi

INTRODUCTION   xiii

I   THE GUIDANCE OF THE WISE: THE W.E.A.
     IN SOUTH WALES   1

II   'MEN OF INTELLECT AND MEN OF ACTION':
     SOUTH WALES AND THE ORIGINS OF
     INDEPENDENT WORKING-CLASS
     EDUCATION   48

III THE WAR AND WORKERS' EDUCATION   101

IV   TAKING SIDES: 1918–1929   142

V   SOUTH WALES AND THE 'NEW LEISURE'   191

EPILOGUE   234

BIBLIOGRAPHY   246

INDEX   263

ACKNOWLEDGEMENTS

Much of this book is derived from work originally undertaken for a Ph.D. thesis submitted to the University of Wales. I am grateful to the staff of the Department of History at University College, Swansea, in particular to Peter Stead my supervisor, for their support and advice whilst I was carrying out the research. I wish also to thank the editors of the present series, Professor Glanmor Williams, Professor Ralph Griffiths and Professor Kenneth O. Morgan who have read the drafts of this book and made valuable suggestions concerning the text, correcting errors and remedying faults of presentation.

In my original research and in preparing this book I have enjoyed the assistance of many librarians and archivists. I am grateful to the staffs of the library of University College, Swansea, Cardiff public libruary, the National Library of Wales, Aberystwyth and the British Newspaper Library at Colindale. I wish particularly to acknowledge the help I received with regard to the N.C.L.C. collection from Mr Iain Maciver, Assistant Keeper of Manuscripts of the National Library of Scotland. My thanks are due to Mr Allan Rogers M.P., formerly the district secretary of the south Wales W.E.A. who gave me unfettered access to the records of the association. I also had much help from the staff at the W.E.A. headquarters at Temple House, London. Special mention ought also to be made of Professor Hywel Francis and the staff of the South Wales Miners' Library, Swansea. Many others shared their recollections with me, but I would particularly like to record my appreciation of the help I received from Dr and Mrs John Thomas, Mr and Mrs J. P. M. Millar, Mr and Mrs Mark Starr, Mr D. T. Guy and Mr Bill Gregory, sadly all now deceased. I would also like to record my appreciation of the assistance I have received from the staff of the University of Wales Press, especially Liz Powell who has treated all my enquiries with tact and understanding.

The tolerance and patience of my wife Ruth, and our children Jennie and Daniel was, of course, essential to the completion of this work. My father Dick Lewis, himself a product of and a contributor to the workers' education movement in south Wales, did much to trigger my interest in this topic. Finally, I would like to dedicate this book to the many thousands of men and women, tutors and students, in south Wales who dedicated their lives to the betterment of their fellow men and women through the various agencies and traditions of the workers' education movement. All errors of fact and interpretation are my own work.

ABBREVIATIONS

A.S.E.	Amalgamated Society of Engineers
A.S.R.S.	Amalgamated Society of Railway Servants
C.L.C.	Central Labour College
C.W.S.	Co-operative Wholesale Society
E.C.	Executive Committee
I.S.T.C.	Iron and Steel Trades Confederation
I.W.C.E.	Independent Working Class Education
L.B.C.	Left Book Club
M.F.G.B.	Miners' Federation of Great Britain
N.C.L.C.	National Council of Labour Colleges
N.E.C.	National Executive Committee
N.L.S.	National Library of Scotland
N.U.G.M.W.	National Union of General and Municipal Workers
N.U.M.	National Union of Mineworkers
N.U.R.	National Union of Railwaymen
S.L.P.	Socialist Labour Party
S.W.D.N.	*South Wales Daily News*
S.W.M.L.	South Wales Miners' Library
S.W.M.F.	South Wales Miners' Federation
T.G.W.U.	Transport and General Workers' Union
T.U.C.	Trades Union Congress
U.R.C.	Unoffocial Reform Committee
W.E.A.	Workers' Educational Association
W.E.T.U.C.	Workers' Educational Trade Union Committee

INTRODUCTION

Advocates of adult or continuing education today tend to stress its value in terms of expanding access to further and higher education by individuals from groups, often defined by race or gender, who were previously under-represented. A concomitant of this context of debate is the concept of empowerment: the equipping of individuals with skills and competencies to fulfil themselves as individuals, whether academically, socially or economically. Often defined as recurrent or lifelong education, the focus of the education is the individual; success is defined in individual terms, though there is also an assumption that society in general will benefit from having a well-educated and, by extension, well-trained workforce. It is a concept which enjoys wide political support as it fits in with radical right-wing notions of fostering individual initiative and self-betterment, but it can also be seen on the left as deeply challenging to the existing social order, in which particular individuals have their life-chances stunted by belonging to under-privileged groups.[1]

The current context of discussion, the focus on race and gender and on the empowerment of individuals, differs significantly from the context in which the advocates of adult educational provision functioned early in this century. Whilst many at the time feared loss of international competitiveness due to the inadequate provision of technical training, adult education was not usually discussed in terms of meeting specific skill shortages through vocational training, or fostering social mobility, but was seen to have a broader and deeper purpose. In the first half of the twentieth century the overriding concern was the function of adult education in the context of the rising aspirations and expectations of working-class people in general and organized labour in particular. It was

---

[1] For a survey of new developments in adult education, see F. Molyneux, G. Low and G. Fowler (eds.), *Learning for Life: Politics and Progress in Recurrent Education* (London, 1988). For a study of the challenge of new pressures on workers' education, see R. Fryer, 'The challenge to working-class education', in B. Simon (ed.), *The Search for Enlightenment: The Working Class and Adult Education in the Twentieth Century* (London, 1990).

concerned with how, in an increasingly democratic age, the responsibilities of full citizenship could be inculcated and how political enfranchisement could be extended to the social and economic enhancement of the working class.[2]

In July 1944, G. D. H. Cole published a brief Fabian pamphlet which sought to analyse the structure of the British working-class movement.[3] He found that it consisted of three elements: the trade unions, the political wing (in effect the Labour Party) and the Co-operative movement. However, in addition to these three major components, he also found a fourth, much smaller but fully important enough to be considered by itself. This section was the workers' education movement. It also consisted of three elements. One was the education service of the Co-operative movement, which like the youth wings of the political parties he felt was too sectional to be seen as a true educational movement. The other two elements were the most significant: namely, the Workers' Educational Association and the National Council of Labour Colleges, representing two quite separate traditions. The one collaborated with the state system of education, and the other stressed its independence of the state and the class interests it represented. Although G. D. H. Cole, as a leading participant in workers' education, was not exactly a detached observer, his point that the workers' education bodies need to be seen not just as adult education agencies but also as integral parts of the labour movement is important in seeking to understand their role. For both movements emerged not just as a response to, but also as a part of, the rise of labour. They also emerged as organized labour was beginning to make an impact on informed public opinion and was forcing a response from the educated classes. The first decade of the twentieth century saw the emergence of labour as a credible political force and also saw organized labour develop as a national force in the economic life of the country. The participation of labour in the government of the nation became a realistic prospect, but also industry-wide

[2] For two distinct interpretations of the movements behind these trends, see B. Simon, *Education and the Labour Movement, 1870–1920* (London, 1965), 60–92 and 296–330; J. F. C. Harrison, *Learning and Living, 1790–1960* (London, 1961), 219–89.
[3] G. D. H. Cole, *The British Working Class Movement* (London, 1944), 17. The recognition of workers' education as a distinct sector is well established amongst adult educationalists: see J. Lowe, *Adult Education in England and Wales: A Critical Survey* (London, 1970), 157.

disputes and the threat of a general strike were no longer confined to the dreams of advanced trade union activities or the
nightmares of the defensively minded bourgeoisie.

In this new context, adult educationalists amongst the
university-educated classes saw both dangers and opportunities. For some, the danger was that the rising power of
labour could outstrip the intellectual capacities of working-
class leaders and that their followers could be seduced by
spurious knowledge and bogus remedies for their grievances.
Yet others, whilst sharing these anxieties, saw in the new situation opportunities to graft the values of a liberal university
education on to those from the working classes placed in positions of trust and responsibility, so that spurious knowledge
and bogus remedies could be detected and rejected by such
leaders and therefore, it was hoped, by their followers. They
advocated a form of adult education which was geared to the
collective nature of organized labour, and which sought to
tackle the problem of the organized working-class movement
by seeing the workers as a group, to be raised not individually
but collectively.

Whilst there were many working-class activities who
welcomed the desire of upper- and middle-class academics to
share their values and experience with them, there were
many trade unionists who were deeply suspicious of the
motives and intentions of progressive academics. Some
demanded that the universities discharge their responsibilities
to the working class by extending their education to the labour-
ing masses; others demanded that the universities, as 'handmaidens of capitalism', should be shunned by the working
class. To the latter, university-based workers' education was a
ruling-class ploy designed to curb the aspirations of the labour
movement: something designed to protect property relations
and the existing social order. Thus, from the outset the concept
of workers' education was riven by two irreconcilable visions of
its nature and purpose. Whilst this division between orthodox
and independent workers' education was real and deep, there
is a coherence in the historical development of workers' education because the two traditions sprang from the same context
and were equally, though not necessarily similarly, affected by
changes in that context over the succeeding decades.

Although the two traditions differed as to the nature and purpose of workers' education, both eschewed any role in helping individuals who wished to rise to higher stations in life. Both sought to raise the working class in general, not to assist those of ability to leave their class background. Yet, despite the rhetoric of both traditions, it was the activist, the bright, the energetic and the visionary elements amongst the working classes that were to be the main targets of workers' education. Inadvertently, but perhaps inevitably, both traditions equipped such people to break out of their social confines and gain higher stations in life, whether as a full-time union official, labour exchange clerk or cabinet minister. Over the years this inherent contradiction led to a reluctant admission that social mobility was an additional benefit of adult education, whilst lip-service was still paid to the older collective objectives of workers' education.

Yet throughout the first half of the century the collectivist ideal of workers' education as a form of adult education provision, which thought of the group first and the individual second, remained a key element in both traditions. It is this collective approach which marks out workers' education as a subset of adult education. A recent study of current provision of workers' education around the world stresses that what distinguishes workers' education from general adult education is the extent to which, quoting Mark Starr, it gives primary importance to 'the person in his group activity'.[4] It is focused on how that person can be a more effective member of his trade union or community through co-operative and collective action. The ideological stance of the organization is largely irrelevant, but in the context of this study the two traditions adopted quite different ideological perspectives when then framed their long-term objectives.

Contemporaries detected a significant attitudinal change within the ranks of organized labour quite early in the process. In December 1907 Professor Henry Jones, the well-known, highly regarded, Welsh-born professor of philosophy at Glasgow University, visited south Wales for the first time

[4] P. G. H. Hopkins, *Workers' Education: An International Perspective* (Milton Keynes, 1985), 18.

for a number of years. He was struck by a new atmosphere, a new stress on social class in political discussion and a new belief that the state was the only agency fitted to tackle social and economic ills.[5] In short, he was alarmed by the spread and penetration of socialistic ideals amongst politically aware young men. His findings were reported extensively in the south Wales press and it is quite evident that he was not alone in finding the trends disturbing. He understood the drift of thought but was also alarmed at the long-term implications. The spectres of spurious knowledge' and 'bogus remedies' reared their heads. For Professor Jones, the challenge had to be met by educating the rising democracy to a proper sense of its duty to build on what existed and not simply to destroy the established order.

The significance of Henry Jones's alarm stems not only from the fact that he felt constrained to change the subject of some of his talks during his south Wales visit from 'True and false citizenship' to 'True and false socialism', but that he was a representative of an important school of philosophical thought which was having a profound effect on the British adult education movement. The influence of T. H. Green and the neo-Hegelian or Idealist school of philosophy on the emergence of a corporatist or ethical critique of crude individualism and utilitarianism is well known.[6] Whilst it would be wrong to overstate its impact, its influence was to seep into the growth of the 'New Liberalism' and the socially radical ideas of Edwardian political Progressivism, which could accommodate a more interventionist state and the collectivist aspirations of organized labour without abandoning the ideals of voluntary action and a market economy. However, its effects on adult education were even more profound. It was the ideals of Green which powered such initiatives as Toynbee Hall and the university settlement movement, which sought to bring to the masses the civilizing cultural and spiritual cement of a university education. By this means the working classes would develop a sense of citizenship and belonging to the nation in

---

[5] *South Wales Daily News* (hereafter *S.W.D.N.*), 12 December 1907.
[6] See P. Gordon and J. White, *Philosophers as Educational Reformers: The Influence of Idealism on British Educational Thought and Practice* (London, 1979); also J. Ree, *Proletarian Philosophers: Problems in Socialist Culture* (Oxford, 1984), 14–20.

which their justified grievances could be resolved in a way that did not threaten civilization itself.

Whilst Green and the Oxford neo-Hegelians of the late nineteenth century left an imprint on British political and educational history through such leading lights as H. H. Asquith, William Beveridge, R. B. Haldane, H. A. L. Fisher, William Temple, Benjamin Jowett, A. D. Lindsay, R. H. Tawney and the founder of the W.E.A., Albert Mansbridge, there was a second fount of Idealist influence in Britain based at Glasgow University.[7] Under Edward Caird and his disciple and successor, Henry Jones, the Scottish Idealists (there were profound differences between the various schools of neo-Hegelian thought but in terms of their general commitment to public service their influence was fairly uniform) who questioned the materialist values of classical economics and sought to carry the treasures of knowledge, by means of 'settlements' and extension lectures, to the huddled masses of the tenements and workshops. A pupil of Henry Jones, and someone who was to play an important role in the development of workers' education in south Wales, Thomas Jones, summed up the Glasgow Idealist philosophy thus: 'Selfishness was not to be overcome by postponing its gratification to the next world but by social service in this. The State was a moral institution and civic duty a spiritual function. This world was not to be spurned, but to be embraced and possessed, for within it there was nothing finally and absolutely secular.'[8] The Idealists denounced the other-worldliness of Scottish and Welsh Calvinism, but equally gave no quarter to purely materialist ideologies of which, in south Wales, Marxism was to be the most challenging. Through J. S. Mackenzie, another product of the Scottish Idealist school, and Thomas Jones, the W.E.A. in south Wales was underpinned by a distinct philosophical commitment to social service and co-operative activity which stayed with it right up to the Second World War. Henry Jones was something of a guru to political 'progressives', those who sought a working electoral alliance between organized labour and popu-

---

[7] For the place of the Scottish Idealists in the development of British philosophy, see J. Passmore, *A Hundred Years of Philosophy* (London, 1970), 51–57.

[8] T. Jones, 'Biographical Sketch', in W. Smart, *Second Thoughts of an Economist* (London, 1924), xxii.

lar liberalism, in south Wales. His words were recorded with due reverence by the mouthpiece of south Wales progressivism, the *South Wales Daily News*. His ideas gave a kind of intellectual coherence to Progressivism[9] which extended beyond those who simply wished to see the old *de facto* alliance between organized labour and popular liberalism sustained. In south Wales, it encompassed many academic and professional men and women who wished to see the rising power of organized labour harnessed to the needs of society and its improvement. In the context of the W.E.A., the values of co-operation and co-partnership fitted, at first, easily with the distinctly Lib-Lab nature of the organization. When the Lib-Lab tradition withered and died, the 'progressive' semi-corporatist ideals remained and became integrated into south Wales socialist Labourism, the W.E.A. playing a part in the process.

Much of the anti-capitalist rhetoric, which distinguished socialist from liberal Labourism, was derived from a Marxian critique of capitalism, which became an integral part of the world view of many working-class activists in south Wales through the separate workers' education tradition associated with the Labour College movement. Drawing on a strong anti-capitalist sentiment within organized labour and an older working-class autodidact tradition, Marxism became an alternative to the collaborationist outlook engendered by the dominant Idealism of the university extension movement.[10] It became not just an economic critique but the basis for an alternative 'proletarian' philosophy which could fill the vacuum left by the rejection of religion and other 'bourgeois' world views. The desire to build this 'independent' working-class educational movement was, like the emergence of the collaborationist W.E.A., closely enmeshed with the rise of organized labour as a political and economic force. The scope for independent working-class action, which the emergence of great trade unions such as the South Wales Miners' Federation created, was felt not just in the fields of collective bargaining and poli-

[9] For a study of the linguistic limitations and failings of South Wales Progressivism, see P. Stead, 'The language of Edwardian politics', in D. Smith (ed.), *A People and a Proletariat: Essays in the History of Wales, 1780–1980* (London, 1980).

[10] The place of the working-class autodidact tradition within the development of British Marxism is examined in two valuable studies: S. Macintyre, *A Proletarian Science: Marxism in Britain, 1917–1933* (Cambridge, 1980), and Ree, op. cit., 7 ff.

tics, but also in education. Marxist economics and history gave an intellectual coherence to this movement and became a force in themselves for the creation of a new attitude amongst activists and subsequently amongst leaders.

The development of workers' education in south Wales is of particular interest because it coincided with fundamental changes in the nature of the labour movement in the region. The extent to which the two traditions of workers' education contributed to this change is the subject of this study, as is the extent to which the changing nature of organized labour called into existence and subsequently shaped the development of adult and workers' education in south Wales. The way that the workers' education movement in south Wales helped to shape organized labour in the region, in terms of leadership and outlook, is also a key element in the study.

South Wales in the Edwardian era was still being transformed by a rapidly expanding coal trade. The coalfield experienced an expansion which resulted in a dilution of its Welshness. The old cultural cement of the Welsh language and the chapel was under attack and this was to have long-term political consequences as the shibboleths of Welsh popular liberalism lost resonance among the youthful, mainly English-speaking, labour activists of the coalfield. Politically, the Liberal Party was still secure, and it felt confident that old ideals of Welsh liberalism could contain or confront the aspirations of organized labour.[11] Yet it failed to prevent the conversion of the miners' union to independent labour politics[12] or the entrenchment of an anti-capitalist ethos among its leadership. The old enemies of Welsh liberalism, the landowners and the Anglican clergy, were replaced in the minds of many politically conscious young men by the capitalists and their hired lackeys, the colliery management—collectively defined as the 'bosses'.

Another and related consequence of the slow, relative decline of the influence of Nonconformity in industrial south Wales and the rise of organized labour was the creation of alternative

---

[11] For the survival of the older 'conservative' Liberalism in South Wales, see K. O. Morgan 'The New Liberalism and the challenge of Labour: The Welsh experience', in *Welsh History Review*, VI (1972–3); also D. Tanner, *Political Change and the Labour Party, 1900–1918* (Cambridge, 1990), 207–8.

[12] R. Gregory, *The Miners and British Politics, 1906–1914* (Oxford, 1968), 125.

routes for the bright young men of the working class to break
out of the drudgery of manual labour. Organized labour,
with its rising demand for officials and, later, full-time politicians, offered opportunities to combine service to fellow workers with an ability to leave the less congenial existence of
the mine, the steel mill or the footplate. The sharp intellects
and organizational skills of men such as Frank Hodges and
Arthur Horner, and even A. J. Cook, were lost to the chapel
and may consequently have assisted in that institution's decline as these former candidates for the ministry sought secular
and earthly salvation for their followers.[13] The workers' education movement was to help them find that alternative route. It
is unwise to overstate the extent of the decline of Nonconformity
before the first world war.[14] The chapel, with its tradition of
adult classes and Sunday schools, its encouragement of
discussion and close textual analysis, may well have provided
the model for more secular forms of learning which were to
be followed by erstwhile members of the Nonconformist
churches.

As a region of the United Kingdom, south Wales was not
only distinguished by its dependence on the coal trade and
the hold of Nonconformity, it was also Welsh. The Welsh
language, the most potent symbol of Welshness, was also under
attack. The most vicious aspects of earlier educational policies
which sought to extirpate the language may have gone by the
Edwardian era, but in their place came a process of Anglicization far more insidious and ultimately, for most of industrial
south Wales, successful, namely, immigration and industrial
development. By 1911 nearly a quarter of all adult males in
Glamorgan were non-Welsh immigrants;[15] the chapels, which

[13] Frank Hodges was rejected for ordination when his trial sermons were judged too
political: F. Hodges, *My Adventures as a Labour Leader* (London, 1925), 19–20. Arthur
Horner had a two-year scholarship to attend a theological college in Birmingham, a
career cut short by political activity: A. Horner, *Incorrigible Rebel* (London, 1960), 14.
For A. J. Cook, see P. Davies, *A. J. Cook* (Manchester, 1987), 2–8.

[14] In 1914, when the W.E.A. could boast of having at most some 500 students attending its classes in Wales, it is estimated that some 158,000 adults were attending the Sunday school classes of just one denomination in Wales, the Calvinistic Methodists.
Ministry of Reconstruction, *Final Report of the Adult Education Committee*, Cmnd. 321
(London, 1919), 282.

[15] J. Parry Lewis, 'The Anglicization of Glamorgan', in *Transactions of the Glamorgan
Local History Society*, 4 (1960), 36.

had been the most effective means of transmitting the language and the culture, could not cope with this process, and the vicious circle was completed as those institutions also declined.[16] By the turn of the century there were parts of industrial south Wales which were, in effect, utterly Anglicized. In Monmouthshire in 1901 only one person in eight claimed to be a Welsh-speaker, in Cardiff only one in twelve.[17]

The cause of this assault on Welshness in its religious, cultural and linguistic forms, was, as stated earlier, the expansion of the coal trade. There was between 1901 and 1911 a 40 per cent expansion of the mining workforce, supplied in no small measure (73 per cent in fact) by immigration from outside Wales.[18] Throughout the Edwardian era south Wales was a society built on the coal trade: most people, directly as miners or managers, or indirectly as railwaymen or seafront workers, or even as shopkeepers and school teachers, gained their live-lihood from coal mining. Only the metalliferous trades offered anything approaching an alternative industrial base, and that was still closely connected with coal. This grotesque over-commitment to one industry was to have dire consequences in the inter-war period when chronic structural unemploy-ment disfigured valley society. But before 1914, south Wales struggled to adjust to the social problems of industrial expan-sion manifested in terms of housing shortage, lack of sani-tation, and a very mobile, often quite young and pre-dominantly male, population. This social ferment bred a political challenge to popular liberalism which was not to mature into a new pattern of political support until after the First World War. The chief agency for this change was the Independent Labour Party (I.L.P.). Deriving its force initially from an ethical critique of capitalism, it was, by the Edwardian era, a broad movement which stretched from the most advanced elements of liberal radicalism, through

---

[16] E. D. Lewis, *The Rhondda Valleys* (London, 1959), 240–7.

[17] *1901 Census: Returns for the County of Monmouth*. Cmnd. No. 1361 (London, 1902), table 40, p. 59; *1901 Census. Returns for the County of Glamorgan*, Cmnd. No. 1212 (London, 1902), table 40, p. 168.

[18] B. Thomas, 'Migration into the Glamorganshire coalfield, 1861–1911', in *Economics*, X (1930), 289. For an assessment of the economic factors behind the 1910–14 industrial strife in the coalfield, see L. J. Williams, 'The road to Tonypandy' in *Llafur*, 1, No. 2 (1973).

Marxism to the outskirts of syndicalism. Its initial impact in south Wales was limited, but by 1906 it had already helped to convert the S.W.M.F. rank and file to independent political action.[19] Working through trades councils and local Labour Representation Committees, 'Labour' became a recognized political label as candidates were elected to Boards of Guardians and county and district councils. The fervour which not long before had driven the messengers of Welsh religious revivals was now redirected as the soap-box missionaries of the I.L.P. 'went into the highways, byways and street corners to preach the gospel of socialism' to the hostile, the indifferent and the (sometimes) receptive audiences of industrial south Wales.[20]

It was this desire for 'independence' that so alarmed many academics and educationalists, and it was a key factor in stimulating the development of the Workers' Educational Association. It was certainly the desire to assert some kind of intellectual hegemony over the rise of labour that lay behind the conference on Oxford and working-class education held in the summer of 1907, when 430 delegates from some 210 organizations, mostly unions, trades councils and co-operative bodies, generally agreed with the shipwright, J. M. Mactavish, later to be Mansbridge's successor as general secretary of the W.E.A., that the time had come for the universities in general and Oxford in particular to minister to the needs of the working classes. For many Oxford dons, especially those like Tawney and Alfred Zimmern imbued with the Idealist vision, the invitation to help shape the rising labour movement was too good to miss. For others, like Sir Robert Morant, the permanent secretary to the Board of Education, the idea was a 'sound political investment'.[21] The work of the conference was consolidated with the publication the following year of the 'Oxford report' on workers' education, which placed the university tutorial class on a pedestal

[19] By 1909 there were 77 branches of the I.L.P. in south Wales east of the River Neath, with five full-time, paid organizers. K. O. Fox, 'The emergence of the political Labour movement in south Wales, 1894–1910' (University of Wales M.A. thesis, 1965), 43.

[20] F. Hodges, op. cit., 24.

[21] B. Jennings, 'The making of the Oxford report', in S. Harrop (ed.), *Oxford and Working Class Education*, new edn. (Nottingham, 1987), 17–18.

and made Oxford academic standards the measure of quality in provision. For by such means the working-class leaders would acquire 'the synoptic mind which Plato says is desirable in Governors'.[22]

The 1907 conference and the 1908 report were also a trigger for opposition to the take-over of the workers' education movement by Oxford. There were many, like Ramsay MacDonald, who felt that Oxford had more to gain from such a development than did Labour.[23] One worker-student from Ruskin College, by the name of Noah Ablett, who attended the Conference wondered 'why the universities have so suddenly come down to help the workers to emancipate themselves'.[24] Ablett also read the report and took this as further evidence of the university's evil intentions. Out of these suspicions grew the movement for independent working-class education (I.W.C.E.) enshrined in the Labour College movement and the Plebs League and magazine, also born in Oxford in 1908.

The close linkage between the movements means that they can be fully understood only if they are studied together, as two disparate elements of the same movement; for the W.E.A. and the Labour College were called into existence by the same set of circumstances' and their subsequent development was shaped by the changes in those circumstances. The great struggle, however, was between the I.W.C.E. and the W.E.A. perceptions of workers' education. Conventional histories of this struggle tend to be written by protagonists of, or those sympathetic towards, one or other of the two outlooks. The result is usually a caricature of the opposing view. The W.E.A. tutors are witting or, more insultingly, unwitting agents of capitalist propaganda. Labour college lecturers are well-meaning propagators of a limited intellectual experience unable to see the wider picture.[25] The struggle between these two traditions in south Wales was a much more subtle and complex story than is allowed by such interpretations.

<hr>

[22] Ibid., 142.

[23] Harrison, op. cit., 268.

[24] Minutes of the Joint Oxford Conference on the Education of Workpeople, 10 Aug. 1907: W.E.A. Headquarters, Temple House, London.

[25] Two contrasting examples are M. Stocks, *The W.E.A.: The First Fifty Years* (London, 1953), 89, and J. P. M., Millar, *The Labour College Movement* (London, 1979), 60.

I

THE GUIDANCE OF THE WISE: THE W.E.A. IN SOUTH WALES, 1906–1915

1. 'WALES IS A CONGENIAL COUNTRY FOR SUCH AN ORGANIZATION'

Tom John, erstwhile president of the National Union of Teachers and a leading figure in the educational life of south Wales, made the above statement whilst seconding the motion by which the W.E.A. was formally established there.[1] It reflected a belief by its supporters that the association would with ease adapt to, and be adopted by, the popular culture of the area. So close were the objectives of the W.E.A. to what were perceived to be the natural aspirations of the people of south Wales that the national annual report of the W.E.A., commenting on the foundation conference of the assocation in south Wales, declared its confidence that the W.E.A. had 'a great future amongst the rapidly expanding population of the valleys'.[2]

This belief that in some way the association was peculiarly able to tap into well-established patterns of popular culture amongst the working people of south Wales also coloured the early histories of its activities in the region. The first, and in some ways the one that established the received wisdom on this matter, was propounded by Daniel Lleufer Thomas, then chairman of the W.E.A. in Wales, at the National Eisteddfod in 1915. For him the association was able to fuse the ideals of a Welsh rural culture and popular education, associated with the work of Griffith Jones, the S.P.C.K. and the eisteddfod, with the English (and Scottish) traditions of the mechanics' institutes, and the Christian socialist and university settlement movements.[3] It was by the confluence of such educational idealism that the W.E.A. could help revive a Welsh ideal of popular culture to counter what Lleufer Thomas saw as the alien

---

[1] *Western Mail*, 8 Oct. 1906.
[2] Workers' Educational Association (hereafter W.E.A.), *Fourth Annual Report, 1906–7*.
[3] D. Lleufer Thomas, 'University tutorial classes for working people', *Transactions of the Honourable Society of Cymmrodorion* (1916), 69–118.

and divisive ideologies which had brought pain and conflict to
the industrial areas of south Wales.[4]

Whilst Lleufer Thomas saw the early history of the W.E.A. in
terms of the flowing together of English and Welsh traditions,
later writers laid greater stress on the centrality of Welsh popular educational traditions. D. Emrys Evans, writing in 1927,
saw a direct line of development from ancient bardic traditions, resistance to Anglicization, and the development of the
eisteddfod, taking on a social context through the work and
ideals of Robert Owen and reaching its most promising form
with the W.E.A.[5] Ben Bowen Thomas, in the most sophisti-
cated account of the development of adult education in early
twentieth-century south Wales, also saw the circulating
schools and Griffith Jones as the initiators of a tradition of
voluntary educational supply whose ideals were best exemplified by, and lived on in, the W.E.A.[6]

The idea, which was prevalent at its inception, that the
W.E.A. was peculiarly well suited to the needs, the aspirations
and traditions of the mass of the Welsh population, and the subsequent historical interpretation of its origins and development,
reflect, of course, both the hopes and the purposes of the authors
and the age in which they spoke and wrote. Few, at the time,
had the will or the need to challenge such assumptions. Only
one commentator close to the association in its early years
chose to puncture the illusion of the intrinsically Welsh roots
of adult education provision in industrial south Wales in general and the W.E.A. in particular. P. S. Thomas, writing in
1931, took evident delight in mocking the idea that the 'erstwhile Calvinists' of the Sunday schools were now the students
of history, economics and philosophy attending the tutorial
classes of the valleys:

> In short Griffith Jones, Llanddowror, has been canonised
> and enshrined as the patron saint of the Adult Education
> movement in Wales. This historical fiction may gratify the
> urge to discover reputable national antecedents of the

[4] Ibid., 94.
[5] D. Emrys Evans, 'Adult education in Wales', *Transactions of the Honourable Society of Cymmrodorion* (1927), 134–42.
[6] B. B. Thomas, *Survey of Adult Education in Wales* (Cardiff, 1940), 7–23.

work, or it may serve as an appropriate background to classes in rural areas, but it would tax the powers of our historians to trace the exact sequence between these essentially Welsh institutions and the modern Tutorial Class in industrialised south Wales.[7]

Despite the fact that P. S. Thomas had issued a powerful corrective to the more simplistic assumption that the W.E.A. had simply established itself in the Principality by being the natural inheritor of an older indigenous popular cultural and educational tradition, this view has persisted. It found expression in the official fiftieth anniversary history of the association in south Wales, issued in 1957, and even in a report prepared in 1970 by the Co-ordinating Committee for Adult Education in Wales.[8]

P. S. Thomas was, however, correct to reject the idea that adult education in industrialized south Wales in the inter-war period owed much to bardic circles, chapel literary societies or eisteddfodau. That was a heritage that was grafted on or was relevant only outside the industrialized valleys and coastal towns. Certainly, there was nothing peculiarly Welsh about the personalities behind the founding of the south Wales district of the association who were present at a conference held at the Cory Hall in Cardiff in early October 1906. They were in essence merely a local extension of a wide network of socially conscious academics, trade unionists and co-operators, mostly, though not exclusively, of the liberal/progressive type, who had joined together to found the W.E.A. only a few years earlier.[9]

The records of the W.E.A. reveal very little about the background to the formation of the south Wales section of the organization. But in a report of the founding conference carried by the *South Wales Daily News*,[10] a list of the 'provisional committee' was published and this, combined with the sparse informa-

---

[7] P. S. Thomas, 'Adult education in Swansea', *Cambria* (Spring 1931).

[8] C. R. Williams, *Jubilee Year. The South Wales District of the Workers' Educational Association* (Cardiff, 1957), 4–7; Co-ordinating Committee for adult education in Wales, 'Report on Adult Education in Wales', May 1970, 2.

[9] There are innumerable accounts of the origins of the W.E.A. One of the most succinct is to be found in T. Kelly, *A History of Adult Education in Great Britain* (Liverpool, 1970), 248–50.

[10] *S.W.D.N.*, 8 Oct. 1906.

Membership list of provisional committee of the South Wales W.E.A., October 1906

1. Chairman	P. W. Raffan	Momouthshire C.C.
2. Hon. Sec.	A. B. Badger	Director of Higher Education, Mon. C.C.
3. Hon. Sec.	Coun. J. Chappell	Cardiff Co-op. Scy.
4. Hon. Sec.	J. Austin Jenkins	Univ. Coll. of South Wales & Mon.
5. Member	Coun. T. W. Allen	Labour Co-partnership Association.
6. Member	G. R. Bennett	Newport N.U.T.
7. Member	Coun. W. H. Brown	C.W.S. & Newport Education Cttee.
8. Member	Prof. R. Burrows	Univ. Coll. of South Wales & Mon.
9. Member	W. Cadogan	Newport Trades Council.
10. Member	S. Fisher	Cardiff Trades Council.
11. Member	Miss E. P. Hughes	Glam. Educ. Cttee.
12. Member	G. W. Moores	Sec. Higher Educ. Cttee. Newport.
13. Member	A. Onions	S.W.M.F.
14. Member	F. W. Pepperell	Cardiff Assistant Teachers Association.
15. Member	L. W. Richards	Blaina Industrial Co-op. Scy.
16. Member	Mr. Seig	Cardiff Co-op. Scy.
17. Member	A. W. Swash	Cardiff N.U.T.
18. Member	A. Steel	Western Section Co-operative Union.
19. Member	Coun. J. Taylor	A.S.R.S.
20. Member	Ald. E. Thomas	Cardiff City Council
21. Member	J. Watt	Cardiff Ruskin Scy.
22. Member	W. T. Whitney	Tredegar Co-op. Scy.
23. Member	Coun. P. Wright	Newport Educ. Cttee.

tion contained in association records and in the press reports of the foundation meeting itself, allows the nature of the personalities and pressures behind the organization to be analysed.

A key personality in the list of the provisional committee and in the conference itself was Professor Ronald Burrows. Professor of Greek at the University College in Cardiff from 1897 to 1908, Burrows was a significant influence on the foundation and development of the early W.E.A. in south Wales. In the first years of the century, there was a small number of academics in Cardiff anxious to see the university develop its links with the community that existed outside its walls. In this regard, two developments, the provision of programmes of extension lectures and the establishment of a university 'settlement', are central to an appreciation of the role of these academics in the early history of the south Wales W.E.A.

Extension lectures had been part of the work of the newly founded Welsh university colleges in the 1870s and 1880s.[11] Initial enthusiasm seems to have waned as the colleges concentrated on building up the undergraduate teaching and research functions of the institutions, and regular extension lecture programmes tended to die out. An influx of new teaching staff into Cardiff in the 1890s from universities with well-established extension and settlement traditions seems to have spurred a new enthusiasm for this work. In Cardiff three academics were particularly keen. In addition to Burrows, Sydney Chapman and Professor J. S. Mackenzie were the leading lights of the settlement/extension movement within the university college.

Chapman, a lecturer in economics, was in Cardiff for only just over one year in 1899–1900, but he brought with him extensive experience of settlement and extension work from Manchester which he diffused amongst his colleagues, students and former graduates of Cardiff to considerable effect. He returned to Manchester at the end of 1900 as professor of economics, and there he was later to play a pivotal role in the early development of the W.E.A. locally and nationally.[12] Addressing a Guild of Graduates meeting in November 1900, called to discuss the establishment of a university settlement in Cardiff, Chapman argued that extension and settlement work were two sides of the same coin. The social work of the settlement must be accompanied by educational work, which would be facilitated by local associations in each locality

[11] B. B. Thomas, op. cit., 14.
[12] M. Stocks, op. cit., 37.
[13] S.W.D.N., 23 Nov. 1900.

connected with the nearest university college.[13] It was a proposal which foreshadowed the development of the W.E.A. along similar lines, and perhaps reflects the contribution that Chapman was to make to the newly formed association.

Whatever Chapman's role in the wider development of workers' education, in south Wales Burrows and Mackenzie were the leading academics involved in the creation of the early W.E.A. Both provided the intellectual muscle that elsewhere was provided by leading divines such as Charles Gore and William Temple, and Oxford dons such as A. D. Lindsay and A. L. Smith. They were all socially conscious intellectuals anxious to see the fruits of scholarship and liberal education used to raise the condition of working people. Equally important, Burrows and Mackenzie brought with them experience of well-established university extension and settlement movements in other university centres.

Ronald Burrows, a brilliant Oxford graduate from a privileged background, shared with Albert Mansbridge a devout adherence to high Anglicanism. It was through his connections with Anglican divines such as Gore and Scott Holland that Burrows became part of that wider community of young, public-spirited academics driven by a desire to convert to practical action the ideals they had learned at the feet of their neo-Hegelian mentors.[14] When he took up an appointment at Glasgow University, Burrows soon threw himself into the social and settlement work connected with the university. He formed close working relationships with local trade unionists and especially with the 'anti-sweating' campaigns of the Glasgow Trades Council, something of which he proudly boasted in one of the very first W.E.A. lectures ever held in south Wales.[15] Although heavily influenced by the social radicalism of Oxford liberal opinion, Burrows was actually something of a Tory paternalist anxious to see translated into modern life 'the friendly personal relations between individuals that did at least something in our villages to sweeten life and blunt the edge of political differences'.[16] He feared the long-term consequences of class conflict and saw education and social work as the means of removing

[14] G. Glasgow, *Ronald Burrows: A Memoir* (London, 1924), 15–16.
[15] *Barry Dock News* (hereafter *B.D.N.*), 17 May 1907.
[16] R. Burrows, 'Evolution or revolution', *Welsh Outlook* (Jan. 1914), 28.

the great causes of class antagonism. In giving the keynote
address to the founding conference of the W.E.A. in south
Wales, Burrows stressed that the organization did not wish to
educate working men out of their class, but to raise the educational sights of those within the class. He praised the values and
efficacy of voluntary effort where state provision was impracti-
cal or inappropriate, pointing to the success of the Cardiff
Settlement as supporting evidence.[17] Radical in his own way,
Burrows always stuck to the values and perceptions of his background and upbringing.[18]

Burrows was an English patrician, Mackenzie a Scottish
meritocrat. John Stuart Mackenzie was much more in the
mainstream of contemporary advanced ideas on social
reform. A disciple of the Scottish neo-Hegelian Idealist,
Edward Caird, it was as an undergraduate at Glasgow University that Mackenzie developed an interest in social reform and
adult education.[19] His philosophical interests, guided by Henry
Jones, centred on the question of how ethics could be used to
influence social policy. He spent a few years in Germany studying Kantian and Hegelian philosophy, returning in 1886 to a
fellowship at Cambridge. Following a period as a lecturer at
Owen's College, Manchester, where he once again became
active in social and extension work, in 1894 he was offered
the chair in philosophy at Cardiff. In Cardiff he established
links with the local labour movement, undertaking for the
local I.L.P. a series of lectures on political economy which
won many local trade unionists to the cause of workers' education.[20] B. B. Thomas, writing in the late 1930s, said that Mackenzie's book, *Introduction to Social Reform*, published in 1890,
which sought to examine the ethical and philosophical basis
of social reform, had a profound impact on many educated
young men in Wales.[21] The Revd M. Watcyn Williams, also
writing in the late 1930s, believed that many of the ministers
of religion who became active in settlement and W.E.A. work

[17] *S.W.D.N.*, 8 Oct. 1906.
[18] Glasgow, op. cit., 87.
[19] M. McKenzie (ed.), *J. S. Mackenzie* (London, 1936), 42.
[20] *Labour Pioneer, Organ of the Cardiff Socialist Society* (Nov. 1900). See also Councillor
Peter Wright's address to the south Wales W.E.A. 1909 annual general meeting,
S.W.D.N., 11 Oct. 1909.
[21] B. B.Thomas, op. cit., 16.

in the depressed areas of inter-war south Wales had been inspired to undertake these activities through the example and teaching of Mackenzie.[22]

A strong supporter of the ideals of co-operation and trade unionism, Mackenzie shared with Burrows the same dread of the effects and consequences of class conflict. For democracy to succeed it had to be under the 'guidance of the wise subject to the criticism and control of all'.[23] The selection of those best fitted to govern depended on a well-educated population, a democracy where true merit would be the sole qualification for office. The politically active working man was therefore a prime target of his extra-mural work. Thus were embodied in Mackenzie all the external (that is, non-Welsh) influences which powered the moves to establish the W.E.A. in south Wales.

The revival of university extension lectures in Cardiff in 1901 seems to have been due in no small measure to Mackenzie's advocacy of them in the college's senate.[24] Yet it was the establishment of a university settlement in the Splott area of Cardiff which seems to have attracted most attention and enthusiasm amongst the socially conscious staff and students of the university college. The ideals which drove this enthusiasm can be seen in an address by the first president of the college's Past Students' Association, Charles Owen, at its annual general meeting in 1902. The heroes were Arnold Toynbee and those university men working in the settlements of the big cities who 'gave up so much to diffuse amongst the dumb and hopeless millions some of the talents and interests which had enriched their own lives'.[25] Owen did not want the students and graduates of Cardiff to stand convicted of being untouched by this social spirit which so 'honourably distinguished' their own age.

The Splott Settlement, where Burrows, along with his wife, took up residence as warden, became a recipient of philanthro-

[22] Cited in Mackenzie, op. cit., 89–90.

[23] Glamorgan Gazette, 1 Nov. 1912.

[24] M. Turner 'The miners' search for self improvement: the history of evening classes in the Rhondda' (University of Wales M.A. thesis, 1966), 201.

[25] C. Owen, Address to the Second Annual General Meeting of the Cardiff University College Past Students' Association (Cardiff, 1900), 4.

pic largesse from such local magnates as Lord Tredegar and also a focal point for socially conscious students and graduates.[26] For the latter it was a point of contact with the realities of life for the working people of Cardiff, but it also opened up channels of communication with the local labour movement and activists. Indeed, Burrows and Mackenzie used the settlement to promote their ideals among the more aware and intellectually able sections of the working class.[27] The 1906–7 annual report of the settlement records satisfaction at the way in which those working men in the area capable of taking an active and intelligent interest in public affairs were being attracted to the lectures and the debates organized by the settlement.[28]

The early history of the W.E.A. in south Wales is characterized by the role and influence of a small group of socially conscious academics anxious to guide the movement. But they did not operate in isolation; they were part of a wider, loose network of progressive opinion which functioned in a twilight zone between the agencies of popular liberalism and the organized labour movement in south Wales. The list of names that made up the provisional committee constituted an influential slice of informed progressive opinion in south-east Wales in 1906. In fact, the committee was almost exclusively drawn from Cardiff and Monmouthshire, the most Anglicized part of the region. The groups and individuals who made up the committee also overlapped in interests and affiliations. The largest single group included those associated with the consumer co-operative societies, a large and influential movement in Edwardian south Wales and one which in some ways most closely embodied the ideals of radical progressivism: collective but voluntary, commercial but not aggressively competitive, socially conscious but imbued with 'self-help', non-capitalist but not anti-capitalist.

Mansbridge, himself a staunch co-operator, clearly used his

---

[26] B. M. Bull, *The University Settlement in Cardiff* (Cardiff, 1965), 7–12.

[27] The East Moors Settlement annual reports for the period 1903–7 record a varied educational programme from temperance talks and advice on furnishing a working man's home, to lectures on 'The ideals of citizenship' by the editor of the *South Wales Daily News* and an address by Adela Pankhurst on 'Why women want votes'.

[28] In 1908 Burrows wrote that he thought one of the main functions of the settlement was to teach the unskilled poor the 'qualities of the artisan', *S.W.D.N.*, 5 Mar. 1908.

contacts to involve the movement in south-east Wales in the
establishment of the association in the area. In this regard, a
key figure was T. W. Allen (later Sir Thomas Allen), a local
councillor from Blaina in the western valley of Monmouthshire.[29] The manager of the Blaina Industrial and Provident
Co-operative Society, he was already well established as a
national figure in the movement. In 1908 Allen was president
of the Co-operative Congress when it met in Newport. Mansbridge attended the Congress and at a meeting held in Blaina
during the Congress spoke of how important Allen and his
co-operative society had been in forming the south Wales
W.E.A.[30] Indeed, Allen and the Blaina Co-operative Society
had been affiliated to the W.E.A. from the outset.[31] Allen, a
radical Liberal in politics and a devout Baptist by religious
affiliation, actually attended the Cory Hall conference as a
representative of the Labour Co-partnership Association,
another of his enthusiasms and a further indication of the attitudinal base upon which the W.E.A. locally was built.

Yet further evidence of the overlapping network of progressive opinion and political activism is represented in two other
personalities on the provisional committee list. The representative of the Newport C.W.S. and local education authority was
Councillor W. H. Brown. Brown had been president of the Co-
operative Congress when it met in Newport in 1900; like Mansbridge and Allen, he was a director of the C.W.S. Brown was a
prominent member of the Liberal Party in Newport from the
mid-1870s until his death in 1907. As well as being a local councillor, he was also a Rechabite and teetoller.[32] At a time when
the divisions between Lib-Labism and independent labour
representation were still not set in concrete, Brown was popularly perceived as a 'labour' man. This is even more the case
with the representative of the Cardiff Co-operative Society,
John Chappell.

Chappell was precisely the kind of labour man whom Mackenzie and Burrows were anxious to influence. An active trade

[29] See the entry on Thomas Allen in J. Saville and J. Bellamy (eds.), *Dictionary of
Labour Biography* (London, 1972), vol. I (hereafter *D.L.B.*).
[30] *South Wales Weekly Argus*, 13 July 1908.
[31] *W.E.A. Second Annual Report, 1904–5*, 11.
[32] Obituary, *South Wales Weekly Argus*, 27 Apr. 1907.

unionist, Chappell made his name in the city as president of the Cardiff, Barry and Penarth Coaltrimmers Union. Holding this office in a key skilled union, at the height of the coal exporting boom, he fought against 'sweating' on the docks, where union organization was difficult and victimization easy. He was returned as a 'labour' representative for the dockland ward of Splott in 1898. Despite the fact that he soon threw in his lot with the local Liberal association,[33] his hard work for the dockers and their families meant that he still received a good press from the local socialist journal.[34] He came in contact with Burrows through the settlement, and it seems that he was initially picked out as the person best fitted to act as secretary to the new association in south Wales. To that end he was awarded a scholarship by the association to attend a Cambridge University Extension Summer School in 1906.[35] However, his civic duties seem to have prevented him from taking up the post of secretary, and Chappell's local authority career blossomed at this time. He became Lord Mayor of Cardiff in 1909.

This pattern of political affiliation is not confined to those on the committee representing the co-operative movement; it is also apparent in those representing the trade union movement. The general secretary of Chappell's union, the Coaltrimmers, was Samuel Fisher. A native of Devon, a devout Baptist, Rechabite and trade unionist, he was hostile to the spread of socialist ideas and resigned as secretary of Cardiff Trades Council (the body he represented on the provisional committee) in 1900 because he felt that body was being manipulated by the advocates of independent labour representation.[36] As late as 1920 he was describing his politics as 'Liberal now Labour'.[37] An influential union in Cardiff and south-east Wales at this time was the Amalgamated Society of Railway Servants; the secretary of one of their Cardiff branches for the previous ten years was James Taylor, who was also a Lib/Lab member of Cardiff city council.[38] Even the S.W.M.F. representative on

[33] K. O. Morgan, *Wales and British Politics* (Cardiff, 1963), 204.
[34] *Labour Pioneer, Organ of the Cardiff Socialist Society* (Oct. 1900).
[35] *W.E.A. Third Annual Report, 1905–6*, 17.
[36] *Labour Pioneer, Organ of the Cardiff Socialist Society* (May 1900).
[37] *Who's Who in Wales* (Cardiff, 1920).
[38] *S.W.D.N.*, 5 Oct. 1911. See also M. J. Daunton, *Coal Metropolis: Cardiff 1870–1914* (Leicester, 1977), 213.

the provisional committee, Alfred Onions, was a man very much in the same mould. The Shropshire-born treasurer of the Federation, Onions was also miners' agent for its Tredegar District. A magistrate, district and county councillor, his political outlook can be judged by the *South Wales Daily News* description of him in 1906 as 'Methodist and progressive of the trade union type'.[39] Like Fisher, he was to come to terms with independent labour politics and he became Labour M.P. for Caerphilly in 1919.

Nowhere is the political orientation of the provisional committee more clearly displayed than in the choice of its chairman, P. Wilson Raffan, the chairman of the new district until a fellow Scot, Mackenzie, succeeded him in office in 1909.

Raffan emigrated to south Wales in the late 1880s to work as a journalist on the *South Wales Gazette*, a weekly newspaper circulating in the western valleys of Monmouthshire. He soon became its editor and then, in 1892, its proprietor.[40] On the radical wing of the Liberal Party, he threw himself into local politics and became both a district and county councillor for Abercarn. Prominent in the 'Welsh revolt' campaign against the terms of the 1902 Education Act, he was also an active campaigner for land reform and taxation, being prominent in the 'land campaign' of 1909.[41] In 1910 he became M.P. for Leigh in Lancashire, where he supported those who advocated a 'progressive alliance' between the Liberal Party and organized labour.[42]

Raffan thus personified the social radicalism that was willing to see the creation of a working progressive alliance between liberalism and labour. Whilst this movement failed to make significant headway within the Liberal political establishment in south Wales, the W.E.A. was to some extent part of an ill-defined attempt to institutionalize a dialogue between a labour movement with rising political ambitions and the agencies of popular liberalism. The network that formed the provisional committee could still, with relative ease, accommodate within its ranks someone such as Peter Wright, a 'labour' councillor

[39] *S.W.D.N.*, 6 Dec. 1906.
[40] Biographical details given on Raffan's election as chairman of Monmouthshire County Council, *S.W.D.N.*, 6 May 1909.
[41] H. V. Emy, *Liberals, Radicals and Social Politics* (Cambridge, 1973), 217.
[42] P. F.Clarke, *Lancashire and the New Liberalism* (Cambridge, 1971), 322.

from Newport, a shipping contractor and trustee of the Seamen's Union, who spoke regularly on I.L.P. platforms. A campaigner for welfare reforms, Wright was also a well-known professional wrestler, earning him what must be a unique accolade from the *South Wales Argus* in 1909 as 'a great wrestler and social reformer'.[43] Heavily influenced by some public lectures delivered by Mackenzie in the late 1890s, he was, like the good professor and Raffan, a Scotsman, and, like Fisher and Brown, a total abstainer. Wright maintained his links with the district association, becoming a vice-chairman when his former academic mentor became chairman of the south Wales W.E.A. in 1909. Wright was someone on the outer edges of radical liberal opinion. Much more in the mainstream was Alderman E. Thomas, one of the few thoroughly Welsh figures involved in the founding of the W.E.A. in south Wales. A staunch liberal and Nonconformist, Thomas was also a strong advocate of the teaching of Welsh in local authority schools. Yet, although he was part of this wider network which made up the provisional committee, he stands out in the list as someone who belongs to a slightly different tradition.[44] There were, for example, no ordained ministers involved in the founding of the association or in its early work in south Wales. Thus one must share P. S. Thomas's scepticism about the lineal descent of this movement from Griffith Jones. The W.E.A. was an English movement, brought into Wales by a network influential in the most Anglicized part of industrial and urban Wales, and in no small measure made up of public figures with English or frequently Scottish backgrounds.

One member of the academic coterie which was to dominate the W.E.A. in Wales in its early years was able to combine all the various strands which constituted this complex and overlapping network. This was the only woman on the provisional committee, Miss Elizabeth Phillips Hughes. The sister of the famous Methodist preacher, Hugh Price Hughes, E. P. Hughes was one of the most remarkable Welsh women of the late nineteenth and early twentieth centuries.[45] After a career in teaching

[43] *South Wales Argus*, 20 Mar. 1909; other biographical details from *Who's Who in Wales* (1920).

[44] See the entry for E. Thomas (*Cochfarf*) in the *Dictionary of Welsh Biography* (hereafter *D.W.B.*).

at Cheltenham Ladies' College, and a period of study at Newn-
ham College, Cambridge, Miss Hughes became the first Principal of Cambridge College for Women Teachers. A formidable
advocate of public education in general and of women in particular, she became acknowledged in Wales as the leading
female authority on the subject. She was the only woman to
sit on the committee which drafted the charter of the University of Wales. An educationalist with an international reputation, she made extensive lecturing tours of Europe and
America and published innumerable articles on education
and the need for higher standards in teacher training. She
even held a visiting professorship at the University of Tokyo,
and thereafter became something of an expert on, and enthusiast for, Japan and the Japanese.

Politically, she was mainly concerned with improved education and welfare provision. A supporter of women's suffrage,
she declared that she understood, but disapproved of, the
direct action tactics of the suffragettes.[46] In 1920 she described
her politics as 'Radical and Democrat'. In 1899 she retired to
her home town of Barry to devote the rest of her life and energy
to unpaid public work. The W.E.A. became one of her enthusiasms and she remained a prominent member of the district
committee well into the inter-war years.

The founding of the W.E.A. in south Wales, as elsewhere,
sprang out of two distinct but related developments which
were not peculiar to the area but a feature of British society
at the turn of the century. The first was the growth of an awareness of social problems and a growing conviction, amongst
informed opinion, that poverty, bad housing and poor education were not the inevitable lot of the toiling masses. Second,
there were the rising political aspirations of organized labour
and the growth in its ranks of socialistic ideas. Both trends
were to surface in the foundation conference, but in the process
they were also to trigger debate and disagreement, foreshadow-
ing the fact that the W.E.A., a 'progressive alliance of the mind'

[45] Biographical details taken from *Who's Who in Wales* (1920) and the entry for E. P.
Hughes in *D.W.B.* Her career as an advocate of female education in Wales is illumi-
nated further in, W. Gareth Evans, *Education and Female Emancipation: the Welsh
Experience, 1847–1914* (Cardiff, 1990).
[46] *B.D.N.* (21 Jan. 1906, 7 June, 7 July 1907).

which the association in effect constituted in south-east Wales, was not going to have an easy ride.

Over 250 separate organizations were represented at the Cory Hall conference, mostly voluntary bodies, together with some local education authorities. It was a triumph of organization, and it seems to have been co-ordinated by the Director of Higher Education for Monmouthshire, and long-standing member of the W.E.A. national executive, A. B. Badger.[47] An otherwise rather shadowy figure,[48] he seems to have shared with his fellow directors of education a desire to maximize the opportunities for post-elementary education granted under the terms of the 1902 Education Act.

The star speaker at the conference[49] was William Brace, vice-president of the S.W.M.F., miners' agent for the Western Valley District and, since the previous January, Lib-Lab M.P. for south Glamorgan: a virtual personification of south Wales progressivism. His speech, though supportive of the new initiative, was bland and dealt in general terms with the desire of the working man for education and the hope that the association could co-ordinate local authority and volun-tary efforts to supply this demand. It was an earlier speech by Burrows, in which he stressed the value of voluntary action in the fields of education and social work, citing the Splott Settle-ment as an example of the good that could be achieved by such efforts, which set the tone of the proceedings and which, when followed up by Principal Griffiths of the University College, triggered the first interjections from the floor. Griffiths com-bined his lauding of voluntary organization with statements about the need to instil in the working class an awareness of their duties as well as their rights in an era when working people stood at the threshold of political power. It was too much for some of the delegates, who rose to assert that the state was the only agency capable of meeting the the educational needs of working people. The platform ran into further trouble

[47] The provisional committee of the south Wales W.E.A. was established in the spring of 1906. W.E.A. executive committee minutes, 5 May 1906, Temple House, London.

[48] Badger was approached to sit on the W.E.A. executive committee as a representa-tive of the Association of Directors of Education. W.E.A. executive committee minutes, 1 Dec. 1904.

[49] The details concerning the Cory Hall conference are drawn from the the the accounts in the *S.W.D.N.* and the *Western Mail* and *W.E.A. Fourth Annual Report, 1906–7*, 30.

with the advocates of independent labour politics over what should have been a formality, namely, the nature of representation on the association's district committee. The inclusion of trades councils provoked debate because in some areas, such as Barry, the functions of a trades council were carried out by local Labour Representation Committees. An amendment proposing the inclusion of L.R.C.s in the list of represented bodies was opposed by the platform, and when it went to a vote the amendment was lost by seventy-three votes to fifty-two. There can be little doubt that it was the overtly political nature of the L.R.C.s which prevented their inclusion. But the point was a fine one. Trades councils put forward endorsed candidates in many local elections, and the miners' union, which was included in the list of represented bodies, had its own electoral machinery. However, this was 1906: the Labour Party was now a recognizable entity in the Commons and not just an *ad hoc* body promoting direct working-class representation. That very day, the south Wales miners were taking part in a ballot to decide whether or not the M.F.G.B. should affiliate to the Labour Party. Although the U.K. result went against affiliation, the south Wales miners voted by a clear majority in favour.[50] The issue, therefore, highlighted the underlying tensions within the south Wales labour movement and also brought into stark relief the dilemma which faced an organization such as the W.E.A., which sought to stress its non-sectarian and non-partisan nature, but which also claimed special links with organized labour just as that movement and its activists were becoming highly political. The platform and the provisional committee may have displayed an impressive tally of established leaders, but on the floor of the conference the new mood was only too apparent.

For Mansbridge and the leading lights of the association, the conference was a qualified success. A district organization existed and at least in south-east Wales the W.E.A. had made itself known amongst the activist element in that complex network which still linked organized labour and popular liberalism in the area. It still had to show that it could establish

---

[50] R. Page Arnot, *South Wales Miners: A History of the South Wales Miners, 1898–1914* (London, 1967), 149.

itself in those areas where a genuinely Welsh culture predomi-
nated, and that it could accommodate the new socialistically
inclined activists of the valleys and the coastal towns. The challenge that faced the association in the region was to find some
formula, some pattern of activity, which would allow it to
meet indigenous educational needs and also to respond to significant changes in popular thought. It has to be said that
those on the provisional committee and on the Cory Hall platform in October 1906 offered little evidence that such a formula
had been discovered. The history of the W.E.A. in south Wales
up to the outbreak of the First World War is, to a large extent, a
story of attempts to manufacture this elusive mixture.

2. 'IF THE WORKERS WILL ONLY ATTEND OUR MEETINGS'

The warning signs were there in the foundation conference that
the intellectual initiative amongst labour activists was passing
to a new perception of politics, one overlaid by an aggressive
rejection of class collaboration and a new confidence in the abilities of organized labour to secure an earthly salvation. The
advocates of state socialism, soon themselves to be challenged
as leaders of advanced opinion in south Wales, were making
the running.

In the councils of the S.W.M.F. this new outlook was finding
more and more support. One of the new breed was A. C. Willis.
An advocate of independent labour representation, he earned a
reputation as a pugnacious orator and critic of Lib-Labism.
'You must be Labour men pure and simple,' he told the Federation patriarchs at a 1906 S.W.M.F. conference. 'You are not to
be Lib-Labs.' Whilst he respected the old leaders, he went on,
'the needs of the present cannot be effectively met by the
methods of the past'.[51] In this brief intervention, Willis encap-
sulated the feelings of many young activists. He believed in the
power and the potential of the working class to solve its own
problems, he believed in the state as an agency to remedy
social wrongs, and he saw voluntary action as an inadequate
substitute for state intervention.[52] Yet in this period, when

[51] *S.W.D.N.*, 13 Mar. 1906, quoted in P. Stead, 'Working-class leadership in south
Wales, 1900–1920', *Welsh History Review*, 6, No. 3 (1973), 336.
[52] *South Wales Weekly Argus*, 13 Feb., 4 Dec. 1909.

popular political activity was still in a very plastic condition, he found little difficulty in working with those who still clung to the older verities; he often could be found on platforms with William Brace, Thomas Allen and P. Wilson Raffan.

It is not clear just how Willis came to be appointed as the district secretary of the newly-formed south Wales W.E.A., but it was a significant choice. The foundation conference had teetered on the edge of becoming a fiasco over the question of L.R.C. representation. The leading lights of the association probably saw in Willis a bridge between themselves and this rising generation of trade unionists. Willis was precisely the type of labour activist who so disturbed the philosophical equanimity of Henry Jones, but he was also exactly the type targeted by the leading figures of the W.E.A. locally and nationally. In addition to being prominent in the Six Bells lodge of the Western Valleys District of the miners' federation (becoming president of the district in 1907), Willis was also a local councillor in Abertillery, chairman of the local education committee and editor of a local Labour journal.[53] He was, however, a very Edwardian type of socialist: a staunch temperance man, a member of the National Vigilance Association and the Social Remedy Campaign, his views on education being reflected in a curious mixture of moral and practical purpose. Speaking at the foundation meeting of the Abertillery branch of the W.E.A., Willis advocated the provision of classes in subjects of practical value to working people such as gardening, the keeping of fowls and political economy. Education could raise the standard of life for working people, but it could also raise their moral condition, especially that of young workers, as he explained to the Consultative Committee on Continuation Classes in 1907.[54] Thus self-improvement shaded almost imperceptibly into moral growth, thence to class improvement and a more effective working-class movement. Willis straddled in

[53] *South Wales Weekly Argus*, 26 Oct. 1907. These biographical details are given in press reports of Willis's appearance before Abertillery Magistrates Court, where he was being prosecuted by the owners of Six Bells (Arael Griffin) Colliery for technical breaches of the Coalmines Act, when there was a strong smell of victimization. Brace acted as his defence counsel and Raffan chaired the bench; the case was dismissed.

[54] *South Wales Gazette*, 29 June 1907; *Board of Education, Report of the Consultative Committee on Attendance, Compulsory or Otherwise, at Continuation Schools*, Cmnd. 4758 (London 1909), vol. II, Minutes of evidence, 425.

attitude the outlook of those progressives of the 'trade union type' who dominated the south Wales provisional committee, and the advocates of independent labour politics who registered their protest at the foundation conference. It is not unreasonable to speculate that that was the reason he was approached to be the honorary district secretary of the W.E.A.

Both Wilson Raffan and Willis, the chairman and the secretary of the newly formed south Wales district of the W.E.A., were profoundly political men who saw clearly the deep political purpose of the association. It was a purpose made explicit in a newspaper report of a district committee meeting held in December 1907, when it was stated that the W.E.A. realized that the 'democracy of this country will in the near future be called upon to play an important part in the affairs of this Empire'. It was essential, the report went on, to ensure that those who assume such power should use it 'wisely' and for the 'greatest good'.[55] Whether Willis and Wilson Raffan would have agreed completely on what constituted wisdom and the greatest good must be considerd doubtful, but it illustrates the temper of the times, the same mixture of enthusiasm and anxiety which impelled those active in the W.E.A. The anxieties and the enthusiasm did not, however, add up to a strategy for workers' education. The nature, and the mechanisms of delivery, of the tuition that would foster wisdom and the greatest good were the issues which confronted the W.E.A. nationally and locally.

The W.E.A. in south Wales began a search for a pattern of activity which would excite the interest and engage the aspirations of the target group, the intelligent, politically aware working class. Nationally, the W.E.A. encouraged an initial tactic based on the formation of a local members' branch of the association. In the context of south Wales, this was not to prove a very successful activity. The experience in south Wales contrasts markedly with that of industrial Yorkshire, where the association was able to tap into a well-established tradition of self-improvement and political awareness associated with semi-religious organizations such as labour churches and

[55] *S.W.D.N.*, 1 Dec. 1907.

mutual improvement societies.[56] These bodies, though they existed in south Wales, never gained the social hold they enjoyed in Yorkshire, and they certainly never became a significant element in the development of the association as they did in south and west Yorkshire. Whereas in Yorkshire the W.E.A. grew out of thriving and lively branches, twenty-five by 1914,[57] in south Wales the main thrust of activity was to come from the district. By 1914 some twelve branches had been founded in south Wales, none west of the Afan Valley,[58] but few had really thrived. With one exception, none of the branches developed a mass membership, and only Cardiff had a continuous history up to 1914. Thus, whilst it is possible to see the history of the W.E.A. in industrial Yorkshire in terms of the development of a genuinely popular surge of support for what the association represented and offered, it is difficult to sustain such an analysis for the movement in south Wales. Here, the W.E.A. was an agency in which the initiative came from a relatively small group of academics, educationalists and trade unionists who operated at a regional level, not from any spontaneous rank and file demands.

The second component of the strategy followed by the W.E.A. in seeking to establish itself in its early years was the attempt to use local authority continuation classes as a vehicle for workers' education. Continuation classes or, as they tended to be called, evening classes were an early attempt to provide post-elementary education, usually, but not exclusively, of a technical or vocational character. State support for such activities, channelled through local education authorities, had grown, especially after the 1902 Education Act, and it was thought by some leading figures in the W.E.A. that local pressure could result in the use of continuation classes as a vehicle for workers' education. Thus did the branch and the continua-

[56] Harrison, op. cit., 249–99.
[57] Ibid., 269. On the other hand, the W.E.A. was far more successful in Wales before 1914 than it was in Scotland, which did not have a fully functioning organization until after 1918. See W. H. Marwick, 'Workers' education in early twentieth century Scotland', *Journal of the Scottish Labour History Society* (1974).
[58] Between 1907 and 1909, W.E.A. branches were founded in Abertillery, Barry, Cwmavon, Cardiff and Pontypridd. In 1909 branches were established at Tredegar, Merthyr and Porth. Between 1911 and 1914 branches were created in Llantwit Major, Abergwynfi, Caerau (Maesteg) and Ynysybwl.

tion class policy come together. It has to be said that, at least as far as south Wales was concerned, the policy was not a success. The factors which account for the failure of the policy are best understood by examining the experience of the branches and their attempts to build a programme of workers' education through the agency of the continuation classes.

If any town in Wales should have been able to sustain a strong W.E.A. branch it was the Principality's only city. A young university town, with a staff and student body with a declared interest in democratizing higher education and its benefits, Cardiff had a large, if somewhat fragmented, labour movement,[59] which might be expected to offer enthusiastic support for the association and its aims. In addition, the local authority had, by the standards of the time, quite a reasonable record in the supply of post-elementary education. Indeed, these three elements were represented at a well-attended and extensively reported foundation meeting in the summer of 1907.[60] The branch officers elected seemed to augur success; the chairman was Ronald Burrows, the vice-chairman was Alderman E. Thomas, a leading Liberal luminary on the city council, and the secretary was Samuel Fisher, a classic 'progressive of the trade union type'. The branch officers personified the same type of alliance between educational and political 'progressivism' that was so dominant in those listed in the provisional committee.

The Cardiff branch of the W.E.A. did not thrive. The reasons for the lack of success seem to fall into three categories: the changing political environment in the city, the nature of educational experiences offered under the auspices of the branch, and, finally, the personalities involved. Through Samuel Fisher, the W.E.A. branch was intimately linked to an older tradition of Labourism which was under challenge in Cardiff, as elsewhere in south Wales, by the bolder, and usually younger, spirits of the I.L.P. Organizationally and intellectually, the initiative was passing out of the hands of men such as Fisher. The branch does not seem to have attracted any of this new breed of activist and remained a rather exclusive set

[59] M. J. Daunton, op. cit., 181.
[60] S.W.D..N., 14 Apr. 1907.

of individuals clustered round the three officers. No trade union, other than Fisher's Coaltrimmers, gave anything but nominal support to the branch.

In line with the general policy of the association, the branch mounted a lecture series in conjunction with the local education authority. The series, entitled 'Wages and what fixes them', given by H. S. Jevons, professor of political economy at the University College, was clearly aimed at the local labour activists. It commenced in a blaze of advertising handbills and newspaper publicity, but the turnout was very poor. Comments by W.E.A. branch officers critical of the apathy and ignorance of local working people in failing to seize a golden opportunity for self-improvement, combined with comments from Jevons in his first lecture to the effect that the popular press was guilty of simplifying and misleading working people as to the true nature of the wages system, brought the wrath of the *South Wales Daily News* down on the heads of Jevons and the officers of the Cardiff W.E.A. They were accused of adopting an 'ivory tower' mentality, and Jevons's approach was contrasted unfavourably with that of Henry Jones, whose recent visit had excited so much interest.[61]

The lecture series was completed, attendances did improve, but the episode damaged the branch, and it never really recovered prior to the First World War. Relations with both the local education authority, which proceeded thereafter to run its own classes on political economy and withdrew financial support for the W.E.A. courses, and the university were soured.[62] Apart from work with the Splott Settlement, very little education was actually provided by the branch in these years. The problems were compounded in 1908 by the departure of Burrows, who does seem to have been the driving force in the branch.[63] But the early experiences of the Cardiff branch reflect recurrent themes in the early history of the W.E.A. in south Wales and the factors behind the failure of the branch and continuation class strategy. The nature of the small cliques that tended to dominate branches, the character of evening

[61] Ibid., 9, 10, 13 Jan. 1908.
[62] Ibid., 6 Feb. 1909, 3 May 1909.
[63] Glasgow, op. cit., 93.

classes looked upon by industrial workers, according to the *South Wales Daily News*, as something for 'office boys and clerks',[64] and the growing ideological tensions between an older labourism and a newer anti-capitalist perspective amongst trade union activists—these all played their part. This is perhaps better illustrated in accounts of two branches in different parts of industrial south Wales, where the formula was tried and applied even more assiduously than in Cardiff.

Barry was essentially a new town, a product of the coal-exporting boom of the late nineteenth century. Its population, like that of most port towns, was rather cosmopolitan, very Anglicized and somewhat transient. It had a vigorous labour movement made politically aware by the fact that an important employer in the town was the Taff Vale Railway Company, whose anti-union activities contributed massively to the rising political ambitions of organized labour.[65] It also had something of a radical political reputation.[66] Unlike some parts of industrial south Wales, it did not have a strong co-operative movement, but it was overwhelmingly working-class and its professional middle class was very small indeed. Amongst this élite, however, there loomed one figure whose presence was felt by everyone in the town, the formidable, redoubtable and amazing Miss E. P. Hughes.

Following her retirement to Barry, Miss Hughes devoted her energies, initially, to the interests of women, especially young women. She established an organization called the Twentieth Century Club, dedicated to instilling in local young women a deeper awareness of their rights and duties as citizens. Echoing the language often used by advocates of workers' education, Miss Hughes argued that the new political responsibilties which women would soon acquire demanded that those about to discharge them should receive a 'solid' knowledge of the system, so that the new power was used correctly and to best

[64] *S.W.D.N.*, 8 Mar. 1909.
[65] In 1907 92 per cent of the staff of the Barry Rail Company were members of the A.S.R.S., and Barry was a centre of the All Grades movement, *B.D.N.*, 13 Sept. 1907.
[66] It was in Barry in the 1890s that the first branch of the Social Democratic Federation was established in Wales. K. O. Fox, op. cit., 22. It was Barry delegates who objected to the exclusion of the L.R.C.s from representation at the W.E.A. Cory Hall conference in October 1906.

effect.[67] However, she also argued in favour of single-sex schooling for girls, because she felt mixed schooling disadvantaged
them, and also she advocated specific training in home craft
for adolescent females.[68] Socially and educationally radical,
she operated above and beyond the level of petty party politics, but she still fitted in well with the 'progressive' tenor of
the provisional committee. Her enthusiasms were wide-
ranging, from Japan and the Japanese to welfare and prison
reform; in 1906, for example, she gave a lecture to the Barry
branch of the I.L.P. on the merits of the American parole
system which she had witnessed first-hand on her many tra-
vels.[69] But education was her forte, her deepest enthusiasm.
She was amongst the first women to be elected to the Central
Welsh Board for Intermediate Education.[70] The scourge of
those who sought to impose a narrow ratepayer mentality on
the existing public provision, she supported more enlightened
teaching methods and the need for the proper training of teachers. Under pressure from E. P. Hughes, Barry became only
the second town in Wales to insist that all potential elementary
teachers must receive some form of secondary education.[71]

The two local weekly papers, the Liberal *Barry Herald* and the
Unionist *Barry Dock News*, opened their columns to Miss
Hughes and were yet another platform from which she cajoled
the people of the town along the paths of social progress. Yet
her relations with those active in the local labour and socialist
movement were ambivalent; she told the workers of Barry
about what they needed, whereas the socialists tried to tell
them about what they wanted. They were never quite on the
same wavelength.

The Barry branch of the W.E.A. was the first in south Wales,
established in the late autumn of 1906 just after the Cory Hall
conference.[72] It followed the usual pattern, the leading lights

[67] Ibid., 7 Dec. 1907.
[68] *Highway*, II, No. 37 (Feb. 1910), 75–6. When the national executive of the W.E.A.
wished to establish a small committee of inquiry into the educational needs of working
women, they approached Mrs Ramsay MacDonald, Mrs Ethel Snowden and Miss E.
P. Hughes. W.E.A., N.E.C. minutes, 13 June 1907, loc. cit.
[69] *B.D.N.*, 16 Mar. 1906.
[70] P. E. Watkins, *A Welshman Remembers* (Cardiff, 1944), 35.
[71] *B.D.N.*, 29 Nov. 1907.
[72] *B.D.N.*, 19 Oct. 1906. There was a formal foundation meeting addressed by E. P.
Hughes the following month. *S.W.D.N.*, 19 Nov. 1906.

were local worthies, councillors, headteachers and a sprinkling of labour men such as the man elected as branch secretary, Pemberton. He was a member of the engineering union and a frequent critic of his fellow workers' indifference to education and self-enlightenment. The branch set itself the limited task of providing, in conjunction with the Barry Evening Class Committee, 'a special course of lectures in matters of historic, scientific and economic interest'.[73] In the winter of 1907–8 the W.E.A. organized eight lectures by local and visiting notables, one by Miss Hughes, almost inevitably on Japan, another by her brother on local government, and several others on history and literature. The programme was tilted towards labour activists by two contributions from the Swansea dockers' leader, James Wignall, who spoke about organized labour in America and from a 'distinguished London labour leader', H. Orbell on 'The life of the poor'.[74] The following year saw a similar series, including a visit from the anarchist Prince Kropotkin, who told his Barry audience about conditions for the working man in Russia.[75]

The speakers were interesting and well-meaning, but they were not making the impact Miss Hughes had expected. Working people were not attending in the numbers she desired, and the W.E.A. and its main supporters were not gaining the intellectual initiative amongst labour activists. As early as the summer of 1907 the branch officers were writing of the 'strong democratic spirit' in the town, but also of the 'lack of unity in their desire for education'.[76] The fact was that the W.E.A. had some severe competition in the single lecture field. The Barry Education Society, established before the arrival of the W.E.A., consisted mainly of teachers and those interested in matters educational. It arranged lectures by outside experts such as Millicent Mackenzie, the wife of J. S. Mackenzie, the head of teacher training at University College, Cardiff. It showed a distinct interest in the question of the 'Higher education of the working classes' and invited the then president of the N.U.T., Marshall Jackman, to address them on this subject in

[73] B.D.N., 18 Jan. 1907.
[74] Ibid., 20 May, 20 Sept. 1907, 28 Feb. 1908.
[75] Ibid., 14 Jan. 1908.
[76] W.E.A. Fourth Annual Report, 1906–7, 32.

early 1907.[77] It was the Education Society and not the W.E.A. which established an Oxford Extension Delegacy course on Victorian poets and novelists in the town in 1909.[78] There was little direct rivalry between the two bodies, and there was overlap of membership and officers, but there was also an evident duplication and blurring of purpose and function. For those interested in education or in self-improvement the Barry Education Society met their needs. For those interested in education for political change, the Barry branch of the I.L.P. put on a very rich fare. In the first six months of 1906, for example, no fewer than thirty-eight meetings were held, many with well-known outside speakers such as the Pankhursts and J. Bruce Glasier.[79] Two men who were later to help make the nature and purpose of workers' education an important issue in the coalfield, Noah Ablett and T. I. Mardy Jones, were also given a platform. The W.E.A. was trading in a crowded market.

Just prior to the beginning of the first series of W.E.A. lectures in the autumn of 1907, the W.E.A. branch officers put out a curious statement which clearly outlined their purpose but also displayed an anxiety about whether the workers would oblige: 'If the workers would only attend our meetings then we will know their requirements and progress to that perfect citizenship which is the ambition of all social reformers.'[80] Miss Hughes realized after the second series of lectures that the W.E.A. was simply not getting the workers to attend, nor were they getting the 'solid' knowledge necessary for 'perfect citizenship'. In the summer of 1909 Miss Hughes and the Barry W.E.A. embarked on a new initiative which tried in a more direct fashion to straddle the need for 'solid' knowledge and the demand for solutions to real problems. The opportunity came with the publication in the summer of 1909 of the reports of the Royal Commission on the Poor Law. Here was the chance for the workers of Barry to study, in depth, a fundamental problem of social reform, to weigh the evidence and make a rational assessment of the merits of the two solutions offered by

[77] B.D.N., 30 Nov. 1906, 1 Nov. 1907.
[78] Ibid., 19 July 1909.
[79] Ibid., 20 Sept. 1906.
[80] Ibid., 29 Sept. 1907.

the majority and minority reports. Miss Hughes arranged for a lecturer from Cardiff's University College to take a series of six classes on the Poor Law and its reform, and she also arranged for copies of the reports to be available in the local public library's reading room. The lecture series was preceded by a lengthy introduction in the local press from Miss Hughes. She stated that the armies of pauperism needed to be disbanded in the shortest possible time. This was, however, 'a very difficult task especially if we wish to produce no fresh damage to society in the process'.[81] Thus she summed up the progressive dilemma: to secure reform but without challenging the fundamental social order. If workers and thinkers could come together, this dilemma could be resolved; hence the attraction to Miss Hughes of the W.E.A., with its direct line to trade union activists. The problem was that many of those now active in the trade union movement, whilst they may have respected Miss Hughes and the public-spirited individuals who worked with her in the W.E.A. and the other local bodies which sought to bring succour and enlightenment to the working people of Barry, felt little need of what Miss Hughes called 'solid' knowledge; they knew what had to be done. On 22 September 1909, three weeks before the W.E.A. course on the Poor Law reports commenced, the Barry branch of the I.L.P. passed a resolution in support of the minority report, with its demand for the break-up of the whole system and its replacement by positive state action to remedy poverty.[82]

By 1909, on paper, the Barry branch was thriving; it had seventy-three individual members and thirteen affiliated bodies, including local branches of the engineering, railwaymen's and dockers' unions.[83] The essentially nominal nature of these affiliations was exposed when, by the end of the following year, the branch had ceased to function. The truth was that the association had still not found a working formula; functioning on the energy, vision and reputation of one remarkable woman and some energetic acolytes was not enough. The branch was revived in 1913, but under a different district regime; it was then able to find a new role and had a greater impact.

[81] *Barry Herald*, 17 Sept. 1909.
[82] Ibid., 24 Sept., 15 Oct. 1909.
[83] *W.E.A., Sixth Annual Report, 1908–9*, 18.

The most sustained and ambitious attempt to make the branch/continuation class strategy succeed in south Wales came in Pontypridd. Situated at the confluence of the Taff, Rhondda and Cynon rivers, Pontypridd was, in the heyday of the steam-coal boom, a rapidly expanding town at the hub of the south Wales economy. It was strategically an important town if the W.E.A. was to establish itself in the mining valleys. The miners' and railwaymen's unions were strong and influential elements in the local labour movement and the association was fortunate to have as its branch secretary a leading light of the railwaymen in the town, Moses L. Jones.

The very embodiment of late Victorian and Edwardian labourism, Moses Jones's early career was typical of that of thousands of trade union activists. He began his working life in 1876 at the age of eleven at the Aberaman brickworks.[84] He first came in contact with trade unionism in the local coal-mines, where he soon took an active part in a number of disputes. Ill-health forced him out of the mines, and eventually, in 1889, he secured a post as a relief signalman with the Taff Vale Railway Company. This was the company whose legal action against the A.S.R.S. was to contribute so much to the early development of the Labour Party. Moses Jones's activity on behalf of the A.S.R.S. resulted in 1900 in his dismissal from the firm. His victimization by the notorious Taff Vale company greatly enhanced his reputation amongst trade unionists, and Moses Jones used his status and notoriety to good effect in local politics. In 1900 he was elected to the Pontypridd School Board, and in 1903 he was returned to the urban district council.

Although a leading labour activist and secretary of the local trades council for several years, Moses Jones was not an active I.L.P. member, but rather a trade unionist who felt impelled to expand the movement into political action. He was another classic example of the radical progressive of the 'trade union type' who so dominated the early W.E.A. in south Wales. His reputation as a trade union militant—he was often a keynote

---

[84] The biographical details are taken from a lengthy report in the *Glamorgan Free Press* (hereafter *G.F.P.*) on the occasion of a presentation by the Trehafod lodge of the True Ivorites, marking his ten years as their secretary. *G.F.P.*, 20 Sept. 1907.

speaker at A.S.R.S. All Grades rallies[85]—belied an essentially orthodox political outlook indistinguishable from that of the majority of his peers. His attitude to local government was characterized as 'to endeavour to secure public convenience without sacrificing the interests of the ratepayer'.[86] He was as far from syndicalism as he was from the directors of the Taff Vale Railway Company—perhaps further. He was a fighter but preferred the arts of industrial peace and harmonious relations between the social classes. This was all reflected in his attitude to workers' education. In promoting it he sought the support of all sections of the local community. The local newspaper, the *Glamorgan Free Press*, opened its columns to this local worthy with even more uncritical enthusiasm than the Barry papers did to E. P. Hughes. It regularly carried Jones's arguments for the W.E.A. in which he denounced the apathy of the mass of working people towards post-elementary education and the attitude which saw it as something only of use to clerks and teachers. Instead, he used the by now standard argument of the need to educate the masses into their new responsibilities as citizens. 'Knowledge', argued Moses Jones, 'is a power for doing good, the more knowledge a person has the more good he can do.' History showed that progress could not be brought about by educating the few: 'to gain perfection the whole community must be educated. With the advance of democracy, the responsibility of the citizen increases, and this means increased happiness if intelligently carried out.'[87]

These ideas were entirely in line with the arguments for workers' education being deployed by the academics and educationalists active in the W.E.A. nationally and in south Wales. They were also arguments which allowed Moses Jones to form an alliance with local middle-class and professional people who were also keen to have a hand in 'perfecting' the citizenship of the local proletariat. Mostly headmasters and teachers, this group tended to pepper their enthusiasm for the W.E.A. and its local schemes with anxieties about the future if the working classes did not avail themselves of the association's services. The

[85] Ibid., 17 May 1907.
[86] Ibid., 20 Sept. 1907.
[87] Ibid., 17 May 1907.

problem of shaping the mind of the post-school adolescent shaded into a deeper fear about the political influences that could play on the untutored minds of labour activists. Mrs Roberts-Rosser, a teacher at a local secondary school, enthused over a W.E.A. continuation class scheme because it would help to prevent 'many innocent young women' from marring and blighting their lives by falling into 'bad company'. By coming into contact with 'superior intelligence', these 'plastic and pliable' minds would be uplifted and set in the right direction.[88] Of more pressing concern to a local secondary school headmaster and W.E.A. supporter in early 1909 was the 'ominous unrest' growing in the ranks of labour. Dr R. D. Chalke warned a W.E.A. branch meeting of the dangers of a 'rampant and unintelligent socialism' which would 'rush madly and blindly into excesses which would never cure the existing industrial and commercial evils'. Instead, through the activities of bodies such as the W.E.A. he envisaged that 'Labour rightly organized and rightly controlled, intelligent Labour would soon rule the destinies of this great empire'.[89] Few middle-class supporters of the association in south Wales expressed their fears so explicitly. Dr Chalke was, however, from Porth, where the more advanced spirits of the movement for independent working-class education were already making their presence felt.

In Pontypridd, Moses Jones had created a coalition of trade unionists and middle-class educationalists which was able to mount the most comprehensive attempt in south Wales to make the continuation class strategy work. Jones initially organized a debate on the issue of continuation/evening classes and whether they should be compulsory for adolescents. In a fascinating and well-reported meeting, Jones spoke strongly in favour of compulsion, but opinion from the floor was more divided and objections ranged from the issue of the threat to the earning power of young people, vital for some families, to the physical strain of long hours at work followed by class attendance. The questions of personal choice and freedom and the

[88] Ibid., 30 Aug. 1907.
[89] Ibid., 5 Mar. 1909. Headmaster of Porth Secondary School, R. D. Chalke was an active Liberal and later contested Rhondda East in 1929 and Swansea East in 1931 in the Liberal interest. *Who's Who in Wales* (London 1937).

competition such classes would offer to mid-week chapel gatherings were also raised by some of the professional people present. There was general agreement that every encouragement should be given to young working-class adolescents, the focal point of most of the anxieties, to attend continuation classes.[90] Moses Jones, though rebuffed in his advocacy of compulsion, seems to have decided that he should lead a campaign to cajole the youth of Pontypridd to attend. The W.E.A. branch thus became a recruiting agency for local authority evening classes. Jones wrote a letter to all school leavers extolling the virtues of class attendance; he addressed them in their schools; he contacted and wrote to employers telling them to encourage their young employees to attend. Local ministers of religion were induced to urge the merits of continuation classes from the pulpit, Moses Jones stressing their value in terms of moral growth. Trade unionists were also pressed to make the benefits of attendance known to their young members. Jones tailored his arguments to each group that he approached, emphasizing the 'getting on' aspects of further study with the employers, while the benefits of acquainting young trade unionists with the subtleties of accounts and balance sheets were stressed to labour leaders. Keen to enlist all elements in the community in his campaign, he used utilitarian arguments to support the extra ratepayer expenditure. For only a small additional charge on ratepayers, a massive loss of talent and ability could be ended. 'Would you rather have a useless product for 15/- or a good product for a £1?' was the question he threw at the chairman of the Pontypridd Education Committee when the latter queried the extra costs.[91]

In the summer of 1907 words were soon translated into action. The W.E.A. branch established ward committees throughout Pontypridd whose task was to visit the homes of school leavers to encourage their attendance at classes. The ward committees retained 25 per cent of the subscriptions of members who joined at ward level. In addition, the committees organized 'treats' at the beginning and the end of terms for all those who agreed to attend classes. The W.E.A. branch

[90] G.F.P., 5 July 1907.
[91] Ibid., 17 May, 19 July, 16, 30 Aug. 1907.

even agreed to underwrite the additional income of teachers at one elementary school (Mill Street) if they agreed to take evening classes.[92] It was felt that the continuity of teaching would encourage higher attendance.

Moses Jones's scheme gained wide publicity; the national W.E.A. promoted it as a model of good practice. It was singled out for mention by Willis to the Board of Education's Consultative Committee on Continuation Classes, and it was lauded in the pages of the W.E.A. journal, the *Highway*.[93] The scheme was to gain wider notice from a big public meeting arranged by the Pontypridd branch in September. On the stage, behind the main speakers, sat 150 school leavers who had agreed to attend continuation classes. Although technically in different political parties, the Lib-Lab M.P. William Brace, who chaired the meeting, and the 'Labour' M.P. David Shackleton, the keynote speaker, spoke of their essential closeness on most political matters and of their enthusiasm for the work of the W.E.A. They represented two progressives of the 'trade union type', casting an interesting reflection on the position of the association in the developing labour politics of the age.[94]

Despite the best efforts of Moses Jones and his associates, the scheme never functioned properly. This was because of inherent difficulties with the continuation class strategy, the apathy of those at whom it was directed, bureaucratic obstructions and jurisdictional jealousies, and the fact that the whole strategy depended on converting a system designed to provide essentially vocational courses which could not cope with the demands of a movement geared to reorientating the world view of the working classes. In the case of Pontypridd, however, matters were made much worse by what was, at the time, an unusual event—a teachers' strike.

It is ironic that Pontypridd, the one area where a determined effort was made to make the continuation class policy work, should have been the place where teachers decided to make a stand against the cheeseparing of the local education author-

---

[92] Ibid., 18 Oct. 1907.

[93] *Board of Education, Report of the Consultative Committee on Attendance, Compulsory or Otherwise, at Continuation Schools*, Cmnd. 4758 (London, 1909), vol. II, Minutes of Evidence, 426; *Highway* (Oct. 1908).

[94] *G.F.P.*, 27 Nov. 1907.

ity. The county council announced that it was not prepared to pay evening-class teachers for the time they spent marking registers.[95] Whereas elsewhere teachers merely complained about such petty parsimony, in Pontypridd they decided to make a stand and boycotted the evening classes. The situation was a nightmare for Jones, whose pet scheme was threatened by industrial action. His sympathies and trade union instincts were with the teachers, yet he saw all his efforts crumble as the dispute dragged on. Initially, he blamed the education authority and pointed to attempts by county council officers to block his scheme,[96] reflecting long-standing conflicts with Glamorgan county council which were to dog the efforts of the association long after this dispute ended. By late October he was asking the teachers to accept service but to press their grievances through other means. In proposing a motion to the trades council asking the teachers to return to normal working, he called into question the value of industrial action, which brought accusations that he and the W.E.A. were anti-trade union.[97] It was an accusation he refuted, but it reflected a growing chasm between men such as Moses Jones and some younger spirits in the movement. When the dispute was resolved, the damage had already been done, and the scheme foundered.[98]

In the years that followed, the branch tended to concentrate on arranging public lectures by leading figures in the association, such as Burrows and Jevons. When, in 1908, Moses Jones replaced Willis as district secretary of the W.E.A., the branch slipped more under the control of the teachers, ministers of religion and doctors. Worthy discussions on the details of educational policy did not prove a great draw to the working people of Pontypridd.[99] Pontypridd also provided one of the

---

[95] Ibid., 13 Sept. 1907.

[96] Ibid., 4 Oct. 1907.

[97] Ibid., 2 Oct. 1907. His growing hostility to industrial action also came out in a speech he made to an A.S.R.S. All Grades rally a few weeks later when he argued against strike action to support a demand for union recognition. Ibid., 5 Nov. 1907.

[98] Ibid., 5 Nov. 1907, 8 May 1908. The dispute was resolved with most of the concessions coming from the teachers' side.

[99] *Highway* (Dec. 1908), 48; *G.F.P.*, 19 Feb. 1909. One of the ward committees set up in 1907 continued to flourish for a while. The Trallwyn ward, dominated by a local cleric, the Revd A. H. H. Organ, had thirty-nine members in 1909. He seems to have used the committee as an extension of his ministry.

first instances of the W.E.A.'s becoming an agency of social mobility, against the will of its founders. E. J. Hookway took over as W.E.A. branch secretary. Something of a protégé of Moses Jones, Hookway was a young activist with the railwaymen and the local trades council. In 1908 he attended the W.E.A. Summer School in Cambridge. The lectures he attended there were reported by him, almost verbatim, in the columns of the *Glamorgan Free Press*.[100] He attended the 1909 Summer School, and the following year he was appointed as a full-time district organizer for the association in the northwest of England.

If the branch/continuation class strategy was going to work anywhere in south Wales, it would be in Pontypridd. It had able and well regarded working-class activists, a body of middle-class and professional supporters and enthusiasts, and the staunch backing of the local press. The branch struggled on until 1911, when it suddenly collapsed despite having a nominal membership of 137 and over eleven affiliated bodies, including the trades council and the railwaymen's union.[101] As with other branches, Pontypridd could not find a formula which captured the interest or enthusiasm of a significant number of the rising generation of labour activists; when Moses Jones and then Hookway left, the branch collapsed. An ill-defined faith in the value of education to social and political progress was not enough.

In 1909 a region-wide propaganda tour by Mansbridge led to attempts to establish branches at Cwmavon, Merthyr and Porth. Only in Merthyr did the branch last for any length of time. Porth struggled against a growing tide of hostility from the advocates of independent working-class education and obstructionism by the local education committee.[102] In truth, by 1909 it was obvious that, in south Wales at least, the mainspring of the W.E.A. conception of workers' education was not to be the branch but the district committee. The branch/conti-

[100] Ibid., 8 Aug., 4, 11 Sept. 1908.
[101] *W.E.A., Eighth Annual Report, 1910–11.*
[102] *Rhondda Leader*, 13 Mar. 1909. Mansbridge addressed the foundation meeting. It was the only one in Wales where there was any vocal opposition to the association. This came from local I.L.P. members, probably associated with the Plebs League. The Rhondda Evening Class Committee's hostility seems to have been jurisdictional. See Turner, op. cit., 206.

nuation class strategy rested on two assumptions: that there was a latent demand by workers for further education and that it could be supplied by co-ordinating existing public educational provision. Both assumptions proved ill-founded. The branches soon slipped into being merely worthy bodies nagging working people about their failures and fecklessness. Those prominent in the branches eschewed the language of class conflict, just as influential elements within the organized working-class movement in industrial south Wales were becoming more class-conscious, more willing to use the rhetoric of class war.

3. 'IN ALL ASPECTS OF W.E.A. WORK "NIL DESPERANDUM" IS A
   GOOD MOTTO'

In an act of significant, but probably inadvertent, symbolism which followed the opening proceedings of the 1909 annual general meeting of the W.E.A. in south Wales, the delegates left the City Hall to reassemble in the newly completed buildings of the University College in Cathays Park in Cardiff.[103] Earlier, the first chairman of the association in south Wales, Wilson Raffan, handed the chair to J. S. Mackenzie. Both actions emphasized the growing predominance of university academics in the work of the association and the failure to build a popular base of support for the W.E.A. through the branch/continuation class strategy. The meeting, which lasted for five hours, was a watershed. Mansbridge focused on the failure of those educationalists and academics and the 'progressives of the trade union type', who dominated the councils of the association in south Wales, to generate any real enthusiasm for the organization's work or objectives amongst the rank and file. He told the assembled delegates that 'the demand for education must come out of south Wales labour in co-operation with those true scholars who did not care whether they co-operated with a dustman's son or a duke's son'.[104] The problem of how that demand could be fostered remained. Mansbridge was there to promote the new university tutorial class ideal given recent prominence by the publication of the Oxford

[103] *S.W.D.N.*, 11 Oct. 1909; *Highway* November (1909).
[104] Wales W.E.A. district committee minutes, 9 Oct. 1909.

report. As early as January 1908, the *South Wales Daily News* was praising the work of the joint committee established by the Oxford extension delegacy and the W.E.A. to bring the university and organized labour together to provide for the educational needs of the latter. For, in the words of the main organ of south Wales progressivism, 'It has been well said that there can be no greater work for a university than to educate men who act in Labour politics (among whom there is a growing desire for increased education) in historic, economic and other liberal subjects.'[105] The report itself, formally entitled *Oxford and Working-Class Education* and published in November 1908, was to have a profound influence, not only on the W.E.A. but also in the process of dissent from the ideals of the W.E.A., which crystallized in 1909 into the movement for independent working-class education.[106] But in the autumn of 1909, for Mansbridge, the university tutorial class on the Oxford model was the vehicle for future development. Links with the university were thus vital, but commitment from labour was equally essential.

The marathon meeting ended with the acceptance of the desirability of university tutorial classes run along Oxford report lines, but with no illusions about the practical obstacles still in the way of success. Some felt that the culture gap between working people and university tutors would be a barrier; others hoped that the tutorial classes would breed a 'spirit of dissatisfaction' which would spur further demands for social reform. The meeting ended with a commitment by the association to organize a series of three conferences in the region on educational topics of interest to working people.

The first of these conferences met in February 1910 and tackled the question of the failure of continuation classes to excite the enthusiasm and support of working people. Henry Davies, the head of mining instruction for Glamorgan County Council and someone whose attitude to the W.E.A. and its ambitions can only be described as ambivalent, argued that there were simply too many counter-attractions available to

[105] *S.W.D.N.*, 14 Jan. 1908.
[106] See B. Jennings, 'The making of the Oxford report', in S. Harrop (ed.), op. cit., 11–29.

young men in their leisure time. He cited skating rinks, 'bright cinematographic shows', music halls, billiards, football and, worst of all, boxing! There was, said Davies, 'more discussion over the Welsh–Driscoll boxing match over the past week than there was over R. J. Campbell's New Theology'.[107] He predicted dire consequences for the character of the young and the commercial health of the nation if this trend continued.

The second and third conferences, which met in April and July 1910, tried to formulate some concrete proposals which would make the continuation classes viable. The final set of proposals, which were agreed in July, involved a uniform leaving age of fourteen, abolition of half-time education before that age and compulsory continuation class attendance between the ages of fourteen and seventeen, with the hours of young workers reduced accordingly. It was, in some ways, a triumph of organization for Moses Jones, and his stamp is on the set of proposals finally agreed. Over forty trade union branches sent delegates to the July conference and many working men took part in the debates.[108] But the W.E.A. was still not consolidating its hold on the region, and by 1911 branch activity had all but ceased. It was soon evident that if the association was to survive at all, some forthright initiative at district level was required. This came in the summer of 1911 with the appointment of a full-time district or, as the position was then known, organizing secretary.

Whilst it is not clear precisely when the decision to appoint was made, it is known that it was J. S. Mackenzie who selected the man for the job. In the spring of 1911 Mackenzie approached John Thomas, an economics undergraduate at Cardiff who was about to complete his studies, to inquire about his career intentions. Mackenzie suggested that he apply for the new full-time post, and he was the only candidate interviewed for the job in July 1911.[109]

John Thomas was born in Aberdare, where he grew up, the son of the caretakers of a Congregational chapel. Active in chapel affairs, Thomas soon also developed an intense interest

[107] *S.W.D.N.*, 7 Feb. 1910; Wales W.E.A. district committee minutes, 5 Feb. 1910.
[108] Ibid., 9 Apr. 1910; *S.W.D.N.*, 25 July 1910.
[109] Wales W.E.A. district committee minutes, 8 July 1911.

in politics, becoming a keen member of the local I.L.P. and a staunch follower of the local Labour M.P., Keir Hardie. Thomas found Hardie's ethical and emotional form of socialism congenial, and he became a well-known activist with the local I.L.P., speaking at its meetings and writing in its journals. He did not, however, find the rising tide of materialist socialism quite so appealing, and he was out of sympathy with the more advanced ideologues associated with the movement for independent working-class education.[110]

The appointment of Thomas triggered a diatribe against the association in the local I.L.P. journal, the *Pioneer*. Written by an ex-Central Labour College (C.L.C.) student, Wil John Edwards, it contained a searing indictment of the W.E.A. as an agency of capitalist propaganda under the guise of its classes in 'political economy'.[111] This attack indicated just how sensitive the local advocates of independent working-class education were about Thomas, and also reflects why Mackenzie selected him. Based in the coalfield with good contacts in the local labour movement, especially with those beyond the 'progressives of the trade union type', Thomas could straddle the divide between young labour activists and the educationalists of the W.E.A.

The appointment of Thomas also marked the point at which the initiative within the W.E.A. in Wales became focused at the district level. In the years just prior to the outbreak of the First World War, a small coterie of academics and educationalists, mostly living in the Cardiff, Penarth and Barry area, became the driving force within the association and engaged it with a network of contacts with other voluntary agencies geared towards social improvement in the region. Meeting regularly, but informally, in these years at the house of Edgar Jones,[112] the headmaster of Barry Grammar School and a close friend of E. P. Hughes and J. S. Mackenzie, the group sought to build

---

[110] Biographical details taken from an interview by the author and Mr Peter Stead with Dr John Thomas, April 1972; brief biography, 'Dr. John Thomas: pioneer in adult education', prepared by Neath W.E.A. branch, n.d. See also J. Thomas, 'The early days of the W.E.A. in Wales', *Cambria* (Spring 1930).

[111] *Pioneer* (hereafter, [*Merthyr*] *Pioneer*), 5 Aug. 1911.

[112] Interview with Dr Illtyd David, 16 May 1972. Dr David lodged in Edgar Jones's house whilst a sixth-form student at Barry Grammar School just prior to the First World War and well remembered the meetings of this informal group. There is also a brief discussion about this coterie in P. Stead, *Coleg Harlech: The First Fifty Years* (Cardiff, 1977), 16–17.

on the progressive spirit engendered by the social reforms of the Asquith government. They also clung to the hope that organized labour could still play a constructive role in the rising democracy, and they were alarmed by the spread of doctrines of class conflict.

A key figure in this regard was the district treasurer from 1911, Thomas Jones. As with many of his generation, Thomas Jones was something of a disciple of Henry Jones.[113] Imbued, whilst studying at Glasgow, with social reforming idealism engendered by the prevailing neo-Hegelianism, Thomas Jones found the association under that other product of Scottish neo-Hegelianism, Mackenzie, a suitable platform for the propagation of his ideals. Jones had also, whilst in Scotland, been a close friend of Ronald Burrows, and they co-operated in an anti-sweating campaign and formed a short-lived university branch of the Fabian Society.[114] He flirted with independent labour politics and openly declared his sympathy with the demands of organized labour. As late as 1914 he could still be lauded in the pages of the leading I.L.P. organ in the coalfield as 'probably the most brilliant of the young Welshmen of today'.[115] He despaired of the ability of orthodox liberalism to confront the real issues of the region, he was more in tune with the outlook of the 'New Liberalism', and it was as secretary of the Welsh Insurance Commission that he built up contacts with Lloyd George. As treasurer of the association, he used his contacts with wealthy benefactors such as the Liberal M.P. and coalowner, David Davies, Lord Tredegar and Lilian Howell to secure donations for the W.E.A. It was only through such contributions that the W.E.A. in Wales survived the period, but they also gave some substance to the accusation from the Labour College supporters that the association was the 'handmaid of capitalism'.[116]

[113] T. Jones, *Welsh Broth* (Aberystwyth, 1950), 4, 22. There is a very full account of the life and influence of Thomas Jones in, E. L. Ellis, *T.J. A life of Dr Thomas Jones, C.H.* (Cardiff, 1992).
[114] T. Jones, op. cit., 28; Glasgow, op. cit., 34.
[115] [*Merthyr*] *Pioneer*, 21 Mar. 1914; for a highly critical interpretation of the role and influence of this 'unofficial Prime Minister of Wales', see David Smith's 'Wales through the looking glass', in D. Smith (ed.), op. cit. 228–33.
[116] Nearly 55 per cent of the Welsh District's income in the 1911–12 session came from wealthy benefactors. Some 20 per cent came from working men's clubs. *W.E.A. for Wales, Fifth Annual Report, 1911–12.*

Others of this circle were Percy Watkins, the registrar of Cardiff University College and later secretary of the Welsh Board of Health and a prominent figure in the life of the Welsh W.E.A., Silyn Roberts, a Calvinistic Methodist minister who later, in the inter-war years, built up the north Wales district of the association, Russell Jones, an economics lecturer, and Edgar Chappell, secretary of the South Wales Garden Cities and Town Planning Association, whose chairman was J. S. Mackenzie and whose treasurer was the man who replaced Mackenzie as chairman of the W.E.A. in Wales, Daniel Lleufer Thomas.[117] Chappell was one of the first editors of a new journal, established by the endeavours of Thomas Jones and funded by the Davies family of Llandinam, called the *Welsh Outlook*, which sought to transmit the ideals and values of this coterie to the opinion-formers of Wales. The first edition, published in early 1914, contained an article by Ronald Burrows which, the editor stated, 'crystallised the aims and desires of the magazine'. The article was an account of a recent address delivered by Burrows at the university settlement in Cardiff where he had formerly been warden. It was a defence of the ideals of the settlement and the W.E.A. at a time when society in general, and south Wales society in particular, seemed to be descending into class warfare. He blamed oppressive employers for breeding bitterness and resentment amongst working people, but he also denounced the 'nihilist spirit as cruel, destructive and relentless as the inhuman industrialism it seeks to destroy', to be found on the other side. He advocated class co-operation, good will and support for the gradualist reforming spirit of the age.[118]

Blood, argued Burrows, was 'thicker than class'. Underlying the ideals of *Welsh Outlook* was a desire to engage nationalist sentiment in support of social reform and against class conflict. It was a strategy which was to be developed most assiduously by another key member of the Cardiff–Barry circle, Daniel (later Sir Daniel) Lleufer Thomas. The impact of Lleufer Thomas was not to be felt until after the outbreak of war, but the attempt to use Welshness as a bridge between

---

[117] [*Merthyr*] *Pioneer*, 5 Sept. 1914.
[118] *The Welsh Outlook* (January 1914), 27–8. See also Gwyn Jenkins, '*The Welsh Outlook*, 1914–33', *National Library of Wales Journal*, xxxiv (Winter, 1986) 463–92.

the social classes was something which was being promoted as a strategy well before Lleufer Thomas made it a key theme in W.E.A. activity. The initiative in this regard came, originally, from Albert Mansbridge who, in April 1909, suggested that the district rename itself as the Welsh district. Later that year he also suggested that the district should issue a report and propaganda leaflets in Welsh.[119] John Thomas spoke Welsh, but in practice little was done to try to tap the work of the association into the cultural underpinnings of Welsh life.

For John Thomas, the practical difficulties of keeping the W.E.A. functioning crowded out the possibility of pursuing any high-minded commitment to marrying social reform to an enlightened Welsh national sentiment. The local education authorities remained indifferent when not actually hostile— Henry Davies became a figure of particular loathing for Thomas.[120] The trade unions, preoccupied in an era of industrial militancy, were now also subject to the anti-W.E.A. propaganda of the Plebs League and Central Labour College. The working men's clubs provided an alternative avenue of approach to the working class of the industrial areas, and it was a route that was used with some success by Thomas in the pre-war period.[121] By the end of 1914, sixteen working men's clubs were affiliated to the district, in addition to the south Wales branch of the Club and Institute Union. These clubs provided venues for 'one-off' lectures, mainly by John Thomas (fifteen out of twenty-four in 1914–15) on broad social and political topics. Edgar Chappell also used them to promote housing reform.[122]

One other initiative of the year just prior to the outbreak of the war was an attempt to increase the lamentably small number of women attending the tutorial classes in Wales: three out of just over 200 students in south Wales in 1911–12. To this end, in 1911 the district committee established a women's section, and over the next few years the numbers did improve with two non-grant-earning classes, one in literature at Barry and

---

[119] South Wales W.E.A. district committee minutes, 3 Apr., 24 July 1909; *S.W.D.N.*, 5 Apr. 1909.
[120] Interview with John Thomas, April 1972.
[121] Ibid.
[122] *W.E.A. for Wales, Eighth Annual Report, 1914–15*.

the other in 'Home problems' at Caerau (Maesteg) being run specifically for women students with female tutors.[123] This initiative, the only one of its kind in the history of the W.E.A. in south Wales before 1940, collapsed on the outbreak of the war, and the specific needs of women remained an area of gross neglect, despite the prominent role played by Miss E. P. Hughes in the affairs of the Welsh association.[124]

The change of direction in 1909 towards university tutorial classes required the whole-hearted co-operation of the University of Wales and its constituent colleges. From the earliest years of its existence there had been a lobby within the ranks of the Welsh educational establishment which favoured the development of a national university system in Wales based on non-residential teaching to part-time students by itinerant tutors. It was described by the doyen of Welsh educationalists, Sir Owen M. Edwards, as a 'University of Dreams',[125] whose classes were to be established in every town and village in the Principality. Its lectures to be delivered in the leisure time of the Welsh workers, it was held up as the ideal for an intrinsically democratic people and culture. Apart from Edwards, its chief advocate was another powerful voice for extra-mural work, R. D. Roberts, secretary of the London University Extension Board and a governor of the University of Wales. Roberts had campaigned in the early 1890s for the creation of a non-residential university geared to part-time attendance, where three years' work would be deemed equivalent to one year's full-time attendance.[126] Roberts was far ahead of his time, and the scheme made no headway. In April 1909 pressure from Roberts led to the creation by the University of Wales of a committee to examine the possibility of creating a university-wide scheme of extra-mural tutorial classes.[127] Its deliberations dragged on until November 1911, when a sub-

---

[123] *W.E.A. for Wales, Fifth Annual Report, 1911–12*; *W.E.A. for Wales, Seventh Annual Report, 1912–13*, 10. Short courses were also arranged with the I.L.P. Women's Guild in Cardiff in 1912 and with the Cardiff Women's Adult School in 1914.

[124] Miss Hughes was vice-chairman of the District from 1911 to 1919.

[125] Published originally in Welsh in the journal *Cymru* in March 1914, O. M. Edwards's article, 'Workers' university', was republished in translation in *Welsh Outlook* (November 1933).

[126] D. Lleufer Thomas, op. cit., 79, 128: For the role of R. D. Roberts in the development of the university extension movement, see Kelly, op. cit., 224–33.

[127] B. B. Thomas, op. cit., 20.; *S.W.D.N.*, 9 Apr. 1909.

committee consisting of Roberts, John Thomas and Principal Reichel of Bangor was given the task of finalizing the details. Roberts died shortly after the subcommittee was established, and the scheme died with him, reflecting the lack of enthusiasm of the constituent colleges for any university-wide scheme of provision.[128]

The constituent colleges did take up tutorial class work, but with varying degrees of enthusiasm and on an *ad hoc* basis. Bangor established tutorial classes in conjunction with the slate quarrymen's union. Aberystwyth established a full scheme in the 1911–12 session with the full involvement of the local authorities and was able to claim the fairly generous grants now available from the Board of Education.[129] Cardiff, however, proved problematic. A joint committee of the college and the association was established in 1912, but the college refused to underwrite the tutorial classes financially, which meant that this was a burden that had to be carried by the W.E.A. and the individual members of the Cardiff Joint Committee for tutorial classes.[130] This compounded the Welsh association's financial difficulties. It also caused the diversion of resources away from its propagandist functions to being an agency for the actual supply of classes. This meant that Thomas had to spend much of his time actually teaching and not promoting the W.E.A. brand of workers' education. The W.E.A. had succeeded by the outbreak of the war in establishing tutorial class work of the Oxford report type as an important feature of adult education in Wales. John Thomas spent much of his time tutoring joint committee classes[131] just as the association was struggling to make a real impact with the south Wales labour movement, where the intellectual initiative appeared to be falling into the hands of those whose perception of the nature and function of workers' education was very different from that of the inner circle that ran the Welsh W.E.A.

---

[128] Lleufer Thomas, op. cit., 101.

[129] Ibid., 102–7.

[130] *Highway* (June 1912). The members of the joint committee, none very wealthy, were severally responsible for an overdraft of £500. S. Watkins, 'Early reminiscences of the W.E.A. in Wales', *Cambria* (Spring 1930), 11.

[131] In the 1914–15 session, the first when the committee was fully functional, John Thomas tutored four of the ten Cardiff joint committee tutorial and pioneer classes, all on the economic aspects of the war. *W.E.A. for Wales, Eighth Annual Report, 1914–15*.

The indifference and hostility encountered by John Thomas in his first year as district secretary provoked the plaintive comment which opens this section of the chapter.[132] Despite his difficulties, the work of the association did expand in the years up to the outbreak of war. Overall, class attendances recorded in the district annual reports grew from 204 in 1912 to over 505 in 1914. The subject orientation indicates the target audience: they were mostly in the areas of economics and industrial history, fifteen out of eighteen in 1914.[133] Yet the impression that the W.E.A. had failed to make a fundamental impact is difficult to avoid. John Thomas and a small number of dedicated lecturers such as Russell Jones and William King tended to dominate the lists of class tutors. Branch activity never matched that to be found in other regions of the U.K. There were only four functioning branches by the end of 1914: Cardiff, Barry, Caerau near Maesteg, and Llanelli in the industrialized part of south Wales. It was only the generosity of wealthy benefactors, especially the Davies family of Llandinam, which prevented the association sinking between 1911 and 1914. One important innovation for adult education in Wales in the years just prior to 1914 was the establishment of the Bangor Summer School, but here again the support of a wealthy benefactor proved vital in making it accessible to south Wales students.[134]

The W.E.A. did not find Wales as congenial a country as Tom John had hoped at the foundation conference. The Welsh traditions of popular culture did not provide the W.E.A. with a ready market for its brand of workers' education. Outside a small band of committed activists, the W.E.A. made little impact before 1914. The labour movement, diverted by industrial strife or, as in the case of the hugely important miners' federation, influenced by critics of the association, displayed little enthusiasm.

The traditions of Welsh Nonconformity, generally hostile to secular endeavours for reform, became defensive and insular as

---

[132] *W.E.A. for Wales, Fifth Annual Report, 1911–12.*

[133] These figures are based on student numbers given in the W.E.A for Wales, fifth and eighth annual reports.

[134] *W.E.A. for Wales, Sixth Annual Report, 1912–13*, 6; interview with John Thomas, April 1972.

chapel attendances began to fall. Shaken by the anti-intellec-
tual hysteria of the Evan Roberts revival of 1904–5, orthodox
Nonconformity was soon to be confronted by a new challenge, the social gospel of the Revd R. J. Campbell's 'new theology'. Stressing the practical application of Christian principles,
it aroused considerable interest in south Wales; one correspondent of a Barry newspaper even claimed in 1907 that 'The New
Theology is the all absorbing topic on the lunch train from
Barry Dock to Barry; on the dockside; in the shops; in the
brakes; along the shore;—everywhere . . .'[135] A recent study
of the relationship between religion and organized Labour in
Edwardian south Wales has indicated the extent to which
R. J. Campbell's ideas were received with considerable enthusiasm by many, as they appeared to create a working relationship between socialism and Christianity.[136] They were also
vehemently opposed by those who wished to stick to traditional theology, and the 'new theology' was denounced as a
departure from the central message of personal salvation and
an alien, English import which fouled the purity of Welsh Nonconformity. The unwillingness of many Nonconformist ministers to come to terms with the social gospel and, furthermore,
their active hostility to it and its advocates, seem to have
been factors in the decision of many young labour activists to
concentrate on secular routes to social improvement through
political and trade union activism. Instead of fighting the
orthodox theology within the chapels, many turned their
backs on the chapel and even on possible careers as ordained
ministers and directed their intellects and energy into the trade
union movement and politics, local and national. James Griffiths was profoundly influenced by Campbell's preaching of
the social gospel; it seems to have shaped his religious outlook, but it also convinced him that he could best serve God
and mankind through the miners' union.[137] In this way the
'new theology' and the intransigent response of orthodox Non-

[135] *B.D.N.*, 28 June 1907.
[136] C. B. Turner, 'Conflicts of faith, religion and labour in Wales, 1890–1914', in
D. R. Hopkin and G. S. Kealey (eds.), *Class, Community and the Labour Movement: Wales
and Canada, 1850–1930* (Cardiff, 1989), 67–85.
[137] On the religious influences on James Griffiths, see his autobiography, *Pages from
Memory* (London, 1969), 11–18; also J. Beverley Smith, 'An appreciation', in J. Beverley Smith (ed.), *James Griffiths and his Times* (Ferndale, 1976), 62–4.

conformity paved the way for many young men and women to leave a chapel-centred view of life—some abandoning religion altogether—and enter one where service to their fellow men and women was the driving sense of mission.

Mansbridge, a deeply religious man himself, but of the high Anglican variety, always asserted the spiritual dimension of the work of the W.E.A. Speaking in Barry in 1909, Mansbridge stated that he did not know where 'education ended and religion began'.[138] Whilst Mansbridge had tried to link the W.E.A. to the well-known religious sentiment of the Welsh people when engaged in his visits to the area, the association did not, initially, seem to attract ordained ministers to activity in its ranks. The neo-Hegelian ideals of Mackenzie did have a long-term and profound effect on many young men who were subsequently to enter the Nonconformist ministry. But even he could incur the hostility of the orthodox when he suggested that moral development need not be confined to church or chapel. When Mackenzie suggested that moral education in schools should be separated from religious instruction, he brought down on himself the wrath of the *South Wales Daily News*, which stated categorically that 'lack of a biblical basis is inimical to moral growth'.[139] The 'chapel' played no direct role in the early history of the W.E.A. in Wales. A few young ministers, such as Silyn Roberts and Herbert Morgan, influenced both by the social gospel and neo-Hegelianism, did become active in the W.E.A. and the extra-mural movement some years later.

Only among the co-operative societies and the working men's clubs did the W.E.A. in Wales assume, as it did in Yorkshire, 'the protective colouring of its social environment'. But this was not enough. In order to fulfil its deeper political purpose the association needed to get at the leading opinion-formers of the labour movement; they were mainly active in the unions and the I.L.P., and too few of them fell under 'the guidance of the wise' in the years before 1914. John Thomas and the Cardiff–Barry coterie struggled to give, and to some extent succeeded in giving, a sense of purpose and direction to the

[138] *B.D.N.*, 30 July 1909.
[139] *S.W.D.N.*, 15 Feb. 1908.

work of the association. The leading lights of the W.E.A. in south Wales hoped that the association would provide the means by which a new spirit of reconciliation could be added to the increasingly volatile political chemistry of the region. The increased use of the language and imagery of class conflict, particularly of the divisions between capital and labour, made such a hope appear pious; reconciliation of opposites was going out of fashion.

II

'MEN OF INTELLECT AND MEN OF ACTION': SOUTH WALES AND THE ORIGINS OF INDEPENDENT WORKING-CLASS EDUCATION

1. 'THE VERY LIGHT OF THE MOVEMENT'

Whatever may have been the arguments about the nature, content and purpose of workers' education between the supporters of the W.E.A. and the Labour College, there were two aspects on which they were in broad agreement. First of all, education was going to play a pivotal role in the development of the organized working-class movement and, secondly, workers' education was for the raising of the whole working class and not for the raising of individuals out of their class. Mansbridge could always get a cheer when he asserted either proposition at any meeting. In the slightly testy atmosphere of the Cory Hall conference in October 1906, they were the only ideas which triggered a universally warm response from the audience. By 1906 it was possible to construct upon the responses to these two related ideas great hopes for a spontaneous growth of support for, and participation in, schemes for the supply of workers' education. In practice, as the experience of the W.E.A. in south Wales demonstrated, the promise was greater than the reality.

When a delegate to the Co-operative Congress, held in Cardiff in 1900, declared that 'Education is the Very light of the movement. It is to social reform what fuel is to the locomotive', his views were enthusiastically endorsed by the local socialist journal and reported as an unquestionable truth.[1] Yet there were few clear signs that the labour movement had a vision of how education would assist the process of social reform. Mansbridge hoped that a spontaneous enthusiasm would see labour rank and file activists pour into the classes of the W.E.A. But, by and large, the imagination of this group was not stirred by the bill of fare offered by the association in south Wales before 1914.

[1] *Labour Pioneer* (Cardiff) (July 1900).

One organization which did seem to trigger a genuine upwelling of interest amongst young labour activists was Ruskin College. It was founded in Oxford in 1899 by two Americans, the wealthy philanthropist Walter Vrooman, and Charles Beard, later to become a distinguished historian of the United States. They believed that the labour movement in the United Kingdom was about to assume major responsibilities of government. They hoped the college would give labour leaders the intellectual equipment to take on the tasks of statesmanship. Both were admirers of the octogenarian critic of unbridled capitalism, John Ruskin, after whom the new college was named. As with the W.E.A., the publicity associated with Ruskin College always stressed that the education supplied was designed to help men to raise, and not to rise out of, their social class.[2] It was hoped that, after a year or two at Ruskin College, the students would return to their community, their trade union and their local authority to act as beacons of enlightenment amongst their fellow workers. Although based in Oxford, Ruskin College had no organizational links with the university, and its curriculum was geared to the perceived needs of worker-students. There was a heavy stress on the social sciences, political economy and history, with additional studies in the structure of local government and public speaking.[3]

After having established this working men's college, Vrooman and Beard returned to the United States and left the institution to fend for itself. A correspondence course department, offering a curriculum similar to that available to residential students, soon opened up links with working people all over Britain, and by 1902 it was claimed that the college had over 3,500 postal course students. In south Wales by 1902 small groups of these students were meeting regularly in Cardiff, Dowlais, Merthyr, Swansea and Ynysybwl, all striving to gain an education 'worthy of a citizen'.[4] In this they were assisted by the courses in public speaking and public work. An additional attraction of the correspondence courses was the existence of

---

[2] P. Yorke, *Ruskin College, 1899–1906* (Oxford, 1977), 1–3; *The Story of Ruskin College* (Oxford, 1949), 4–15.

[3] Yorke, op. cit., 5.

[4] *Labour Pioneer* (Sept. 1902).

a small number of scholarships tenable at Ruskin College for suitable candidates amongst the postal students. It was through this route that the first south Wales students reached Ruskin College.

From the outset, however, Ruskin College was plagued by financial worries, and the need to spread an awareness of its existence amongst labour activists and for organized labour to assume a responsibility for its funding were combined in the various visits to the area of the first principal, Dennis Hird. Of all the extraordinary personalities associated with the development of British workers' education in this century, Hird is without doubt the most idiosyncratic. A graduate of Oxford, he became ordained as a curate in the Church of England in 1885. In 1887 he moved to a parish in Battersea where he was soon influenced by the Social Democratic Federation, which he joined in 1893, triggering a conflict with the church authorities which was resolved only when Hird renounced holy orders. The author of a number of trenchant satires on English society in general and orthodox religion in particular, Hird was already a controversial figure when he was appointed principal of the newly founded Ruskin College. He was also a strong advocate of the study of sociology when the discipline was in its infancy and still not formally recognized by the University of Oxford.[5] He combined this with a profound interest in Darwin's theory of evolution, which he regarded as the most important intellectual development of modern times. As were many of his contemporaries, he was concerned with how Darwinism could be applied in fields outside biology and zoology. Indeed, it was as a lecturer on the subject of the theory of evolution and its application to social development that he travelled the country speaking to I.L.P. groups and working men's clubs and institutes. This was a time when the ideas of Darwin and Huxley were making an impact amongst the politically active elements in the working class through the circulation of cheap editions of their works. Herbert Spencer's attempts to apply the scientific method and evolutionary principles to the problems of society were also making an impact amongst those growing sceptical of, and restive with,

[5] W. W. Craik, *Central Labour College* (London, 1964), 37–9.

the explanations of the pulpit and the Bible class, even if his anti-collectivist conclusions were less acceptable.

In 1906, when Hird made a short tour of south Wales, he was already well known as a lecturer and as the principal of Oxford's working men's college. His lectures stressed the need for the workers to acquire knowledge of their society, and how it was ruled by the economic imperatives of capitalism and not by some inexorable law of nature. Hird emphasized how the workers could, through understanding their conditions, challenge them and create a 'scientific morality'[6] in which reason would be the guiding light and a new order created. It was a message that appealed to many young activists, but it was couched in terms which, reinforced by his status and learning, did not at first occasion any criticism from more orthodox quarters. Thus, Ruskin College, and its principal, gained wider publicity and support.

By 1906 the financial needs of the college required more than could be supplied by the erratic and unreliable sources so far tapped. The executive committee decided to establish a scheme of union-sponsored scholarships, and the S.W.M.F., at the time one of the biggest unions in the country with over 120,000 members, was a prime target of the secretary of the college, Bertram Wilson. When the letter which he sent to the executive committee of the Federation was passed on to its constituent district committees,[7] Wilson decided that it would be necessary to campaign for the college through the good offices of active members of the union who had connections with the college. In this regard he was fortunate to have two ex-students of Ruskin who made themselves available for the task: one was J. L. Rees from the Swansea Valley and the other, far and away the more effective of the two, was T. I. Mardy Jones from Ferndale in the Rhondda.[8]

In selling the idea of residential scholarships to trade unionists the supporters of Ruskin College had, inevitably, to stress

[6] *Merthyr Express*, 3 Nov. 1906.

[7] S.W.M.F. Rhondda No. 1 district committee minutes (hereafter Rhondda No. 1 minutes), 5 Mar. 1906. Power within the S.W.M.F. was dispersed amongst the constituent districts, which varied in size from the huge Rhondda No.1, which in 1906 had just over 28,000 members, to the Saundersfoot District, which had only 276. R. Page Arnot, op. cit., Appendix I.

[8] Rhondda No. 1 minutes, 5 Mar. 1906.

the value of an education there to the labour movement in general and their own union in particular. It was a major departure for any union to use funds for this purpose, and officials were always fearful of litigation by an aggrieved member if union money were used for any function which a court could deem illegal. On top of this, there would always be resentment amongst members if it were thought that membership fees were being used for personal advancement rather than for the benefit of the whole membership. Thus the campaign for support of scholarships tenable at Ruskin was conducted along lines which stressed its value as a 'labour' college which would assist the organized working class as well as the members of the supporting union in achieving their objectives of improved wages and conditions of employment, as well as wider social reform. The greater involvement of organized labour in the processes of national and local government gave another angle of attack on those who might oppose such expenditure. One of the first unions to support sponsored scholarships to Ruskin was the tightly organized British Steel Smelters' Association, a union which had significant support in parts of industrial south Wales. In 1905 the general secretary of the Steel Smelters, John Hodge, justified the union's decision to send its two full-time organizers, J. T. Macpherson and Tom Griffiths (later M.P. for Pontypool, 1918–35), in the following way:

> I kept before our members the idea that industrial battles must be fought around board tables, municipal councils and all local administrative bodies as well as in parliament and urged that those whose place it was to lead ought therefore to be equipped with good learning and sound economic doctrine, and succeeded in having our two organizers, Messrs. Griffiths and Macpherson sent to Ruskin College ... It has repaid us.[9]

It was a pattern of argument which was to be used time and again in the following year when supporters of Ruskin College were endeavouring to persuade the district committees of the S.W.M.F. to establish scholarships there. In addition to the immediate and direct benefits of a stay at Ruskin, it was

[9] *S.W.D.N.*, 29 Mar. 1906.

stressed that such scholarships would be for those who would commit their lives to the service of their fellow workers, and not for those who wished for places in the 'overstocked professions'. W. H. Stevenson, a Ruskin student from the anthracite district of south Wales, writing in 1906 about the benefits of union scholarships, stated clearly that Ruskin would equip worker-students with 'a sound knowledge of social and economic questions, and they shall return to the mine, the factory and the workshop whence they came to use their knowledge in the uplifting of their fellow men'.[10]

Stevenson's article was an opening shot in Ruskin's campaign for the support of the S.W.M.F. The main burden of this campaign, however, fell on the shoulders of T. I. Mardy Jones, the most able of the Welsh worker-students to attend Ruskin before 1906. Mardy Jones went to Ruskin on a correspondence scholarship between 1902 and 1904. His intellectual gifts soon attracted the attention of the vice-principal, H. B. Lees-Smith. Mardy Jones became a protégé of the vice-principal who supervised some work he prepared on mining royalties. This was subsequently published in the *Economic Review* and he was made a Fellow of the Royal Economic Society.[11] An academic career might have followed, but Mardy Jones returned to the coalfield and soon became enmeshed in trade union and political work. Elected checkweighman at Maerdy Colliery in the Rhondda, he also soon became chairman of the lodge committee and of the local I.L.P. branch. What was interesting about Mardy Jones was that he also felt impelled to use his academic gifts for the benefit of his fellow workmen. Shortly after his return from Oxford, he arranged some classes in economics under the auspices of Rhondda's Evening Class Committee. Financial support was withdrawn, however, when one local councillor complained that Mardy Jones's classes were producing nothing but 'socialists and infidels'.[12] Thus Mardy Jones was seen locally as a member of the more advanced wing of the local labour movement and not, as he was portrayed by supporters of the Labour College movement

---

[10] Ibid. W. H. Stevenson was later to become a journalist with the *Daily Herald*; James Griffiths, op. cit., 16.

[11] *Llais Llafur*, 24 July 1909.

[12] *G.F.P.*, 18 Oct. 1906.

in the years after the 1909 split, as simply the mouthpiece of educational orthodoxy.

For Mardy Jones the campaign to secure scholarships at Ruskin from the miners' union for their members was a mission which he conducted with stupendous energy and enthusiasm. During 1906 he addressed over one hundred different lodge, district and other meetings in the coalfield in support of Ruskin College. It was a campaign of which he was so proud that he still made reference to it when he was M.P. for Aberdare many years later.[13] Mardy Jones was the archetypal target of workers' education, a real 'man of intellect and action', dedicated to the labour movement but with the ability to influence large numbers of his fellow workers through his intellectual gifts and skills of communication. Mardy Jones knew exactly what arguments to deploy in support of Ruskin College. He knew the appeal had to be couched in terms of equipping union activists with the knowledge and skills necessary for the more effective conduct of union business. In large public meetings Mardy Jones would combine the specific trade union benefits with Ruskin College's role in the larger process of democratizing the supply of education and improving the conditions of the working class.[14]

The greatest success achieved by Mardy Jones in 1906 was to persuade his own district committee, the large and influential Rhondda No. 1 District, to establish two annual scholarships, each worth £65 per annum, at Ruskin College. Using arguments which stressed its role as a 'labour' college, his case was most clearly summed up by another, unnamed delegate who said: 'We have to contend with the masters, who have men thoroughly versed in the laws of supply and demand and we want to bring into our ranks young men educated in these matters at Ruskin College, able to hold their own against all comers.'[15]

The debate at district and lodge level was not just about the nature and purpose of the education supplied at Ruskin; it was also about the legality of spending money on scholarships. In

---

[13] See his entry in S. V. Bracher, *Herald Book of Labour Members* (London, 1922).
[14] See his address to the Aberdare miners on 6 Oct. 1906, the same day as the W.E.A. foundation conference in Cardiff. *Merthyr Express*, 8 Oct. 1906.
[15] Rhondda No. 1 minutes, 15 Oct. 1906.

the case of the Rhondda No. 1 District, this was resolved by establishing a separate fund made up of special levies on the constituent lodges. What exercised the delegates more than the question of the legality of the expenditure was the issue of who would be eligible for scholarships. At one district meeting it was alleged that some young men were entering the industry and joining the union to be able to apply for the scholarships. The allegation triggered a response from another delegate which won general approval: 'They [the scholarships] will be for those who have done most for trade unionism in their district; men who have their heart and soul in the business, and the well-being of trade unionism; not for those who are looking simply after their own interest.'[16]

In order to prevent abuse of the scholarships, the district established a complex system of selection. Candidates had to be between eighteen and thirty-five years of age, with at least twelve months' membership of the union. They had to have a record of active union membership which had to be attested by one of their lodge officers; their moral character had to be confirmed by a testimonial from a local clergyman or person of similar standing. After the self-seekers were weeded out, the candidates were allowed to proceed to a written examination. This consisted of a test in arithmetic and an essay of between 150 and 200 words on the subject, 'Wealth, capital and labour: the relationship of the three'. The written test was followed by an oral examination on topics such as general knowledge, knowledge of colliery work, knowledge of the Compensation Acts and of trade union work.[17] Clearly, the system was designed both to select those whose commitment was to using their time at Ruskin in the interests of their fellow workers and to exclude those whose personal ambitions lay outside the labour movement. Mardy Jones was chairman of the Rhondda No. 1 District by the time that the first scholarships were awarded to two well-known and staunch members of the union, Noah Rees and Tom Evans. Speaking from the chair, he emphasized once again how the men going to Ruskin were not going to become 'professional men, lawyers, journal-

---

[16] Ibid., 10 Dec. 1906.
[17] Ibid., 31 Dec. 1906.

ists and doctors but to enable them [by means of education] to
uplift and generally benefit their fellow miners'. He also spoke
of his pleasure in seeing the way in which the miners were wak-
ing up to the great need for 'education as a means of the betterment of their class'.[18] Thus Mardy Jones once again reinforced
the dual themes of workers' education which the two emerging
traditions were to share.

By 1906 the first products of Ruskin College had already
trickled back to the coalfield. One of the first to attend on the
basis of a correspondence course scholarship was Edmund
Stonelake, a miner from Aberdare. Upon his return he became
secretary of the Aberdare Trades Council, and in 1904 a member of the local district council. In his unpublished memoirs, he
recalls how his time in Oxford soon made him something of a
local celebrity and he was expected to make contributions to
discussions of all types.[19] Another former student called Casey
was elected to Newport Board of Guardians shortly after
returning from Ruskin.[20] Even in these very early years much
was expected and much was demanded from the products of
Oxford's 'working man's college'. Stonelake recalls how
Oxford was remote from the minds and experience of working
people, though most associated it with a great seat of learning
and anyone who attended an Oxford 'college' was regarded
as a man of great ability. 'Consequently', writes Stonelake, 'I
had greatness thrust upon me.' It was an image he further fostered by a lantern-slide show of views of Oxford, which he
played to gatherings of all types in the Aberdare area.[21]

There was also set in train a process of marking out these men
as different, special, whom a career of union or public service
inevitably began to tug away from the day-to-day realities of
working-class life in the coalfield. Full-time posts as union officials, even election to parliament, were to undermine the pris-
tine purity of their intentions when they went to Oxford. It was
a process that was to be given a bitter edge later when victimization of the products of the 'labour' colleges was often to make

[18] Loc cit.
[19] E. Stonelake, 'Autobiography' (unpublished MS, University College of Swansea
Library), ch. 10, 1–2.
[20] S.W.D.N., 29 Mar. 1906.
[21] Stonelake, op. cit., 2.

it impossible for them to serve their fellow workers in the manner originally intended. Mardy Jones's experience with the Rhondda evening classes committee was perhaps one of the very first incidents of this regrettable phenomenon.

The road to Ruskin College was not easy for the early students from south Wales. The correspondence course scholarships were small, and few could go to the college without making great personal sacrifices. Edmund Stonelake recalls how his wife had to use a 'nest egg' which she had saved over the previous six years in order for him to finish his studies.[22] This was common for married students; Jack Lawson from the north-east of England had to see his wife go into domestic service in Oxford to finance his stay at Ruskin.[23] Even for single men the experience was often a hard one financially. Wil John Edwards was unable to complete his two-year stay at Oxford when his personal savings ran out, and Mardy Jones also had severe financial difficulties whilst at Ruskin College.[24]

These severe financial problems were compounded by the nature of the Oxford 'experience' for these worker-students. Most of the early students seem to have found the time inspiring and uplifting, and the contact with the very different social groups that inhabited the city interesting and enlightening. Yet many students displayed a love–hate attitude towards the place. Stonelake shows this in another comment on his time at Ruskin: 'At Oxford my environment was so changed that I soon realised that there were two distinct worlds on the face of this earth. One, the world of Education, beauty and culture; of music and art; and the other where the working class people just exist ...'[25] W. H. Stevenson, the anthracite miner and Ruskin student, writing in 1906, saw contact with the higher social strata as beneficial. He welcomed the social gatherings at the college, arranged by Lees-Smith, the vice-principal, where the students met sympathetic dons and undergraduates: 'Most of them belong to a higher social grade than ourselves and from them we learn that politeness is not always

[22] Ibid., ch. 7, 3–4.
[23] J. Lawson, *A Man's Life* (London, 1932), 163.
[24] W. J. Edwards, *From the Valley I Came* (London, 1956), 198
[25] Stonelake, op. cit., ch. 7, 1.

a weakness.' Contact with such people, he wrote, widens intellectual horizons and teaches that 'not all the leisured classes are indifferent to schemes for social reform'.[26] It was a viewpoint which would have warmed the heart of men like Mansbridge, Mackenzie and Burrows, and if this outlook was shared by those inclined to go to Ruskin College it augured well for the development of yet another progressive alliance of the mind where 'men of intellect and men of action' amongst the working classes of south Wales would willingly be subject to the 'guidance of the wise'. Yet just as the route to Oxford for such men was being made a little less stony, the atmosphere was beginning to change. A growing tension within the college amongst the teaching staff and between some of the staff and certain students was compounded by the fact that Oxford in the first decade of this century could be a hostile place for politically active members of the working classes. The 'ragging' of socialist and suffragette speakers by the heartier type of undergraduate did not always endear the place to the young men sent there to serve their fellow workers. There were regular running fights between Ruskin students and undergraduates after meetings and demonstrations, when the verbal abuse hurled at the undergraduates was met with physical abuse thrown at the worker-students of Ruskin College.[27] Jack Lawson recalled that he and his fellow students at Ruskin were never allowed to forget that they were in a hostile centre.[28] Stevenson's description of a warm relationship between the worker-students of Ruskin and the university may have been an accurate reflection in 1906, but it was soon to become less valid. Oxford, for many of the 'men of intellect and men of action' from the coalfield, especially those selected by their district committees to attend Ruskin College, soon came to symbolize not some idyllic haven where they could receive an education which they could use to uplift their fellow workers, but a place where their consciousness and commitment could be imbued with ruling

---

[26] *S.W.D.N.*, 29 Mar. 1906.
[27] See Stonelake, op. cit., ch. 7, 16; Hodges, op. cit., 29–32; Edwards, op. cit., 184. Hodges recalls that following a meeting addressed by Keir Hardie, undergraduates laid siege to Ruskin College, smashing all the windows; Ruskin students replied by pouring boiling water over the assailants.
[28] Lawson, op. cit., 163. Lawson also admits that the Ruskin students could be deliberately provocative in their dress and demeanour.

class ideas, to entrench the élite and maintain the existing economic and social order.

2. 'SOME OF THE WILDEST AND MOST REVOLUTIONARY YOUNG MEN IN THE COUNTRY'

Writing about the events which led to the Ruskin College 'strike' of 1909, H. Sanderson Furniss had no doubt about the pivotal role played by a significant number of the student body who were imbued with revolutionary socialist and syndic-alist ideas. Furniss was the lecturer in economics at the college. Appointed in 1908 with an orthodox Oxford education and, by his own admission, possessing the standard outlook of a middle-class liberal of the age, he soon fell foul of several of the south Wales students. They were, he said, '... constantly discussing socialism with me, and their essays were full of criticisms of capitalism, suggestions for its overthrow and schemes for its replacement. In fact I had to spend much of my time in my correction of their essays in pointing out the irrelevance of much that was introduced.'[29] It was the arrival of Furniss as a lecturer in the highly sensitive subject of economics, and the increased friction between him and some of the south Wales students, which seem to have triggered a steady decline in relations between the student body and the college authorities. In this regard Hird's role is ambiguous. He and his lectures, a curious mixture of social Darwinism and Marxism, were undoubtedly popular with the students, especially those whom Furniss described as 'wild' and 'revolutionary'. However, the arrival of Furniss and a new vice-principal, Charles Sydney Buxton, eldest son of a Liberal cabinet minister, whose limited knowledge of his subject and of working-class life matched that of Furniss, seems to have started the process which culminated in the so-called strike of 1909. The former vice-principal, T. I. Mardy Jones's mentor, Lees-Smith, who in 1907 had become Professor of Economics at Bristol, decided to strengthen his influence over Ruskin College, and in his new capacity as chairman of Ruskin's executive committee embarked on a programme of curriculum reform.[30] As these reforms were

[29] H. Sanderson Furniss, *Memories of Sixty Years* (London, 1931), 84, 86, 136.
[30] B. Jennings, 'Revolting students: the Ruskin College dispute, 1908/09', *Studies in Adult Education*, IX (1977), 8–9.

aimed at Hird's teaching and sought to strengthen the teaching of orthodox economic ideas, they were promoted in the teeth of hostility from Hird and the more radical students.

There seems to be little doubt that the new teaching appointments, combined with Lees-Smith's attempts to check Hird's influence over the student body, were key factors in the breakdown in relations that culminated in the 'strike' of 1909. However, there were also deeper factors which transcended personalities. Many of the leading figures on Ruskin's governing council were also leading figures in the W.E.A., and Mansbridge took a keen interest in the college. At the time of the dispute, Mansbridge confided privately his belief that the main cause of the conflict was Hird's deliberate fostering of the students' sense of class-consciousness, which was further embittered by the 'gorgeous panorama ever before them of an Oxford in which they have no part'.[31]

The generation of students who came to Ruskin after 1906 seem to have found the city less enchanting than did their predecessors. The men of Ruskin appear to have adopted a more challenging stance; they were more willing to go down to the Martyrs' Memorial and there harangue undergraduates from a 'higher social grade' about the imminent demise of their class and its rule. Ruskin College students began to earn a reputation in Oxford and outside as revolutionaries and extremists. When some of the south Wales students tried to organize opposition to a S.W.M.F. contribution to the new School of Mines in Pontypridd, they were roundly condemned by the *Western Mail*. They were, said the editorial, advocates of a tyranny of ignorance, 'the blackness of the Middle Ages returning in the gaudy sheen of socialism'.[32] Nor were the students arousing only the hostility of the 'capitalist' press. By the autumn of 1908 complaints were being sent from lodge officials to the Rhondda No. 1 District that Ruskin students were returning to the area and spreading syndicalistic hostility to the Federation and orthodox trade unionism.[33] It was an allegation which the Ruskin men

[33] Ibid., 12.
[32] *Western Mail*, 28 June 1907. The seven students concerned, including Ablett, Gill and Noah Rees, were forced to sign a letter to the *Western Mail* dissociating the college from their campaign against the School of Mines. Ibid., 5 July 1907.
[33] Rhondda No. 1 minutes, 3 Oct., 28 Nov. 1908.

denied, but it did reflect the way in which a number of the students were challenging the assumptions of trade union activity, and it led to the assertion at the time that the Ruskin 'strikers' of 1909 were led or influenced by syndicalist ideas and organizations. That some of the leading figures in the unrest at the college had links with syndicalist groups there is no doubt,[34] but there is no evidence which can sustain the assertion that all the leading figures were under such influence or that these links were the most significant factor in the unrest. What seems to have been of greater importance was the fact that the men attending Ruskin, especially those from south Wales, were imbued with a highly developed sense of class-consciousness and a deep sense of hostility to capitalism, and that they reacted negatively to anything (or anyone) that appeared to be operating in its defence. This trend was undoubtedly reinforced by the careful selection procedures adopted by unions to weed out self-seekers and careerists from those who sought scholarships to Ruskin College.

Even before 1906, the bulk of students attending Ruskin tended to share similar political perspectives. Stevenson, writing in 1906, stated that most of the students were socialists. There was, he wrote, often great difficulty in obtaining a speaker for and against a particular motion in student debates, as there was such unanimity on most of the major political issues of the time. Stevenson also stated that it came as a great shock to new arrivals at Ruskin to be told that there could be two sides to every question.[35] The heightened sense of class-consciousness to which Mansbridge referred is also attested in the memoirs of Wil John Edwards: 'Ruskin men had all been concerned with the class struggle ... it had become part of us and a big enough part to crowd out any suspicion that any of our opponents might have a point of view.'[36]

It is the deep sense of class-consciousness, the abiding anti-capitalist ethos, rather than any strong syndicalist influence

[34] M. G. Woodhouse 'Rank and file movements among the miners of south Wales, 1910–26' (University of Oxford D.Phil. thesis, 1970), 40; B. Holton, *British Syndicalism, 1900–1914*, (London, 1976), 48; see also the entry on Ablett in the *D.L.B.*, vol. III.

[35] *S.W.D.N.*, 29 Mar. 1906; though Jennings suggests that in its earliest years socialist students were very much in the minority at Ruskin. Jennings, op. cit., 6.

[36] Edwards, op. cit., 172.

that is the key to understanding the 1909 'strike' and the origins of independent working-class education. In 1907 there were thirteen south Wales miners in residence at Ruskin College, the largest single regional and occupational grouping amongst the fifty-three students then in residence.[37] Of the thirteen, ten had held offices in the miners' union, some of them substantial posts such as checkweigher, lodge or district secretary. Several were also active with their local trades council and/or were members of a local authority. The south Wales students after 1906 were thus a significant group within the student body: men of experience touched by that spirit of the age which so disturbed Henry Jones. According to Wil John Edwards, the Ruskin men were already so deeply concerned with the class struggle that it bred in them a profound hostility to their class enemies and their apologists in the University of Oxford.

The attitude of the newly appointed staff to the interest and enthusiasm some of the students displayed for Marxist economic and historical theories became another point of tension. The students responded by organizing their own economics classes based on Marx's *Capital*. A key figure in this departure was Noah Ablett,[38] a Rhondda No. 1 District scholarship student whose political development had taken him from considering a career in the Nonconformist ministry to becoming the foremost advocate of independent working-class education (I.W.C.E). Ablett possessed both a powerful personality and a sharp intellect. In Ruskin College he won a number of converts to Marxian economics and history. He also had links, whilst at Oxford, with the syndicalist group, the British Advocates of Industrial Unionism. As the leading figure in the establishment of student-led study groups in Marxian economics, Ablett played a key role in the emergence of a strong body of student opinion hostile to the direction the college appeared to be taking under the influence of Lees-Smith and his protégés, Buxton and Furniss. At the time of the dispute and in subsequent writings on the subject, the role of the

---

[37] Details taken from a list of students resident at Ruskin College in 1907, held at Ruskin College Library and also reproduced in Yorke, op. cit, 38–9. It is not clear how many of the south Wales students were in receipt of district scholarships; only the Rhondda men, four in 1907, were there on a regular scheme.
[38] See entry on Ablett in *D.L.B.*, vol. III.

'revolutionary' and 'syndicalist' students at the college has been emphasized by both supporters and critics of the Ruskin authorities. Whilst it is true that Ablett and some of his close allies were heavily influenced by the new syndicalistic ideas, it is an inadequate explanation to see this as the key factor in the dispute. Most of the students with a political background seem to have been I.L.P. supporters whose attitude towards the classes on Marxism varied from finding them beacons of enlightenment to regarding them as mires of incomprehensibility. One account by a recently returned Ruskin student, published in south Wales at the time of the 1909 dispute, reports students as being 'subjected' to a course of studies on Marx. He wrote that he could think of no more arduous task than 'attempting to wade through a chapter of Marx ... for some students the ordeal would be too much and copies of Marx would be thrown across bedrooms'. [39] Ablett admitted many years later that he had found it initially difficult to overcome the aversion many Ruskin students felt towards Marxian theories. The dismissive and contemptuous attitude of Buxton and Furniss, however, assisted Ablett in this regard, but it was 'the more intractable of the students' who found in Marx an 'efficient armoury' against the professors of orthodox economics and history.[40]

Thus, whilst the 'wild' and 'revolutionary' young men played an important role in the Ruskin dispute, this does not explain why the critics enjoyed support beyond that group in the student body and especially amongst the students sent on scholarships from south Wales. The anonymous student who wrote of copies of Marx being hurled across bedrooms also laid emphasis on conditions at Ruskin before the strike. The students worked an eight- to ten-hour day and had to contribute to the housework of the college.[41] Their perpetual poverty rankled in a city in which the conspicuous wealth of the privileged classes was flaunted. The college year lasted forty-eight weeks, and thus contact was perpetual and petty conflicts

[39] *Llais Llafur*, 5 June 1909.
[40] *[Merthyr] Pioneer*, 28 Apr. 1917.
[41] *Llais Llafur*, 5 June 1909. Tom Evans complained about the excessive amount of housework at the college to the Rhondda No. 1 District. Rhondda No. 1 minutes, 28 Nov. 1909.

were magnified.[42] Above all, the students from south Wales, men of mature years, often married and with extensive trade union experience, resented being treated as if they were adolescents.[43] The critics of the Ruskin authorities were able to focus these feelings of resentment against the university; the feelings of warmth towards the university felt by earlier cohorts changed to simmering resentment by those who came after 1906. Ablett and the critics of the Ruskin authorities found an effective weapon in the suggestion that Ruskin's function as a 'labour' college was being subverted by those who wished to link it more closely with the university.

In the evolution of that set of ideas and principles which added up to 'independent working-class education', the belief that Oxford University was actively seeking to control Ruskin and, by extension, all workers' education became a key element. It was an idea first articulated by Ablett at the conference on Oxford and working-class education held in the summer of 1907. Whilst many of the working-class delegates voiced criticisms of Oxford and other universities for failing to meet the educational needs of the working class, Ablett attacked the motivation of the universities, stating that he and the 'trade unionists whom I represent view the movement with suspicion [Hear! Hear!]. They wonder why the universities have so suddenly come down to help the workers emancipate themselves.'[44] For Ablett and his supporters, the universities in general, and Oxford in particular, were mainly concerned with inculcating ruling-class ideas in the minds of labour leaders at a time when organized labour was about to take on a much more prominent role in the government of the country. Only a break with the universities and all the orthodox agencies of education, especially those funded by the capitalist state, could guarantee that the working class could be educated for emancipation. In this regard, Marxist economics and history played a key role in virtually guaranteeing that the education was geared to the needs of the working

[42] Furniss, op. cit., 86–7.
[43] Rhondda No 1 minutes, 27 Jan. 1908.
[44] Minutes of the Joint Oxford Conference on the Education of Workpeople, 10 Aug. 1907, held at W.E.A. headquarters, Temple House, London. Ablett was listed as representing Ruskin College's Marxian Society.

class, as no agency of capitalist indoctrination could tolerate Marxism on the curriculum. Marx in the curriculum took on an almost talismanic quality, an 'efficient armoury' against the 'plausible arguments of those trained scholars' who could so easily seduce the intelligent working-class activist away from the true path of emancipation. Thus, in the minds of the supporters of I.W.C.E., the defence of Ruskin as a 'labour' college and the defence of Marx in the curriculum were inextricably bound together.

Whilst there is no concrete evidence that the university, or any part of it, was seeking to subvert Ruskin, Ablett found in the Oxford conference and the subsequent report ample evidence of a conspiracy. The limited links being proposed by Lees-Smith and others were further proof, but the enforced resignation of Dennis Hird was the last straw and triggered the boycott of lectures which became known as the Ruskin College strike. The supporters of I.W.C.E., now joined together in the Plebs League, founded in the autumn of 1908 with the stated aim of ensuring an effective link between organized labour and Ruskin College, were able to appear as the defenders of Ruskin College's position as a 'labour' college against those who wished to link it more closely with the university. The Ruskin authorities were portrayed as the aggressors, the innovators, and the Plebs supporters as the custodians of the 'labour' college. It was a stance Ablett and his allies were to exploit to great effect in the years to come.

The simmering discontent at Ruskin was known about in trade union circles in south Wales well before the outbreak of the 'strike'. As early as January 1908, Noah Rees and John Evans, the first Rhondda No. 1 District scholars, told their district of the need for the trade union movement and the miners in particular to 'capture' the college to ensure that the teachers and the subjects taught were sympathetic to the labour movement.[45] In May 1908 Mardy Jones paid a visit to the college and heard the fears of the south Wales students that it faced a take-over by the university.[46] By October 1908 the Rhondda No. 1. District was told that there was 'practically a strike' at

[45] Rhondda No. 1 minutes, 27 Jan. 1908.
[46] S.W.D.N., 27 Apr. 1909.

the college, with students boycotting certain lectures and refusing to take examinations.[47] Furniss became the focus of complaints to the district by the scholars at Ruskin, who demanded a 'better teacher' of economics and one who would teach 'economics of a more advanced kind'.[48] By the end of 1908 the issues which were to be highlighted during the 'strike', and subsequently in the debates over the creation of a new 'labour' college, were already being discussed in lodges and districts of the S.W.M.F. The depth of conflict within Ruskin by the end of 1908 was highlighted in the Rhondda No. 1. District by receipt of college reports on Ablett and Tom Evans, who were described as insubordinate and as unsatisfactory in their work. Initially, the district was willing to dismiss the reports as the product of a deep personality clash between Ablett and Furniss; even the district's 'honorary' agent, the Lib-Lab M.P. William Abraham, 'Mabon', saw it in these terms.[49] As the two students were about to complete their stay at Ruskin, the matter might have lapsed. However, in February 1909, the district received a letter from Hird dissociating himself from the adverse reports on Ablett and Evans and praising both men; there was also a letter signed by fourteen second-year Ruskin students defending and supporting Ablett and Evans.[50] Both letters referred to the issues of principle involved in the conflict; thus explanations which seemed to see the matter simply as a personality clash were no longer tenable; the debate was about Ruskin's status as a 'labour' college and the nature and content of the teaching in a true 'labour' college.

The south Wales branch of the Plebs League was founded at a meeting in the York Hotel in Cardiff on 2 January 1909.[51] The League had been created by dissident Ruskin students a few months earlier to 'bring about a definite and more satisfactory connection between Ruskin College and the labour move-

---

[47] Rhondda No. 1 minutes, 3 Oct. 1908.

[48] Letter to Rhondda No. 1 District from Ablett, Tom Evans and John Evans, read into Rhondda No. 1 District minutes, 5 Jan. 1909.

[49] Ibid.

[50] Rhondda No. 1 minutes, 22 Feb. 1909.

[51] Plebs (February 1909). Present were past and present students of Ruskin College, including Ablett, Gill, T. Evans, W. H. Stevenson, A. Jenkins, W. Davies, S. Morgan and W. W. Craik. Ablett was elected chairman, with Evans as secretary.

ment'.[52] To facilitate this objective, local branches were to be established by former students and sympathizers and, through the publication of the *Plebs* magazine, the most important and influential organ of the movement for independent working-class education, a national campaign for I.W.C.E. was begun. It was in the first editions of the magazine that Ablett and another former south Wales Ruskin student, Ted Gill, laid down the priciples of the I.W.C.E. movement. Ablett's contribution is well known and much quoted. In the article in the first edition of the *Plebs*, Ablett denounced any links with the universities, which he portrayed as purveyors of capitalist ideas. He also stressed the central need for a residential college to create a cadre of trained activists, men 'scientifically trained' with a knowledge of 'labour economics' and 'the ability of speech and pen'. For, Ablett contended, in the 'present loose democracy of the trade unions, individuals count for much'.[53] In seeking to appreciate Ablett's role and contribution to the development of the I.W.C.E. movement, it is necessary to understand the centrality of his commitment to the residential college and his belief in the need for such an institution in the creation of an élite of leaders and teachers who would apprise the workers of their historical mission to challenge and overthrow the capitalist system. Ablett wrote of how this group would 'naturally be expected to wield great influence in their respective localities. Gathered together in a little community for one or two years; the inter-change of ideas, the various methods of improving conditions; the lessons to be learned by successes and failures; these things constitute advantages of too great and unique a character to be overlooked.'[54] In putting forward the case for a residential college, Ablett was, of course, also criticizing the shortcomings of the existing union leadership. What he wanted was a new leadership imbued with a new world view, one which saw capitalism not as something from which to seek concessions but something to be challenged and overthrown. A true 'labour' college would assist in the emergence of this new leadership ethos; the existing regime

---

[52] Craik, op. cit., 60–3.
[53] *Plebs* (Feb. 1909).
[54] Loc. cit.

at Ruskin was geared to perpetuating the ideals of collaboration with capitalism, and therefore either that regime had to
be removed or a new institution had to be created.

In seeking to understand why so many of the south Wales
students supported Ablett's view about the nature of a true
'labour' college whilst few of them shared his more advanced
perceptions, it is perhaps more useful to look at the views of
Ted Gill. Gill, a scholarship student at Ruskin from the Western Valleys Miners' Council of Monmouthshire, had, like
Ablett, just completed his stay at Oxford. He always rejected
the idea that syndicalist ideas had played any significant role
in the troubles at the college, and instead he stressed the failures of the Ruskin authorities to ensure that the education provided met the needs of the working-class student. In an article
in the second edition of the *Plebs* magazine, Gill gave a revealing insight into why he supported the break with Ruskin and
the creation of the I.W.C.E. movement. He suggested that
much of the existing tuition tended to deny the reality of the
class struggle and the reality of deep divisions in society. He
argued that the 'Grecian' or Idealist philosophy which underpinned much of the Ruskin and the W.E.A. teaching was at
best irrelevant, or was intended to mask the class bias of the universities and what they propagated. 'The working-class student', wrote Gill, 'has no time to listen to the elaborate
apologies made on behalf of the oppressing class. Neither has
he time to listen to effusions on the weaknesses of his own
class.' What was required was knowledge of the 'social forces
operating in society, and how best they can be utilised for the
benefit of the people'. The theories of men who 'dedicated
their lives to the Workers' cause, should be interpreted to him
in a sympathetic and efficient manner'.[55] This was a clear
assault on the Ruskin curriculum as it was being recast by
Lees-Smith, and also on the teaching styles of Furniss and Buxton. It clearly displays the hostility the south Wales students felt
towards what they sensed to be Ruskin's shortcomings as a
'labour' college. Its prime function was to assist in the perfection of organized labour, not the intellectual development of
individuals drawn from the labour movement. For the work-

[55] *Plebs* (Mar. 1909).

ing-class student, wrote Gill, the 'workings of his own organization should be his special interest in order to detect possible
defects, the removal of which would lead to greater unity'.[56]

Gill's article is important because it came from someone who
was in the mainstream of the south Wales labour movement,
unlike Ablett, whose syndicalist links and sympathies placed
him at its most advanced reaches. It gives clues as to why so
many activists within the Federation were prepared to countenance a break with Ruskin when news of Hird's enforced resignation arrived in south Wales. Hird's stock amongst trade
unionists and I.L.P. activists there was high, following a tour
of the area he conducted in the early spring of 1909, and it
was reinforced by the activities of Plebs supporters in the coalfield. Thus the actual dismissal came as a profound shock.

The lecture boycott, which was originally designed to secure
Hird's reinstatement, soon changed into a campaign for the
creation of a new 'labour' college to which trade unions would
transfer their allegiance. The Plebs League and its organ now
became the co-ordinating agency for this demand, and its leading lights in south Wales became preoccupied with this issue as
the question of Hird's dismissal changed from whether he
deserved reinstatement to whether the action of the Ruskin
authorities justified a break with that institution and the creation of a new 'labour' college. The idea of a new college seems to
have been under discussion prior to the 'strike'. At the March
meeting of the Rhondda Plebs, a proposal to establish a
'Plebs' college in south Wales had been discussed.[57] No details
as to the nature of such an institution were given, but it indicates that a break with Ruskin was already being contemplated before Hird's removal.

It was the proposal to create a new 'labour' college which
actually triggered the 'civil war' in British workers' education
that was to drag on for the next fifty years. At the outset the
centre of this conflict was Oxford, where two rival colleges
vied for the support of the organized working class. However,
the real theatre of war was to be found in the industrial
areas, and in 1909 the most important battlefield was the south

[56] Ibid. See also W. H. Seed, *The Burning Question of Education* (Oxford, 1909), 7.
[57] *Plebs* (Apr. 1909).

Wales coalfield. The S.W.M.F. was big enough to make or break any new college, and both sides knew this. Great efforts were made by each to convince the districts of the Federation of the righteousness of its cause. South Wales was already being cited in the press as the stronghold of the Plebs League, and it was reported that five branches of the League were already in existence, three in the Rhondda, one at Aberdare and another at Blaenavon, all the home areas of some of the returned students.[58] Support for a break with Ruskin and the establishment of a new 'labour' college was strong amongst the cohort of students that attended Ruskin on Federation money after 1906. This was to prove a significant factor in weakening Ruskin's position in the Federation, for these men, selected for their commitment to the Federation and its work, questioned Ruskin's credentials and effectiveness as a 'labour' college. In addition, from the early stages of the conflict, the advocates of a break enjoyed the active support of two miners' agents, the very influential full-time officials of the districts, James Winstone and George Barker of the western and eastern valleys of Monmouthshire respectively.[59] Both men were I.L.P. supporters and were regarded, at the time, as being politically the most advanced of the full-time officers of the Federation, but the very fact of their public support was crucial to the Plebs campaign. For it was one thing to secure condemnation of Hird's dismissal;[60] it was quite another to persuade the districts to switch their allegiance to a new 'labour' college. The conflict inevitably provided ammunition for those who opposed, or were sceptical about, using union money for scholarships in the first place.[61]

For Ruskin College the problem was different. Unlike the

[58] S.W.D.N., 9 Apr. 1909.

[59] Ibid., 14 Apr. 1909. It was reported that at a meeting of the South Wales Plebs group held on 10 Apr. 1909, both Barker and Winstone declared their support for a new college, with Hird at its head.

[60] Reports of Hird's enforced resignation appeared in the south Wales press on 30 Mar. 1909. The first response was a resolution demanding his reinstatement, passed by the Mid-Rhondda Trades and Labour Council on 2 Apr. 1909. Similar resolutions were passed by various bodies in the region in the following weeks. S.W.D.N., 30 Mar., 1909, 3 Apr. 1909; Rhondda Leader, 10 Apr. 1909; Free Press of Monmouthshire, 23 Apr. 1909; South Wales Weekly Argus, 10 Apr. 1909.

[61] Because of the adverse reports on Ablett and Evans, the Rhondda No. 1 District had delayed a decision on whether or not to send more students to Ruskin. Thus, ironically, no Rhondda students took part in the 'strike'.

Plebs League, Ruskin did not have a tightlyknit body of active supporters in the coalfield. The activities of the Ruskin authorities seem to have alienated the majority of those sent there on district scholarships, none of whom seems openly to have backed the authorities during the 'strike'. Some non-scholarship south Wales students did stay loyal, but their chief weapon in the coalfield was T. I. Mardy Jones, the protégé of Hird's deadly rival, Lees-Smith, who seems to have been in close contact with the Ruskin authorities throughout the period of the dispute.

W. W. Craik, in his account of the 'strike', argued that the decision by the Ruskin authorities to send students home on an enforced fortnight's holiday was crucial to the creation of a new college because it allowed the malcontents to engage in propaganda in their home areas at a crucial time.[62] In fact, the influence of the 'strikers' was not critical in south Wales. It was the returned ex-students, in particular Ablett and Gill, who played the key role in promoting the idea of a new college.

The focal point of the dispute was the Rhondda No. 1 District, the biggest and richest in the coalfield. It was also where the chief advocate of the new college, Noah Ablett, and the chief spokesman for the Ruskin authorities, T. I. Mardy Jones, were based. The South Wales Plebs League, with Ablett as its chairman, had the bulk of its supporters in the district, and it enjoyed the support of all the ex-district students at Ruskin including Noah Rees, Tom Evans and John Evans. It also enjoyed vocal support from some of the younger and more militant delegates to the district meetings, such as George Dolling, who happened to be the chairman of the district in the early part of 1909.

Mardy Jones had less direct support, but he enjoyed the sympathy of some of the older delegates, such as Councillor W. H. Morgan, and he could play on the hostility displayed towards the syndicalistic ideas of Ablett and some of his allies. Also, the district agent, D. Watts Morgan, played a rather ambivalent role during the debates over the proposed new college. Less than sympathetic to Ablett and Tom Evans over the bad reports from Ruskin the previous year, he refused to allow the

---

[62] Craik, op. cit., 78.

issues of Hird's dismissal and support for the new college to be separated after Ablett had, in a tactical blunder, linked them early in the dispute.[63] Watts Morgan was later induced to join the Plebs League and was even invited to chair the founding conference of the Labour College, which he declined because the district had yet to decide whether to support the new college; the invitation was a blatant attempt to bounce the district into backing the Central Labour College.[64]

The personal duel between Ablett and Mardy Jones—for that is what it became—started on 19 April 1909 at the monthly meeting of the Rhondda No. 1. District at Porth. It was at this meeting that an attempt to condemn Hird's dismissal was linked with an attempt to secure the support of the district for a new college. As the agent immediately pointed out, this proposal raised a number of new issues. Besides that, the Ruskin authorities had written to the district with their side of the dispute and countered the most damaging accusations about links with the university and of removing relevant subjects from the curriculum of the college. Ablett, however, used the occasion to attack the Ruskin case. He cited the alleged removal of sociology from the curriculum as evidence of the attempt to subvert Ruskin as a 'labour' college. The student body had resisted this change and now the Ruskin authorities were seeking to remove the teacher of sociology which, he stated, 'gives from a scientific standpoint the causes of poverty, and helps us find a remedy'.[65] Hird's removal was yet more evidence of the attempt to link Ruskin with Oxford University. After a few testy exchanges between Ablett and Watts Morgan, the meeting decided, in line with usual practice, to refer the matter to the lodges. The spring and summer of 1909 saw Ablett and Mardy Jones debating the issue before the lodges of the district and in the letter columns of the local and regional press. The debate tended to focus on the action of the Ruskin authorities, whether they were justified in removing Hird and whether these actions reflected a desire to tie the college more closely to the university, and thereby undermine

---

[63] Rhondda No. 1 minutes, 19 Apr. 1909.
[64] *Plebs* (Sept. 1908).
[65] Rhondda No. 1 minutes, 19 Apr. 1909.

Ruskin's claim to be a 'labour' college. Only occasionally did the deeper issues over the nature, purpose and content of workers' education intrude into the recriminatory ramblings that appeared in the press.

Mardy Jones was from the outset in close touch with the Ruskin authorities and in particular with Lees-Smith, whom he visited at Bristol on several occasions, even claiming travelling expenses from the Ruskin authorities for these trips. He told the secretary of Ruskin College, Bertram Wilson, that 'South Wales was being made the cock-pit of the dispute'.[66] Mardy Jones made it clear in correspondence with Wilson that his links with the college should not be made known in the coalfield; though Ablett suggested on several occasions that Mardy Jones was just a 'front man' for the Ruskin authorities.

These contacts proved invaluable for Mardy Jones, as he was able to counter specific allegations and cast doubt on others, seriously weakening Ablett's case against Ruskin. One notable example was the 'Winterstoke affair'. In order to prove that Hird's dismissal was part of a long-term plot to link Ruskin more closely with the university and to make its curriculum more acceptable to wealthy benefactors, Ablett claimed that the heir to the Wills tobacco fortune, Lord Winterstoke, had offered £10,000 to the college if the necessary changes were made. This offer was made, Ablett alleged, through Winterstoke's daughter who was married to Sanderson Furniss, the much-disliked economics lecturer at Ruskin.[67] If true, this story would be very damaging to the Ruskin authorities. But unfortunately for Ablett there was one serious flaw in the tale which undermined the whole claim: Furniss was not married to Winterstoke's daughter.[68] There was no other evidence that such an offer was ever made, and so the whole story rebounded on Ablett and his allies.

The debates, particularly in the press, soon degenerated into

---

[66] Mardy Jones to Wilson, 27 Apr. 1909. Evidence for these contacts is contained in a collection of letters from Mardy Jones to the secretary of Ruskin College, Bertram Wilson, held in Ruskin College Library. Mardy Jones to B. Wilson, 3, 5, 10, 25 May 1909.

[67] Rhondda No. 1 minutes, 19 Apr. 1909.

[68] Ibid., 24 May 1909; Furniss, op. cit., 93–4. Furniss believed that Hird might have started this particular rumour.

a series of highly personalized attacks, Ablett even denouncing Mardy Jones's F.R.E.S. as a badge of 'hopeless orthodoxy' in economic thought.[69] Mardy Jones responded by pointing out that this honour was held by such notable socialists as Ramsay MacDonald, a more useful rebuttal in 1909 than it would have been just over twenty years later.[70] Mardy Jones, by exposing the factual errors in the case made by Ablett and his allies, was able to obscure the substance of their criticism of the Ruskin authorities. At the May meeting of the Rhondda No. 1 District, both Ablett and Mardy Jones were present, and Mardy Jones seems to have won the debate on points, the issue being referred back to the lodges.[71] Again in July the issue came up at the district meeting and again Mardy Jones successfully argued for delay. Following the July meeting, Mardy Jones wrote to Bertram Wilson confident that he would 'vindicate the case for Ruskin College by a handsome majority of Lodge votes in the final decision'.[72] His judgement was premature but not totally ill-founded. It was not until January 1910 that the issue was settled. It went to a card vote, and Ruskin won a narrow victory, but later it was found that two delegates had voted against their lodge mandate, and so a compromise was agreed by which one student would be sent to Ruskin and another to the newly founded Central Labour College.[73] It was not until the summer of 1911, by which time Mardy Jones had been appointed electoral registration agent for the Federation districts of the Rhondda and Aberdare and his energies had been redirected, that Ablett and his allies finally persuaded the district to break completely with Ruskin College.[74]

Ablett's strategy had been to avoid direct discussion about the ideological dimension of the dispute with the Ruskin authorities, and instead to seek to portray the latter as the aggressors

[69] *S.W.D.N.*, 4 May 1909.
[70] Ibid., 11, 17 May 1909.
[71] Rhondda No. 1 minutes, 24 May 1909.
[72] Mardy Jones to Wilson, 13 July 1909.
[73] Rhondda No. 1. minutes, 10 January 1910; *Plebs* (February 1910). By the summer of 1909 many district delegates were already becoming irritated by the dispute. One, only half jokingly, even proposed the abolition of all education, a statement which was met with sympathetic laughter. Ibid., 14 June 1909.
[74] *Llais Llafur*, 24 July 1909. Noah Ablett replaced his rival as checkweigher for Maerdy colliery; Rhondda No. 1 minutes, 12 Sept. 1911.

and the Ruskin rebels as the defenders of the labour interest.
Mardy Jones found it relatively easy to counter the detailed
allegations and then to play on the fund of ill-will which Ablett
and his allies had created in the previous couple of years over
the mining school, the bad reports incident and their syndicalistic utterances. Both Ablett and Mardy Jones were guilty of
trivializing the debates and, instead of confronting the issue
of the nature and purpose of workers' education, engaged in
a campaign of denunciation and distortion. It was, however,
eloquent testimony to Ablett's belief that in the 'loose democracy' of the miners' union 'individuals counted for much.'
The issue was ultimately resolved by the vagaries of personality, popularity and by whoever happened to turn up to the district meetings. Mardy Jones narrowly won the debates, but
Ablett eventually won the argument and, almost by accident,
the district, believing it was supporting a 'labour' college,
became committed to independent working-class education.

Despite mid-Rhondda's reputation as a hotbed of Plebs League activity, the first victory for the new Central Labour College came in the western valleys of Monmouthshire. The key
figure here was Ted Gill who, like Ablett, had just returned
from Ruskin College and was busy re-establishing himself in
the ranks of local union activists. A shrewd operator, not
tainted by any hints of unorthodoxy, he displayed tactical judgement superior to Ablett's by securing a condemnation of
Hird's dismissal before raising the issue of the new college. In
April the Western Valleys District passed a resolution con-
demning Hird's enforced resignation. Gill persuaded the district that Hird's resignation threatened Ruskin's status as a
'labour' college and that, in the words of the resolution that
was passed, 'it would be little short of a calamity in the cause
of the workers to in any way link Ruskin College with the University, as only to the degree that the students were encouraged
to return to their ordinary work and become teachers among
their fellow workmen the College justified its existence'.[75] Gill
shrewdly played on the anxiety that the union might be spending money to facilitate the social mobility of a few members
rather than the interests of the wider membership. He then

[75] *South Wales Weekly Argus*, 10 Apr. 1909.

engaged in a clever campaign in the local press to denigrate the
Ruskin authorities by eulogizing Hird as a firm but kind head
of the college and a faithful friend of organized labour.[76] So
effective were Gill's tactics that even the Lib-Lab M.P. and
an agent for the district, William Brace, denounced Hird's dismissal; Hird was, in Brace's words, a person who had '. . . laid
himself out to teach the students their duty to their fellow workers under the title of sociology'.[77] To the accusation that he
seemed to be supporting the creation of a socialist college he
gave the emphatic reply, 'I am not, nor ever have been a socialist to my knowledge.'[78] Gill had successfully separated the issue
of the content of the teaching from the purpose of the teaching,
and the Western Valleys District drifted into support for the
new college and of I.W.C.E. without debating the deeper
issues involved. Thus, in a personal triumph for Gill, the district voted unanimously in June 1909 to support the new college.[79] Gill had certain advantages over Ablett. He did not
have any effective opposition within the district, he did not
have a reputation for making syndicalistic noises, and he had
the open support of the district agent, George Barker, a socialist anxious to court advanced opinion amongst the rank and
file.

The decision of the Western Valleys District horrified the
Ruskin authorities; they feared it was a precedent which would
trigger an avalanche of support from other districts. An urgent
appeal went out from the Ruskin authorities for an opportunity
to put their case before the district. The request was granted.[80]
It resulted in the only public confrontation in the dispute
between Hird and representatives of the executive committee
that dismissed him.

Prior to the confrontation, the Ruskin authorities launched a
campaign in the local press against the rebels and their allies. It
was quite different in tone from the campaign conducted in the
Rhondda by Mardy Jones, which rested on his ability to expose

[76] South Wales Gazette, 23 Apr. 1909.
[77] Free Press of Monmouthshire, 25 June 1909.
[78] Western Mail, 12 May 1909.
[79] South Wales Weekly Argus, 12 June 1909; Plebs (July 1909). Both Brace and Barker
were present.
[80] South Wales Gazette, 2 July 1909.

and ridicule the faults in the Plebs supporters' case. A loyal Ruskin student by the name of O. T. Hopkins (of whom little is known) wrote a series of letters to the press accusing the Plebs supporters of being syndicalists and supporters of the I.W.W.[81] They were, wrote Hopkins, hostile to orthodox trade unionism. When the attempt to portray Gill as a wild-eyed revolutionary did not seem to find any resonance amongst the district delegates, a circular was put round the district, apparently from the loyal Ruskin students, accusing Hird of inducing the students to strike and of preaching a 'dogmatic atheism' which offended the religious sensibilities of many Ruskin students.[82]

The extent to which Mardy Jones had a hand in these tactics is unknown; he certainly advised Lees-Smith and Wilson on how to handle the issue in the coalfield. [83] And he was present at the meeting between Hird and C. W. Bowerman M.P., who represented the Ruskin executive, held at the Tillery Institute in Abertillery on Monday, 26 July 1909. In addition to Bowerman and Mardy Jones, from the college there were two loyal Ruskin students by the names of R. Bowman and T. H. Haywood, who were soon criticized for the circular and the accusations contained within it, which they repeated at the meeting. Bowerman restated the charges against Hird. Hird, however, handled the meeting with great aplomb, ridiculing many of the sillier charges against him, for example, that he encouraged students to sing 'The Red Flag', which brought laughter from the delegates present. When the meeting was thrown open to contributions from the floor, it was quite evident that the meeting had gone Hird's way, and it was no surprise when some time later the district confirmed its earlier decision.[84]

The debate over the Ruskin 'strike' and the creation of a new labour college continued in the coalfield well into the autumn and winter. The anthracite miners transferred their allegiance

[81] Ibid., 9 July 1909; *Free Press of Monmouthshire*, 25 June 1909. The American-based Industrial Workers of the World was the leading syndicalist organization in the English-speaking world.

[82] *Free Press of Monmouthshire*, 13 Aug. 1909.

[83] Mardy Jones to Wilson, 22, 24 July 1909, loc. cit.

[84] *South Wales Gazette*, 30 July, 3 Sept. 1909.

to the C.L.C. in September,[85] but the eastern valley miners, despite the support of Winstone, declined to send a student to either college, as did the Blaenavon miners.[86] This was hardly a ringing endorsement for the 'strikers' and the new college. The 'strikers' had portrayed the new college as a 'labour' not a socialist college, and certainly not a syndicalist college. The commitment to I.W.C.E. was very shallow; the western valley miners appeared to have no difficulty in agreeing, at the same meeting, to send Frank Hodges to the C.L.C. and to affiliate to the south Wales W.E.A.[87]

Whilst Furniss felt that the 'strike' and its aftermath sprang from the influence of a group of extreme socialist agitators, many of them from the south Wales coalfield and resident at Ruskin at the time of his appointment, it is less the influence of this relatively small number of men but rather the alienation of the slightly wider group of trade union activists, such as Ted Gill, that is the real key to understanding the 'strike' and the creation of the new labour college. The insensitive treatment of their ideas, the dismissive way in which their anxieties about what appeared to be moves to draw Ruskin College closer to the university and further from the trade union movement were treated, was the real cause of the conflict. Lees-Smith, Buxton and Furniss inadvertently did much to create a demand for 'independent' working-class education amongst the rank and file activists sent to Ruskin from the south Wales coalfield after 1906. It is significant that the generation of activists carefully selected by their districts for Ruskin College were already converts to independent political action by organized labour; it required only a small dose of insensitivity to convert these men to independence in the sphere of workers' education. Possessing already a generalized and often unfocused hostility to the prevailing capitalist economic system, they were willing to be convinced that organized labour needed to break free from the ideological underpinnings of that system. Though they may not have accepted, or even understood, the full-blown Marxian critique of capitalism, it was accessible, and

[85] *Llais Llafur*, 11 Sept. 1909.
[86] Blaenavon District minute book, 24 Nov. 1909. Held at University College of Swansea library.
[87] *South Wales Argus*, 30 Oct. 1909.

its teaching could be seen to reinforce the credentials of a truly independent 'labour' college. The rise of an anti-capitalist ethos amongst labour activists was already a trigger for action in the sphere of workers' education by progressively minded academics. This concern was to be given a further boost in the years between the Ruskin College 'strike' and the outbreak of the First World War, when a well-reported upsurge of trade union militancy was seen to be connected with the spread of a particularly virulent form of anti-capitalist ideology amongst labour activists, especially in the south Wales coalfield.

3. THE BRAINS BEHIND THE LABOUR REVOLT?

As the products of the Central Labour College returned to the coalfield, they were acutely aware that they were living through a period of unprecedented trade union militancy. Whilst statistically it is possible to show that the period between 1911 and 1914 was not, at least as far as south Wales is concerned, characterized by any significant increase in the scale of industrial unrest,[88] contemporary observers were convinced that something qualitatively different was taking place in the industrial life of Britain generally and in the storm centre of the south Wales coalfield in particular. This unrest was also characterized by social violence, the incidents at Tonypandy/ Llwynypia in November 1910 and Llanelli in August 1911, when strikers were killed, being the most gruesome examples. It was also noted that the militancy reflected the emergence of a new breed of labour activist imbued with a mental outlook which challenged not just the economic, social and political hegemony of the capitalist system but its intellectual domination as well. For many contemporary observers, and for many historians since, this was one of the most intriguing features of the period. It was also, for some, the most disturbing. Any assessment of the actual impact of Independent Working-Class Education (I.W.C.E.) on the leadership of the miners is, however, bedevilled by a legacy of contemporary and subsequent evaluations which tend to see the close involvement of those

---

[88] See D. R. Hopkin 'The great unrest in Wales, 1910–1913: questions of evidence' in D. R. Hopkin and G. S. Kealey (eds.), op. cit., 249–75.

associated with the Labour College movement with the Cambrian Combine dispute, the Unofficial Reform Committee, the S.W.M.F. centralization campaign and, above all, with the publication of *The Miners' Next Step*, as evidence that they were a force of profound significance in the rising militancy of the period.[89]

The Cambrian Combine dispute, of which the Tonypandy/ Llwynypia disturbances were part, exposed for many young activists the true nature of capitalism and the capitalist state. Declining productivity and new methods of cost accounting led to a more robust attitude towards man-management by the coal owners, triggering a bitter conflict in the Rhondda Valley and other parts of the coalfield, which was to last for a year and involve up to 30,000 strikers. It ended in bloodshed, and a community scarred by social conflict. The use of the police and the army to protect the property of the coal owners gave substance, in the eyes of many young activists, to the idea that the coercive powers of the state existed only for the benefit of the capitalist class. Class-war rhetoric suddenly seemed to express the realities of life in the Rhondda, both in the mines and in the wider community, rather more eloquently than the vocabulary of conciliation still used by the Lib-Labs and progressives.[90] Among those who rose to prominence during the Cambrian Combine dispute were Noah Rees, the ex-Ruskin ally of Ablett, and W. H. Mainwaring, later to be a C.L.C. scholar and lecturer. But the links between the advocates of direct action and workers' control, the 'syndicalist' element in the militancy, and the Labour College movement have tended to obscure the deeper significance of the I.W.C.E. movement in the coalfield. The Labour College classes helped to change the way that many activists within the mining union viewed their position, but most were not converts to syndicalism. One recent study has called in question the hitherto assumed reality of the sense of relative impoverishment, of

[89] A classic contemporary example is Rowland Kenney's 'The brains behind the labour revolt', *English Review*, March 1912, 691–4. Recent examples can be found in Bob Holton, *British Syndicalism* (London, 1976), 168–70; R. Challinor, *The Origins of British Bolshevism* (London, 1977), 115–17.

[90] For an assessment of the deeper social significance of the Tonypandy disturbances, see D. Smith, 'Tonypandy 1910: definitions of community', *Past and Present*, No. 87 (1980), 158–84.

declining real earnings and worsening conditions of employment among the miners of south Wales. Such beliefs, it is argued, cannot be sustained by the quantitative evidence available; they were illusions. That the miners of south Wales had such feelings reflects 'the consequence of the changing socio-political filters through which miners viewed the contemporary distribution of income and wealth'.[91] Explanations of the militancy of the 1910–14 period that focus on declining real wages and declining productivity are inadequate if they do not take account also of the role of ideas, ideology and consciousness. The development of the Labour College movement, one of the changing 'socio-political filters' in industrial south Wales, can be seen as both a symptom and a contributory cause of this rising consciousness. The world view of many young, active trade unionists in the coalfield was being framed by the C.L.C. and its local classes. Yet the outlook that was produced was not uniform; it certainly was not consistently 'syndicalistic' or hostile to political action. The only consistent theme was that it gave its students a 'scientific' critique of capitalism, and thus helped to create and reinforce the increasingly anti-capitalist ethos of the south Wales labour movement. The trend towards capitalist combination, and what appeared to be related attempts to erode the conditions of work in the pits, invested with realism the theoretical critique of capitalism taught by the Labour College classes. But more importantly, the Cambrian Combine dispute marked the point at which the ideas which bubbled out of the C.L.C., and its local classes, began to be absorbed by what one historian has called the 'secondary leaders' of the unions,[92] the branch secretaries and the lodge committee men. They were the key element between the rank and file and the organization's main leadership: the people who made the organizations actually work. It was this element which was to perform a key role in opinion formation among the rank and file, and it was here that the rising anti-capitalist ethos, reinforced by the I.W.C.E. classes, was to have its most abiding effect.

[91] R. Church, 'Edwardian labour unrest and coalfield militancy, 1890–1914', *The Historical Journal*, 30, No. 4 (1987), 850.
[92] D. Smith, 'What does history know of nail biting?' *Llafur*, 1, No. 2 (1973), 35.

As in the opening years of the century, the widespread belief
amongst trade unionists in the value of education to the labour
movement remained strong. Some local union leaders, especially those whose commitment to independent labour representation led them to challenge the supremacy of the older
Lib-Lab officials of the S.W.M.F., were happy to associate
with the products of the C.L.C. In the process they tended to
lionize and overstate the role these men had played and were
playing in the development of a more militant stance by the
union. Typical of such figures were miners' agents like George
Barker, James Winstone, C. B. Stanton and Vernon Hartshorn.
Hartshorn, a figure of respectable Labour orthodoxy by the
early inter-war years, was regarded as a socialist militant by
Liberal critics in the pre-war era. He was perhaps the most
successful of the new generation of miners' agents in combining
many of the leadership values of the old Labourists with the
socialist and class solidaristic vocabulary of the new Labourism.[93] In 1910, echoing in some ways Ablett's belief in the
need to create a cadre of trained and educated union leaders,
Hartshorn suggested that the S.W.M.F. should establish an
education department. This department would organize
classes in which ordinary rank and file members would be
taught, by union officers and officials, as a normal part of
their job, that it was a social and moral duty to their families
and fellow workers to be active trade unionists.[94] In 1911
Hartshorn claimed that Dennis Hird was the 'real creator,
the silent worker behind the scenes of the great changes
wrought in the opinions of the miners of South Wales'.[95] In
1912 Hartshorn invited Ted Gill and Frank Hodges to share
the platform with him at a mass meeting of Maesteg miners,
at which they were introduced by him as 'young men keenly
interested in the welfare of the workers and brimming with
enthusiasm for the workers' cause'. The two men delivered
talks which called for a more class-orientated industrial policy
for the Federation, and the need for the workers to have a

[93] P. Stead, 'Working class leadership in south Wales, 1900–1920' *The Welsh History Review*, 6, No. 3 (1973) 339–40. See also *idem*. 'Vernon Hartshorn: miners' agent and cabinet minister', in S. Williams (ed.), *Glamorgan Historian*, 6 (1969), 83–94.
[94] *Llais Llafur*, 9 July 1910.
[95] Ibid., 18 Nov. 1911.

theoretical understanding of their position.[96] What is significant, and what seemed significant to astute contemporary
observers, was that the language, the rhetoric of class
struggle and historical materialism, became a commonplace
of Federation platforms. This does not mean that all the
listeners, or even a large number of them, fully understood
or agreed with the ideas of the platform, but it was now not
seen as out of place for such ideas to be presented on such
occasions.[97] It was the willingness of men such as Hartshorn
to collaborate with that new generation of Labour College
advocates that convinced many contemporary observers
that this was the key to what was different about the
industrial strife of the years just prior to the First World
War. Yet, despite the conviction among many contemporary
observers and later writers that the south Wales coalfield, the
'industrial cockpit' of Britain in the 1910–14 period, was also
the throbbing heart of the I.W.C.E. movement, the story of
the Labour College movement is one of limited achievement
overlaid by a perpetual struggle for survival.

From the moment of its creation to the day that it finally
closed its doors, the Central Labour College was utterly
dependent on support from the miners of south Wales. If Ted
Gill had not succeeded in persuading the western valley miners
to support the college it is quite possible that the whole scheme
would have collapsed at the outset. Ruskin College, quickly
learning the lesson of the 'strike', reformed itself, formalized
its links with organized labour and distanced itself from the
university sufficiently to make it credible as a 'labour' college.
At the same time, Ruskin developed an arm's-length working
relationship with the University of Oxford, acting as a catalyst
for gradual curricular change and reform of admissions policy
within the university.[98] Looked on favourably by the T.U.C.

[96] *Glamorgan Gazette*, 1 Nov. 1912.
[97] Another example would be C.L.C. student Arthur Jenkins's address to the annual
demonstration of the eastern valley miners where, in a long speech, he called for the
socialization of the means of production, distribution and exchange. *Free Press of Monmouthshire*, 24 Sept. 1909.
[98] Jennings, op. cit., 13–14. Actually these proposals were along lines orginally
drafted by T. I. Mardy Jones in consultation with Lees-Smith, *S.W.D.N.* 27 Apr.
1909; Mardy Jones to Wilson, 30 Apr. 1909, loc. cit. For the impact of Ruskin College
on Oxford University see B. Harrison, 'Oxford and the labour movement', *Twentieth
Century British History*, 2, No. 3 (1991), 231–40.

mandarins, it was to be a powerful rival to the C.L.C. for the affections of the organized working class.

The struggle in south Wales was to secure the affiliation of the Federation's districts. By 1911 five of the districts, five of the biggest in terms of membership, were supporting the C.L.C., but this was the maximum in the years before the Federation, with the National Union of Railwaymen, took over formal responsibility for the college.[99] Ablett, in particular, devoted a vast amount of energy to promoting the college in the coalfield, often struggling against a welter of hostility and indifference to the C.L.C., its objectives and its products. Typical was his experience in the Western District of Miners in 1911. In 1910 the district had agreed to send their retiring chairman, Gwilym Davies, to Ruskin College.[100] This was to be a 'one-off' arrangement, not a scholarship scheme, but it alarmed the C.L.C. supporters, and the following year a campaign was started to try to win the district over to the Labour College.[101] This campaign culminated in a debate between Ablett and a representative of Ruskin College held in December 1911. The discussion focused on Ruskin's links with the university and its limited accountability to the rank and file members of supporting unions. When the issue was thrown open to the floor, Ablett came under intense questioning about the political nature of C.L.C. teaching and whether it was not, in fact, a 'revolutionary' college. Ablett responded by stressing the theoretical rather than the political nature of the teaching and pointed to the presence on the board of governors of Watts Morgan, a 'non-socialist' miners' agent as evidence of the 'labour' rather than socialist character of the C.L.C. Not all the delegates were convinced, and one remarked that if education was going to produce 'revolutionary methods' it was better to do without education.[102] The district committee decided to take no action, and this reflected a 'plague upon both your houses' mentality which was to dog both traditions of workers' education whenever the conflict between them surfaced in the councils of organized labour.

[99] Western Valley Miners, Rhondda No. 1., Anthracite, Maesteg and Rhondda No. 2 (Pontypridd).
[100] *Llais Llafur*, 5 Feb. 1910.
[101] Ibid., 8, 12 July 1911.
[102] Ibid., 30 Dec. 1911.

Ablett's work for the C.L.C. was not confined to the south
Wales miners. Along with Gill and Frank Hodges, he took a
prominent part in the campaign which secured the transfer of
the support of the Amalgamated Society of Railway Servants
(A.S.R.S.) from Ruskin College to the C.L.C. at their annual
conference in Barry in 1910.[103] In 1911 he attended the Trades
Union Congress in Newcastle to fight off an attempt by prominent Ruskin supporters on the Parliamentary Committee, such
as Bowerman, to establish T.U.C. scholarships at Ruskin College. With the support of Barker and Winstone, he organized
a protest meeting for delegates following which the idea seems
to have been quietly dropped.[104]

Ablett's almost obsessive dedication to the C.L.C. probably
contributed massively to its survival, for in its early years the
C.L.C. clung to existence only through the enthusiasm of a
few supporters, Ablett being the most committed. He was a
member of the provisional committee which ran the C.L.C.
until it moved to London in 1911, when he became a member
of the newly constituted governing board of the college. Only
Gill attended the meetings of the governing body anything
like as regularly as Ablett.[105] On several occasions in its early
years the governing body consisted only of Ablett, Gill and a
representative of the A.S.R.S. Far from there being any substantial groundswell of support for the C.L.C. amongst south
Wales miners, only the Rhondda No. 1. District and Gill's
Western Valley District maintained consistent support from
its inception until it was formally taken over by the
S.W.M.F. and the N.U.R. in 1914. The Tredegar Valley,
Eastern Valley and Maesteg Districts sent only one student
and then withdrew support. The Pontypridd District sent
A. J. Cook in 1911 and maintained support thereafter, but that
was unusual. This lack of reliable financial support was due in
part to the vagaries of changing personnel at district meetings

---

[103] *Plebs*, Nov. 1910.
[104] Letter from Ablett to W. W. Craik, n.d., N.C.L.C. collection, National Library of
Scotland (N.L.S.), Acc. 5120, Box 2; *Plebs* (Nov. 1911).
[105] The minute book of the early years of C.L.C., 1909–1915, is held at the W.E.A.
headquarters, Temple House, London. The contents are partially reproduced on a the-
matic basis in J. Atkins, *Neither Crumbs nor Condescension: The Central Labour College, 1909–
1915* (Aberdeen, 1981).

and the pressure on district funds during periods of industrial strife, a situation compounded by the failure of the S.W.M.F. centralization scheme in 1912. The college was in a state of perpetual financial crisis. In February 1910, when the C.L.C. seemed likely to lose its Oxford premises, Ablett initiated an attempt at compromise with Ruskin College, but the negotiations foundered when the reinstatement of Hird was laid down as an absolute requirement by the C.L.C.[106] On two occasions in 1911 the college seemed about to close. In February, faced with what appeared to be an unpayable debt, Ablett actually proposed that the C.L.C. would have to close.[107] That crisis passed, only to be followed in late summer by notice to quit from the college's landlords.

It was at this point that the most exotic and unlikely figure in the annals of British workers' education made his appearance. George Davison made his fortune out of the growing market for snapshot photography, but he was a philosophic anarchist by political persuasion. Ablett had little time for the ideas of Davison and his anarchist friends—a 'sausage mush' is how he described their views to Craik[108]—but he was attracted by the thickness of Davison's wallet, and the wealthy benefactor stood surety for the overdraft which allowed the college to set up home at its new London premises. In 1912 another wealthy friend of Hird provided security for further credit for the college.[109] The irony of wealthy benefactors keeping alive Ablett's C.L.C., a practice he had found so unacceptable when it applied to Ruskin College, could not have been lost on him. He is likely to have been even more disturbed by the recurring student unrest which afflicted the C.L.C. in the early years of its existence.

As early as 1912 there were complaints from south Wales students about the administration and the teaching of the college. George Daggar from Abertillery, D. R. Owen from the anthracite district, and an N.U.R. student from south Wales called Kinsella, made formal protests about the quality of the teach-

[106] C.L.C. provisional committee minutes, 24 Feb. 1910, loc. cit.

[107] C.L.C. Board of Governors' minutes, 7 July 1911; see also Barker's speech to the Aug. meeting of the Plebs League (*Plebs*, Sept. 1910).

[108] Ablett to Craik, loc. cit.

[109] C.L.C. Board of Governors' minutes, 5 Nov. 1912.

ing and what they regarded as gross mismanagement of college resources.[110] The students even asked to be allowed to arrange their own classes in Marxian economics. After initially ignoring the students, Ablett and his colleagues on the governing body took a hard line and pilloried their complaints and denounced their motives in the Plebs magazine.[111] Daggar pressed for an inquiry by his district, the Western Valley. This it agreed to undertake, but, with Ablett and Gill participating as members of the inquiry team, it was heavily weighted against the complainants and, not surprisingly found against Daggar.[112]

The college ran into further trouble in 1913 when the student from the Anthracite District, J. Griffiths, complained to his district committee on lines similar to those of Daggar.[113] The district withdrew its support from the college. Davison was in touch with Griffiths, and he withdrew his backing for the college, denouncing its teaching as 'reactionary and mischievous' and its administration as 'uneconomical'.[114] Student trouble burst out again in 1914 with reports of an actual 'strike' at the C.L.C. appearing in the press. Only fear of jeopardizing delicate negotiations between the college and the executive committees of the N.U.R. and the S.W.M.F. persuaded the students from going public with their grievances, which were largely the same as those voiced by Daggar and his supporters in 1912.[115]

Whilst it is undoubtedly true that much of the student trouble stemmed from the difficult financial position of the college, much blame must attach to Ablett and his failure to keep a firm grip on what was happening there. He had a sharp tongue for his enemies and he seems to have had a tendency to have favourites and cronies. George Sims, the economics lecturer and the focus of much student criticism, seems to have been

[110] Ibid., 17 June 1912.

[111] Ibid., 6, 30 Nov., 12 Dec. 1912; *Plebs* (Jan. 1913).

[112] Opton Purnell (secretary of the Western Valley Miners' Committee) to George Sims (C.L.C. secretary), 18 Nov. 1913, C.L.C. Board of Governors' minutes. See also C.L.C. House Committee minutes, 21, 30 Oct. 1912, C.L.C. Collection, N.L.S., Acc. 5120, Box 69. For Daggar's subsequent career, see his entry in *D.L.B.*, vol. III.

[113] C.L.C. Board of Governors' minutes, 6 Nov. 1912.

[114] Davison to Hird, C.L.C. Board of Governors' minutes, 3 Nov. 1913.

[115] See agreement between C.L.C. staff and dissenting students, 27 Mar. 1914. N.C.L.C. collection, N.L.S., Acc. 5120, Box 2, fo. 1914.

protected by Ablett. Some student protégés of Ablett, such as Reynolds from Ynys-hir, were appointed to the staff of the C.L.C. despite its financial plight. For the dedicated young men, selected because of a sense of commitment to the cause of labour, this seemed to be irresponsible. The heavy domestic as well as academic workload, the 11.00 o'clock curfew, the restrictions on public speaking, all served to alienate many students from the leadership of the C.L.C. just as from Ruskin College.

Whilst there were parallels between the student unrest which afflicted the C.L.C. and that which triggered the Ruskin dispute of 1909, there was one fundamental difference: there was no dispute between the C.L.C. authorities and the students over the purpose of the teaching. Staff and students were united in their commitment to a genuinely independent 'labour' college. That is not to say that there were not deep political differences between or amongst the staff, the students and the governing body. The Central Labour College's reputation as a hothouse of syndicalism is not borne out by the records. According to Gill, in 1909, fewer than seven out of over 400 Plebs League members could be regarded as 'industrial unionists'.[116] He most certainly was not. In 1912 he seconded George Barker's defence of nationalization as the way to eliminate capitalism from the coal industry against fellow C.L.C. governor Ablett and his ally, Frank Hodges, who advocated direct action and workers' control.[117] Nor do the records of the C.L.C. students' debating society support the idea that the Labour College produced a large crop of syndicalist activists. In February 1910 a motion that workers should not support 'palliatives' was rejected. In November 1911 the students supported a motion in support of nationalization, against the pleadings of C. L. Gibbons, another Ablett protégé. In the same month the students supported a motion in favour of 'political action' by six votes to four. In March 1912 they agreed, by a larger margin, that 'Political action is essential to the interests of the working class', this time against the advocacy of A. J.

---

[116] *South Wales Gazette*, 17 Oct. 1909.

[117] A verbatim account of this debate is reprinted in K. O. Morgan, 'Socialism versus syndicalism: the Welsh miners' debate, 1912', Society for the Study of Labour History, *Bulletin*, No. 30, (Spring 1975), 22–36.

Cook.[118] The picture is consistent; the student body had a small vociferous minority of industrial unionists, many associated with Ablett, but the majority were, as Gill suggested, socialist critics of the capitalist order but committed to political action and social reform.

In the process of changing the dominant political outlook of the leadership of the miners of south Wales from liberal Labourism to socialist Labourism, the C.L.C.'s role has perhaps been misunderstood by those who wished to give prominence to a revolutionary mentality that inspired a few key figures but made little impact on the bulk of activists. Support for the C.L.C. reflected and, in part, reinforced the drift to an anti-capitalist mentality amongst the miners' leadership. The willingness of men like Hartshorn, Barker and Winstone to work closely with the products of the C.L.C. reflected their view that the more advanced ideas were symptoms of a desire to question old ways, but did not necessarily offer practical solutions. Speaking at the Labour College A.G.M. in 1911, Winstone warned the young iconoclasts that it was 'bad tactics for the advanced guard of any army to go too far ahead of the main body'.[119] The C.L.C. survived because men like Winstone, Barker and Hartshorn found it a useful ally in their battles against the older type of Federation leader. What distinguished the new leadership from the old was its rejection of the logic of the capitalist system. Winstone stated the issue bluntly: the Federation, he argued, 'Instead of trying to reconcile capitalism and labour ... should show the impossibility of such a reconciliation.'[120] The college also found support because its outlook met a need for an anti-capitalist intellectual framework craved by many young activists. The Marxian critique of capitalism taught at the C.L.C., wrote C. L. Gibbons, supplied them with 'proofs' that the interests of the workers and those of the capitalists were absolutely opposed. 'The lesson was constantly driven home that the workers could

[118] Minutes of the C.L.C. Debating Society, 18 Oct., 7 Feb., 14 Mar. 1910, 6, 23 Nov. 1911, 14, 28 Mar. 1912. C.L.C. collection, N.L.S., Acc. 5120, Box 69. C. L. Gibbons wrote in 1913 that the C.L.C. Debating Society was the main means by which the students sought to relate their theoretical studies to current issues. *South Wales Worker*, 5 July 1913.
[119] *Llais Llafur*, 18 Nov. 1911.
[120] Quoted in Winstone's entry in *D.L.B.*, vol I.

only rely on victory by strong and efficient organization, by building up a fighting organization, and not a compromising, conciliatory and arbitrating one.'[121] It was not difficult for most young activists, imbued with a strong anti-capitalist ethos, to find that message very acceptable. Marxian economics and industrial history became weapons in the battle against a dissembling educational orthodoxy, whose underlying purpose was to infect the minds of working-class leaders with pro-capitalist ideas.

It was the alliance with the newer breed of miners' leader, and the hold that the anti-capitalist ideas propagated by the C.L.C. had amongst a growing number of Federation activists, that made it possible for Ablett and Gill to secure the take-over of the C.L.C. by the S.W.M.F., in conjunction with the N.U.R. At a delegate conference held in July 1914, addressed by Dennis Hird, the nominal head of the college and still held in high esteem in south Wales, the motion went through by 115 votes to 44.[122] Protracted and tortuous negotiations with the N.U.R., complicated by legal difficulties, and the suspicion that not all the senior officials of the railwaymen's union had their hearts in the venture, dogged the scheme, so that the C.L.C. was not formally acquired by the two unions until the following year, by which time the European war was changing the nature of south Wales industrial and political life in a way that was to give a new urgency to the issue of workers' education.

If the prominence of a fairly small number of individuals associated with the C.L.C. has tended to distort the picture of its influence and success prior to 1914, the same, in many ways, applies to the spread and impact of local classes associated with the I.W.C.E. movement. For Ablett, the Labour College was the spawning ground of a new breed of union leader who would regard the conduct of classes in Marxian economics and industrial history as an integral part of the work

[121] *South Wales Worker*, 5 July 1912; this is also quoted in J. A. Cartwright, 'A study in British syndicalism: the miners of South Wales, 1906–14' (University of Wales M.Sc. thesis, 1969), 90.
[122] S.W.M.F. Special Conference minutes, 13 July 1914; letter from Tom Richards (general secretary, S.W.M.F.) to George Sims, 23 July 1914, C.L.C. Board of Governors' minutes; *Llais Llafur*, 18 July 1914.

of himself and his organization. There was no suggestion that the class work should be, or could be, carried out by another body. The Plebs League's function in Ablett's eyes was as a propagandist body for the C.L.C. and for I.W.C.E. It was also a kind of ideological watchdog for the Labour College movement. It was not intended to be an agency for the provision of local I.W.C.E. classes. Ablett would not have regarded such a role as at all healthy, so convinced was he of the need to integrate all Labour College work into that of the trade union movement. Whilst Ablett supported the local Labour College class movement, his dedication to the survival of the C.L.C. made this a matter of secondary importance to him, and his personal role in the establishment of local class groups has perhaps been exaggerated in the past.[123] For Ablett, the C.L.C. was the centre from which everything else in the I.W.C.E. movement sprang. The attendance of promising young activists at the college was essential; that is why he was so angry when a relatively youthful marriage prevented Arthur Horner from going to the C.L.C.[124]

In the Rhondda Valley, Ablett's circle of young activists, operating out of the Plebs Club and Institute in Tonypandy, did establish local class groups shortly after the Ruskin dispute, but systematic class work seems to have been delayed by the Cambrian Combine dispute. In the winter of 1911–12 attempts, initiated by Ablett's own lodge, Maerdy, to secure district support were partially successful, but no financial aid was forthcoming at district level.[125] Nevertheless, voluntary contributions and some grants of money from individual lodges secured the appointment of W. F. Hay as a full-time tutor. In the winter session of 1912–13, with the organizational energy of A. J. Cook as class secretary, a twenty-lecture class scheme on Marxian economics and industrial history was established at five centres within the Rhondda Valley, with class group sizes varying from twelve to thirty-five.[126] There was further expansion in the following session. Thus, by the

---

[123] See, for example, Ablett's entry in the *D.L.B.*, vol. III, where he is described as being 'indefatigable' in setting up local Marxist classes in the coalfield.
[124] Horner, op. cit., 22.
[125] Rhondda No. 1. minutes, 30 Jan. 1912.
[126] *Rhondda Socialist*, 12 Oct. 1912.

outbreak of the war, the Rhondda Valley had quite an extensive network of classes, formally endorsed by the local Federation district but still not enjoying direct financial support.

The teaching in the Rhondda classes was uncompromising in
its propagation of Marxian economic and historical theory. By
1910, through the *Plebs* magazine, Ablett had provided the
Labour College movement with a readable introduction to
Marxist economics and in particular the opening parts of
Marx's *Capital*.[127] Under Ablett's influence, I.W.C.E. teaching
in the Rhondda laid great emphasis on the nature of the exploi-
tation suffered by the working class, the real wealth producers.
Particular attention was paid to the way in which the workers
were deprived by the capitalist class of the value produced by
their labour. This economic critique of capitalism was combined with what was described as the materialist conception
of history (frequently abbreviated to M.C.H.), which stressed
the historical mission of the proletariat to overthrow the capitalist system. A report on a Labour College class held at
Ynys-hir in March 1912 conveys a flavour of the tuition:

> All history since the dissolution of tribal society is the history
> of class struggles, contests between exploiting and exploited,
> ruling and oppressed classes ... the history of these struggles
> forms a series [*sic*] of evolution, which nowadays has reached
> the stage where the exploited class, the proletariat, cannot
> achieve its own emancipation from the bourgeoisie without
> emancipating itself and society at large from all exploita-
> tion, class distinction and class struggles.[128]

There were in Edwardian Rhondda a significant number of
young activists who found in the messages of the Labour
College classes a coherent intellectual framework which gave
them a sense of purpose and mission that they did not find elsewhere. In giving these key individuals a new 'world view' the
Labour College classes in the Rhondda also helped to change
the 'socio-political' filters through which a wider group of
activists, the 'secondary leadership', viewed their condition.

---

[127] N. Ablett, *Easy Outlines of Economics* (London, 1910), originally a series of articles
published in *Plebs* magazine (April 1909–January 1910) and republished in 1919.
[128] *Rhondda Socialist*, 16 Mar. 1912. This is from a lengthy report on an industrial
history course held at Ynys-hir in March 1912.

The Rhondda was different. Nowhere else in the coalfield was there quite the intense concentration of single-industry employment, nor was capitalist combination quite so much a feature of the industry, nor were the social pressures such as housing and a high birth rate made more pronounced by the sheer scale of problems. In addition, there were a large number of younger men employed in the Rhondda coalmines, and a recent study of the industrial strife of the 1910–14 period has shown a close correlation between the youth of workers and their propensity to engage in disputes in the coal industry.[129] It would seem reasonable to assume that these pressures would also make them more susceptible to the type of message being propagated by the I.W.C.E. movement. It may also explain why the Rhondda classes mark a more emphatic conceptual break with earlier traditions of radical thought in the coalfield, which still were only beginning to shake off ties with Nonconformity, moral reform and an ethical (that is, a non-'scientific') critique of capitalism.

The development of I.W.C.E. teaching in the western valleys of Monmouthshire does not display the same kind of conceptual rupture which is so marked in the Rhondda. The Abertillery area already enjoyed a strong local culture of working-class self-improvement. There were active adult Bible classes and Sunday schools attached to the Nonconformist chapels. There were Pleasant Sunday Afternoons groups and literary and debating societies. Meshed into this Dissenting tradition of self-help and improvement was the strong local co-operative movement which, under T. W. Allen, had contributed so much to the introduction of the W.E.A. in south Wales. The strong local I.L.P. branches also acted as focal points in this culture of debate. This reflected a long radical tradition which had thrown up many of the leading lights of mining trade unionism from William Brace, through Tom Richards and Alfred Onions, to Vernon Hartshorn, Ted Gill and Frank Hodges. It was an open-minded culture in which people of very different outlooks could engage in controversial discussions without a breakdown in dialogue. When Hird visited the area in January 1909 he spoke at a meeting of the Abertillery

I.L.P. branch, chaired by A. C. Willis, on the topic 'What evolution means for socialism'. He spoke on the same topic the following night at Blaina, where T. W. Allen acted as chairman. The same month the lively Abertillery literary and debating society discussed whether socialism and progress were compatible. Willis moved and Ted Gill, recently returned from Ruskin, seconded the proposition that they were.[130]

Yet beneath this culture of debate there were tensions which were forcing change. In 1907 the Pleasant Sunday Afternoons group was evicted from one Primitive Methodist Hall after being accused of preaching socialism.[131] These tensions within Welsh Nonconformity, between those who wished to cling to a rigid gospel of personal salvation and those who wished to incorporate a social conscience element in the teaching of their chapels, came to a head in the western valleys of Monmouthshire at about the same time as the Ruskin College dispute. When R. J. Campbell addressed a packed meeting in Abertillery in 1908, it provoked a public argument over the nature of the Nonconformist ministry between two local Baptist preachers, T. T. Evans, who maintained an orthodox stance, and J. Morris Evans, who advocated a more socially aware Christianity. Heavily influenced by forms of social gospel then being developed in the United States, where he spent most of his youth and early manhood, Morris Evans preached a gospel which argued that personal salvation was achievable only in a reformed social and economic order free from the evils of poverty and deprivation. It was a message that was collectivist and anti-capitalist in its outlook. When the deacons of King Street Baptist Chapel in Abertillery sought the dismissal of their radical pastor, the local labour and socialist movements came to his aid, with Ted Gill, A. C. Willis and George Barker his most prominent supporters.[132]

The result of Morris Evans's removal was an attempt to marry the social gospel with the culture of debate and self-improvement in the Abertillery area. An organization calling itself the New Era Union was founded in July 1909. This

---

[130] *South Wales Gazette*, 8, 15, 22 Jan. 1909.
[131] Ibid., 6 Dec. 1907.
[132] *South Wales Weekly Argus*, 10 July 1909; *Llais Llafur*, 25 Sept. 1909.

body, which was established with the support of one hundred volunteers, offering one shilling per week in its support, sought to combine education, social work and some spiritual guidance on a non-sectarian and non-party basis. Morris Evans was the 'superintendent', whilst Willis was in charge of Sunday work, Gill was in charge of social work and George Barker of publicity. The New Era Union was a curious organization designed, in the words of its early publicity, to help through 'true thought, and Scientific methods' to bring in a healthier and juster society. It rejected 'dogmatic creeds'; instead it sought to make 'intelligence victorious over unreason, universal love over individual selfishness, true civilization over brutality and savagery however disguised'.[133] The strong ethical and spiritual content of the New Era Union, with the references to 'scientific' methods, meant that I.W.C.E. teaching was introduced to the Abertillery area through the agency of a body which had a different outlook from the rigid materialism of the Rhondda Valley Plebs. Another difference conveyed in reports is that the New Era Union continued to foster the culture of debate, whilst the Rhondda Plebs tended to foster a culture of indoctrination in the Marxian revelation. Christian and Marxian speakers found a platform (Hird addressed the Union in late 1909),[134] but the vocabulary used by speakers often reflected the semi-religious basis of the organization. For example, Frank Hodges spoke to the Union in July 1910 under the title, 'The religion of social democracy', a creed which would give the working class a 'Kingdom' of social democracy on earth; its redeemer would be the 'conscious social organization of Labour'.[135] In the previous month a Nonconformist minister from Cardiff spoke against the doctrine of total depravity to a 'large and appreciative audience'.[136] The Union continued its existence up to the outbreak of war, with a rather odd mixture of social gospellers and Marxist speakers. For example, in one week in 1913 the Union was treated to a talk from a Bristol vicar who argued that the Established church could be a vehicle for socialism if it could be rescued

[133] Ibid.
[134] *South Wales Weekly Argus*, 27 Nov. 1909.
[135] Ibid., 2 July 1910.
[136] Ibid., 18 June 1910.

from the grip of 'Mammon', while the next week Guy Bowman argued that political action of any sort was a waste of time and that capitalism would be overthrown only by 'sabotage' by the workers themselves.[137]

Despite the strong whiff of Christian socialism which surrounded the New Era Union, Gill used this body to introduce Labour College-type teaching to the Abertillery area, initially making little or no attempt to establish a separate Plebs or Labour College group.[138] In the autumn of 1910, Labour College-type classes were run under the aegis of the New Era Union, with Morris Evans taking a class in industrial history using Engels's *Origins of the Family*, and Ted Gill taking a class in economics using Ernest Untermann's *Marxian Economics* as the main text. These classes continued for the next few years, with Frank Hodges and later Sydney Jones acting as tutors.[139]

In the Abertillery area, where the classes grew out of an older semi-religious and ethical tradition of socialist radicalism, they evolved in a lively culture of debate and discussion. There was a similar background to the emergence of I.W.C.E. classes in the western part of the coalfield. A small group of workers in the Ammanford area, initially heavily influenced by local preachers who were advocates of the social gospel, came together to discuss and debate in a workers' forum.[140] This group gradually organized its own classes on I.W.C.E. lines under the guidance of returned C.L.C. students such as D. R. Owen. Following a visit to their forum by George Davison, the wealthy Labour College benefactor, they were able to acquire their own property known as the White House, which became the centre of I.W.C.E. activity in the anthracite district until the 1920s. It was almost certainly this venture which prompted Davison to withdraw financial support from the C.L.C.; relations between the White House group and the mainstream of the I.W.C.E. movement were, to say the least, strained.

Elsewhere in the coalfield local class work was sporadic. Much depended on the availability of suitable tutors. Also,

---

[137] *South Wales Worker*, 12 Apr. 1913.
[138] *Plebs* (Oct. 1910).
[139] Ibid. (Dec. 1910).
[140] See T. Brennan, 'The White House', *The Cambridge Journal*, VII, No. 4 (1954); also J. Beverley Smith, op. cit., 71–4.

much depended on the personal magnetism of a particular tutor. In Pontardawe in the Swansea Valley, Nun Nicholas, a checkweigher at a local colliery, built up a local class group in Marxian economics which was reported in early 1912 to have over seventy members. When Nicholas left the area to take up a full-time tutor's position with a Labour College class group on Merseyside, class work in the Swansea Valley seems to have collapsed.[141] A similar pattern existed in the Garw, where Hodges, following the Ablett model, sought to make class work an integral part of his duties as the newly elected miners' agent. Hodges established class groups in Tondu and then at Blaengarw, but pressure of work forced him to curtail his activities in this area, and the class work collapsed. The inability to find tutors and the apparent unwillingness of many ex-C.L.C. students to take up class work were cited by Leyshon Williams, the secretary/organizer of Hodges's classes in the Garw Valley, as the main constraint on the establishment of successful I.W.C.E. classes in the coalfield.[142] Only in the Rhondda, where class groups were large enough to sustain the occasional full-time tutor and where they could draw on a large group of ex-C.L.C. men, was class work really sustained prior to 1914.

Ironically, south Wales was one of the main sources for I.W.C.E. tutors in other areas of the U.K. In addition to Nicholas, W. F. Hay and C. L. Gibbons went to the north-west of England as paid I.W.C.E. tutors.[143] In those parts of industrial south Wales which were outside the coalfield, the record of I.W.C.E. class work was even more sporadic. Only in Barry, an N.U.R. stronghold, was there any significant provision. [144]

There was one attempt made by the C.L.C. to try to overcome the problem of tutor shortage. In 1914, W. W. Craik, by then the *de facto* head of the college, tried to establish formal class groups, funded by the Rhymney Valley District of the S.W.M.F., which would operate around a C.L.C. correspondence course with quarterly visits by Craik to discuss the class

[141] *Llais Llafur*, 20 Jan. 1912. See also E. and R. Frow, 'The spark of independent working-class education', in B. Simon (ed.) *The Search for Enlightenment: The Working Class and Adult Education in the Twentieth Century* (London, 1990), 75, 86.
[142] *Plebs* (June 1913).
[143] Ibid. (May 1913). In Rochdale in 1913 Gibbons debated with E. J. Hookway from Pontypridd on the issue of W.E.A. *versus* Labour College-type workers' education.
[144] *Plebs* (Sept. 1914).

group's work and progress. How successful this scheme was is not known and it does not seem to have been tried elsewhere.[145]

The scale of Labour College-type local classes in south Wales prior to 1914 was thus very limited. Of course, there may well have been a number of informal groups meeting on a regular basis which were never reported in the local press or the *Plebs* magazine, though the latter was always anxious to report any advance in I.W.C.E. teaching. There are also some discrepancies between the contemporary record and the claims made later about the scale of class activity. The Aberdare area is a case in point. W. J. Edwards claimed in his autobiography that he organized regular classes in Marxian economics in the Aberdare Valley which, with a brief interlude during the Aberdare strike of 1910, continued into the 1920s, when they were formally taken over by the local miners' district committee.[146] This may well be true but there are no reports of it in *Plebs* or in the local press. In fact, the Aberdare Valley was something of a W.E.A. stronghold in the period around the outbreak of the First World War. Significant numbers of Labour College classes did not appear in the Aberdare Valley until after 1916.

Although the record of I.W.C.E. classes in the coalfield in the years before the outbreak of war is not very impressive, it also has to be said that the Labour College movement succeeded in establishing a place and a role for itself in the south Wales labour movement in a way which continued to elude the W.E.A. However, this was less to do with the extent of class work than with the way in which the movement created an impact on the outlook and perceptions of key elements in the rank and file of the miners' federation. By 1914 Ablett, Gill, Noah Rees and Frank Hodges were names known in every lodge in the coalfield, but no one active in the W.E.A. in south Wales had such renown. The willingness of some of the newer elements in the leadership of the miners' union to associate with, and support, those connected with the I.W.C.E. movement also helped to raise its status and certainly contributed to the idea that the C.L.C. was a key factor in the militancy

---

[145] C.L.C. Board of Governors' minutes, 29 Nov. 1913.
[146] Edwards, op. cit., 211–29, 243, 250.

of the south Wales coalfield. However, the significance of the Labour College movement in general and of the local classes in particular in the development of the 'labour revolt' was overstated by contemporaries and has tended to be overrated by subsequent writers. The I.W.C.E. movement was part of the general drift of anti-capitalist sentiment in the ranks of organized labour, particularly in the south Wales coalfield. It is true that the C.L.C. and the local classes helped to reinforce the trend by giving it an intellectual coherence it might not otherwise have possessed, and in the process helped to create a new outlook amongst a rising generation of activists within the mining industry. The I.W.C.E. movement in south Wales was not rigidly dogmatic; it certainly was not uniformly syndicalist in its outlook. There were deep differences, as was reflected in the debates over the issue of nationalization versus workers' control; the state socialists probably remained the dominant group. It was because those behind the I.W.C.E. movement were clearly men of 'intellect and action' that many contemporary observers found the development very disturbing. When A. J. Jenkinson, a young Oxford economist of the progressive type, read a copy of *The Miners' Next Step*, he was struck by the fact that the authors displayed 'a genius for leadership, men of intellect and men of action. It seems a grievous pity that such energy and ability should be mis-directed', into activities which would lead to the 'cataracts of class-warfare fatal alike to Capitalism and Labour'. What was needed was 'to make clear the identity of interest between Capital and Labour in the mining villages of South Wales'.[147] Such views only served to convince the leading lights of the Plebs League that they did indeed hold 'the current situation in their hands';[148] that they were indeed the authors of the great attitudinal change that seemed to be sweeping the rank and file activists of the Federation. In truth, they were symptom, not cause. The evolution of the S.W.M.F. had reached the point where it was feeling strong enough to challenge the employers at a new

---

[147] A. J. Jenkinson, 'Reflections on a pamphlet entitled, "The miners' next step" ', *Economic Review*, 22 (July 1912). Jenkinson was given a copy of the pamphlet by D. A. Thomas, Liberal M.P. for Merthyr and managing director of Cambrian Combine Collieries.

[148] *Rhondda Socialist*, 9 Mar. 1912.

level, to assert the full independence of the movement from the social, economic and political hold of the 'bosses'. It was a process that was to be greatly assisted by the improvement in bargaining power occasioned by a total war.

III

THE WAR AND WORKERS' EDUCATION

1. THE WELSH IDEAL OF POPULAR CULTURE

The war was to bring dramatic change to the very fabric of Welsh society. There were few areas of Welsh life which remained untouched by the collectivist pressures of total war. Food rationing, rent controls and, above all, the state control of the coal industry and the railways were to give the working people of Wales practical experience of government intervention. The changes were, on balance, beneficial to the bulk of the Welsh working classes, and they undoubtedly made more credible the increasingly anti-capitalist and pro-socialist attitudes and outlook of organized labour. The long-term consequences for the Liberal Party in industrial south Wales were dire. But, especially in the early years of the war, the future looked far from grim. The ominous pre-war growth of revolutionary ideas amongst some sections of the trade union movement seemed checked by a spontaneous upsurge of patriotic fervour, the south Wales miners displaying as much enthusiasm for the war effort as any other group of workers in Britain. Miners' agents became army recruiting agents. Watts Morgan raised a battalion of Welsh colliers for the western front, earned a commission and later a DSO. More surprising was the response of some of the more radical spirits of the 1910–14 era, such as Charles Butt Stanton of Aberdare, the most theatrical of the new breed of socialist miners' leaders. He soon became the scourge of pacifists and anti-war activists and helped, in his own inimitable way, to drive the heart-broken Keir Hardie to an early grave. Most labour leaders, even active I.L.P. men such as James Winstone, felt obliged to endorse the war effort, and, in its early stages, open hostility to the conflict by south Wales labour leaders was rare.

The war greatly enhanced the bargaining position of organized labour. The war effort saw a revival of the old staples of Welsh industry, everything from old ironworks to slate quarries and lead mines went through an Indian summer of prosperity. Nowhere was this new economic buoyancy felt more strongly than in the coalfields. Welsh steam and coking coal was vital for the war effort; the miners knew it, and they knew that the government knew it. Industrial relations were transformed as organized labour flexed its muscles and, as the initial patriotic fervour waned, demands were formulated that would have been regarded as extravagant even in the militant pre-war years. In this context workers' education took on a much more profound significance.[1]

However, the initial impact of the war on both traditions of workers' education was far from beneficial. As with other sections of the labour movement, there were divisions over whether or not to support the war; both traditions embraced those who accepted the conflict as inevitable in the face of German aggression and, on the other hand, those who saw the war as a feature of capitalist imperialism. John Thomas, the W.E.A. district secretary, opposed the war on ethical grounds and became closely associated with anti-war elements in the south Wales I.L.P. Ted Gill, on the other hand, joined the army, was given a commission and raised a unit of south Wales miners to fight on the western front.[2] Others, including Ablett, were somewhat ambivalent in their attitude.[3] Initially, for both the Labour College and the W.E.A., the war created further problems and further pretexts for supporting bodies to cut financial support or put off decisions which might have put such support on a firmer footing.

Yet, from early in the war, there were those in both traditions who believed that it would create new opportunities, raise new issues and foster new appetites for understanding and change. Amongst the supporters of the W.E.A., this took the form of a belief that the war might result in a desire to create a social

---

[1] For an overview of the social, economic and political consequences of the First World War for Wales, see Kenneth O. Morgan, *Rebirth of a Nation: Wales 1880–1980* (Oxford and Cardiff, 1981), 159–79.

[2] *Glamorgan Free Press*, 4 Feb. 1915.

[3] Woodhouse, op. cit., 130.

order in which class conflict would be replaced by an educated and responsible democracy, and state and voluntary effort would be co-ordinated under the guidance of wise leaders selected by a well-informed population. Equally, amongst the supporters of the Labour College there were those who believed that the war would eventually expose the true nature of capitalism, which would be overwhelmed by the very violence it had created. Out of the ashes of the old society would arise a new socialist order, created by a people made conscious of their historical mission. As the war dragged on, year after year, as its effects began to touch every aspect of the lives of the people, the sense of urgency to seek to channel and direct thought and opinion became greater. Workers' education acquired a greater saliency and became a matter of concern for those who had hitherto paid it little attention.

Despite the failure of the W.E.A. in the pre-war years to entrench itself in the life of working-class south Wales, the energy of John Thomas and the backing of a small coterie of academics and professional people, such as Mackenzie, allowed the association to maintain a rather precarious existence. The trade union movement remained aloof: only three out of twenty-five bodies affiliated to the association in south Wales in 1914 were union branches; the rest were mainly working men's clubs.[4] The association remained heavily dependent on private support and, in particular, large subventions from the Davies family of Llandinam. Yet despite this rather meagre catalogue of success, John Thomas himself managed to create a body of support amongst the working-class activists of the Aberdare Valley. This he achieved by going with the grain of the growing anti-capitalist sentiment in the coalfield. Thomas always stressed that he was seeking to give a balanced picture of economics in his classes, but he never disguised his satisfaction at the decided views of his students. In his classes, criticisms of the capitalist system were as strident as in any Labour College group. Anyone invited to address Thomas's class who was anything less than highly condemnatory of the existing social and economic order, or who sought to defend the war as anything other than a conspiracy of capitalist financiers, was subjected

---

[4] *W.E.A. for Wales, Eighth Annual Report*, May 1915, 11.

to the most rigorous and hostile cross-questioning.[5] In this way Thomas managed to outflank the Plebs League, and as late as 1917 the *Plebs* magazine had to admit that the Aberdare area was something of a stronghold for the W.E.A.[6] Many young activists found in Thomas's classes the kind of intellectual grounding they were seeking for work in the ranks of organized labour. George Hall, later a Labour M.P., and, more surprisingly, Mark Starr, later a leading influence on the development of the I.W.C.E. movement in the early inter-war years, started their careers in one of Thomas's wartime classes.[7]

Thomas's strategy was not one which could always sit well with the outlook of the dominant group which ran the association in south Wales. In particular, the rejection of the language of 'class war' by those like Burrows rang hollow in the ears of many workers who attended Thomas's classes. Following the publication of the article by Ronald Burrows on settlement ideals by *Welsh Outlook* in January 1914, the following edition carried a letter from a Penrhiwceiber student in one of Thomas's classes, under the pen-name of 'One of the property-less'. The letter attacked the glib assertion by Burrows that class conflict could be wished away if the workers lived up to the ideals of citizenship. 'We workers who believe that the Class War exists, do not make it but only note that it is so, and point it out to others ... To abolish the Class War we must establish a Co-operative Commonwealth which, I believe, will be the result of organization and education of the working people.'[8]

The leading figures within the south Wales W.E.A. could live with the anti-capitalist tenor of Thomas's classes when the effects were to win over to the association those who would otherwise be recruited by the I.W.C.E. classes. Phil Thomas, a leading I.L.P figure in the Aberdare area, admitted that he had been very suspicious of the W.E.A. until the teaching of John Thomas had convinced him that the association genuinely sought the emancipation of the workers by enlightening them.[9]

[5] [*Merthyr*] *Pioneer*, 25 July, 6, 13, 20 Sept., 4 Dec. 1915. See also Thomas's views on the study of economics as an 'antidote to fatalism' amongst the workers. [*Merthyr*] *Pioneer*, 18 Dec. 1915.

[6] *Plebs* (Jan. 1917).

[7] Interview, Apr. 1972; Neath W.E.A., op. cit.; interview by the author with Mark Starr, 5 Sept. 1983. For George Hall's subsequent career, see his entry in *D.L.B.*, vol. II.

[8] *Welsh Outlook* (Feb. 1914).

Phil Thomas was precisely the type that the W.E.A. was aiming
to win over to its perception of workers' education. The ruling
coterie could live with anti-capitalist rhetoric from John
Thomas; anti-war activity was less easily accommodated. By
the autumn of 1915, Thomas Jones told Thomas that his views
and activities were damaging the association; Thomas also
encountered the sustained hostility of those on the executive
committee of the south Wales W.E.A. who were enthusiasts
for the war effort. He singled out Miss E. P. Hughes as a
leading critic of his activities: 'a bloody-minded warrior of the
worst type', is how he described her nearly sixty years later.[10]
Despite enjoying the patronage of Mackenzie and Lleufer
Thomas, John Thomas was forced to resign in October 1915.
Freed of the need to consider the association, Thomas became
an even more outspoken critic of the war, and his political views
drifted further to the left. In April 1916 he was granted the
status of conscientious objector.[11]

Thomas represented an approach to workers' education
which could have given the association a role in the labour
movement in the region for which it was searching, but that
would have produced tensions within the association which
would have torn it apart. Yet the anxieties over the drift of sentiment amongst working-class activists in south Wales towards
class-war attitudes were only reinforced by what was emanating from the classes of John Thomas. The need for a formula
which would attract working-class activists but detach them
from class-war ideas remained.

Daniel Lleufer Thomas made the most determined effort of
all the leading figures within the Welsh W.E.A. to tackle this

[9] [*Merthyr*] *Pioneer*, 8 Jan. 1915.
[10] Interview, Apr. 1972. The district council of the W.E.A. in Wales does seem to
have been very unsympathetic in its attitude towards the plight of conscientious objec-
tors in its ranks. Dan Griffiths, a teacher and a member of the district council, was subjected to a campaign of blatant discrimination by the authorities. This led to a public
protest campaign, actively supported by the national executive of the W.E.A.; it was
ignored by the Welsh district council and executive. W.E.A. executive committee minutes, 19 May 1917; *Western Mail*, 9 July 1917. See also a pamphlet by the Dan Griffiths
Defence Committee, E. L. Chappell papers, Box 4, National Library of Wales.
[11] Interview, Apr. 1972; W.E.A. Wales, district committee minutes, 15 Oct. 1915;
[*Merthyr*] *Pioneer*, 1 Apr. 1916. Initially he became an elementary school teacher and
then, because of his anti-war activity, he was forced by the military authorities to take
up war work no closer than fifty miles from Aberdare. He went to Singleton Park Farm,
Swansea, as a labourer.

issue. A lawyer by profession and an archetypal Edwardian progressive by inclination, he developed an interest in the labour and trade union movements in the years just before the turn of the century.[12] A strong believer in co-operation and co-partnership, he was also a supporter of the social gospel and had helped to bring R. J. Campbell to south Wales.[13] His concern about the drift of thought within the ranks of organized labour was given an additional boost when, as stipendiary magistrate for Pontypridd, he presided over the trials of those accused of intimidating blacklegs in the Cambrian Combine dispute. He found the willingness of the Federation to throw its cloak over the accused, and its decision to pay the fines of those found guilty, to be a disturbing break with the older practices of trade unionism that eschewed lawlessness. He saw the episode as evidence of serious deterioration in the fabric of society in industrial south Wales. Reviled by many on the left as a lackey of the coal owners, he was regarded by senior officials at the Home Office as unduly lenient in his handling of the Tonypandy rioters.[14]

A leading figure in the Cardiff–Barry coterie, Lleufer Thomas threw himself into social and educational work. With Edgar Chappell, he founded the South Wales Garden Cities and Town Planning Association. With H. S. Jevons, he was active in some housing experiments in Cardiff.[15] His most important initiative was the establishment of the Welsh Council of Social Service. An overtly religious body, it sprang from a paper Lleufer Thomas delivered to the annual assembly of Welsh Independents at Lampeter in 1910, in which he argued that Welsh churches had to move into the area of social service and break away from the world-rejecting Calvinism of orthodox theology.[16] He believed in 'corporate thinking' of networks of like-minded persons of influence investing their society with high ideals and clear social objectives—the School

---

[12] For further biographical details, see his entry in the *Dictionary of Welsh Biography*.

[13] *Llais Llafur*, 20 Oct. 1909.

[14] His comments on the disturbances are reprinted in D. Evans, *Labour Strife in the South Wales Coalfield, 1910–1911* (Cardiff, 1963), Appendix C, 245–7. For the views of Home Office officials on Lleufer Thomas's handling of cases linked to the Tonypandy disturbances, see Jane Morgan, *Conflict and Order: The Police and Labour Disputes in England and Wales, 1900–1939* (Oxford, 1987), 161,196.

[15] *[Merthyr] Pioneer*, 5 Sept. 1914.

[16] G. Davies, *Welsh School of Social Service, 1911–1925* (Cardiff, 1926), *passim*.

of Social Service was such a 'Collegium'. Without such a departure, Lleufer Thomas feared that the Welsh people might swing
from a soul-obsessed spirituality to a soulless materialism in one
generation. Yet he also believed that the key to winning the
minds of the leaders of thought amongst Welsh workers was
through education, and he saw the W.E.A. as the best available vehicle for his ideas.

Lleufer Thomas replaced Mackenzie as chairman of the
Welsh W.E.A. in July 1915. The following month he addressed
the Honourable Society of Cymmrodorion at the National Eisteddfod at Bangor on the subject of 'University tutorial classes
for working people'. In part a history of adult and workers' education in Britain in general and Wales in particular, it was also
an attempt to give an intellectual framework to the movement
in Wales. He saw the W.E.A. and the tutorial class movement
as the direct successor of an older peasant popular culture
which was available to all, irrespective of rank, class or occupation. The ideals of religion and nationality had been rudely dis-
rupted by industrialization and the immigration of non-Welsh
elements. The result of these intrusions into the older culture
was the danger of a repudiation of the ideals of nationality
and religion, and their replacement by an 'illusory ideal of a
cosmopolitan, and perhaps to some extent materialistic brotherhood'.[17] His answer to the problem of recreating the ideal
of popular culture was a comprehensive programme of adult
education, at the centre of which would be the University of
Wales and its constituent colleges. Harking back to an earlier
ideal, of R. D. Roberts and Owen M. Edwards, of a university
which was woven into the popular culture of the Welsh nation,
Lleufer Thomas stated that the task of the University of Wales
was to 'effect a reconciliation of individualism and socialism—
opposite, yet complementary, standpoints, both deeply rooted
in the character and the life of the people; both must find scope
in the new conception of the freedom of civic and national
life'.[18]

The theological colleges would be given the specific task of
fostering philosophical discussions in the tutorial classes to

[17] Lleufer Thomas, op. cit., 94.
[18] Ibid., 95.

counterbalance the dominance of economics as a subject. By this means working people would begin to see that many of their problems are 'philosophical as well as economic'. Voluntary agencies such as the Y.M.C.A., the Co-operative movement and local literary societies would all be integrated into the scheme under the general guidance of the university.

For the W.E.A., its sense of purpose in Wales would be established by becoming the repository and propagator of the Welsh ideal of popular culture, a 'democratic culture and of a human brotherhood based on a frank recognition of nationality'.[19] This recognition would be applied to all studies and all subjects, a sense of nationality overlaid by a commitment to social and public service. The English W.E.A. in Wales would be changed into a Welsh national institution geared to countering the corrosive effects of an internationalist and materialist ideology. In that way the W.E.A. would become the true heir of Griffith Jones.

As chairman of the Welsh W.E.A., Lleufer Thomas had a profound influence over the contents of the written submission of the Welsh W.E.A. to the Royal Commission on University Education in Wales, established in 1916 and chaired by Viscount Haldane (hereafter the Haldane Commission). The statement of the W.E.A. Welsh district committee contained a copy of Lleufer Thomas's address to the Bangor Eisteddfod as well as a statement specially prepared by the district committee. The W.E.A. submission echoed many of the ideas contained in the Bangor address. The University of Wales would assume the main role of provider of tutorial classes, with scholarships being created for extra-mural students to attend summer schools and, in some cases, to become full-time students at the university. The bulk of the funds for this scheme (75 per cent) would come directly from the Board of Education.[20] It was a bold set of proposals which reflected the increasingly radical atmosphere of the period in which it

---

[19] Ibid., 96.
[20] *Statement of the Views of the Council, Workers' Educational Association, Welsh District, to the Royal Commission on University Education in Wales* (Cardiff, 1916), submitted by D. Lleufer Thomas, Philip Thomas (Workers' Representative, Cardiff Joint Tutorial Committee) and Stanley Watkins, hon. secretary, Wales W.E.A.

was produced and submitted, the spring of 1917. In the evidence presented to the commission, the W.E.A. deputation stressed that the tutorial classes should be democratic in tone and organization, with the selection of subject, and, to some extent, the tutor, being in the hands of the class group itself.

Lleufer Thomas led the W.E.A. deputation which gave evidence to the Haldane Commission in March 1917. Very soon the questioning focused on a section of the W.E.A. statement which spoke about the rapid rise in industrial south Wales of a demand by workers for education in politically sensitive subjects. The W.E.A. statement emphasized how this demand was, in the absence of a major programme of orthodox tutorial classes, being met by the Labour College movement: 'Last year [1916] about 500 students were attending these classes.'[21] Lleufer Thomas supplied additional information during the interview about the further growth of I.W.C.E.-type teaching in the coalfield and other industrial centres of the region. The W.E.A. deputation responded to questioning about this issue by arguing that it was the cutbacks in the university tutorial class movement which explained this astonishing growth, and that the Labour College movement was filling a vacuum. In the session 1915–16 no recognized tutorial classes were being provided in south Wales by either the W.E.A. or the joint committees. The enlistment of tutors had led to the virtual collapse of orthodox workers' education in south Wales, and the university colleges had utterly failed to respond to the war-created emergency by redirecting their staff towards extra-mural work.[22] The result was that the class-war teaching of the Labour College movement was expanding unchecked by the W.E.A. form of workers' education, which sought to foster a different world view, one based on nationality, a socially conscious religious outlook and a sense of social and community service. Lleufer Thomas was fully aware that the tutors used by the Labour College classes were individuals who possessed acute intelligence.[23] Thus, only

[21] Ibid., 7.

[22] Viscount Haldane, *Royal Commission on University Education in Wales, Final Report. Appendix III, Minutes of Evidence.* Cmnd. 8993 (London, 1917), 66–76.

[23] Ibid., Q. 12,058 and 12,168, 68–72. See also the note added later to the minutes of evidence by Lleufer Thomas, in response to Q. 12,170, 72.

tutors of equal intellect could controvert or, better still, convert them. The key was the selection and training of suitable tutors. Lleufer Thomas did not see the necessity of seeking to shape or control the teaching beyond the selection of tutors.

For Lleufer Thomas the crisis in orthodox workers' education was made worse by the utter unwillingness of some sections of the university, local authority, business and commercial establishment to see the need for non-vocational education for working people, especially at a time when the nation would be struggling to pay for the war effort.[24] The struggle was thus not just against the challenge of I.W.C.E., but also against the 'ratepayer' mentality which felt that there had to be a tangible economic return for the investment made in education. The clamour for technical and vocational education at the expense of the liberalizing and humanizing disciplines was short-sighted and politically counter-productive as it left a demand which would be satisfied by the advocates of class-war ideas. Whilst Lleufer Thomas was genuinely anxious about the rapid increase of Labour College classes in south Wales in the later war years, it is also true that it was a very useful bogey to scare those who were hostile or indifferent to workers' education, rather in the way that advocates of workers' education were able to use the arrival of thirty Labour M.P.s in the Commons in 1906 as a lever to elicit a governmental commitment to university tutorial classes. It was, however, a very difficult strategy to pursue successfully. There was already a body of opinion amongst employers that believed that all forms of workers' education were subversive of their interests. Efforts to allay such fears ran the risk of confirming in the minds of ordinary rank and file activists the Labour College assertion that the W.E.A. and university form of workers' education were geared to preserving capitalism and the interests of the employing classes. It was a Scylla and Charybdis which would have tested the most skilled navigator, and Lleufer Thomas was a supremely competent pilot, but the task was ultimately to prove too difficult even for him.

The 'Welsh ideal of popular culture' was an attempt to

[24] See Lleufer Thomas's introduction to the *W.E.A. Wales, Eleventh Annual Report, 1917–18.*

synthesize all the various strands which had gone to make up the W.E.A./university form of workers' education in south Wales since 1906 and overlay them with a Welsh cultural consciousness. It was, however, an ideal driven and promoted in the context of anxiety: the desire to displace the hitherto rather nebulous aims of the W.E.A. in south Wales with this new and more coherent ideal. Consciously or unconsciously, Lleufer Thomas sought to turn the W.E.A. into a mirror image of what Ablett desired for the Labour College movement. The association, rather like the Plebs League, would be both a propagator of the ideal and a watchdog which would ensure the ideological purity of the movement. Great stress was laid on selecting and training first-rate teachers, men and women who could be trusted to impart a view of the world which would help to achieve a new order of society. If Ablett was more directly concerned with content than was Lleufer Thomas, it was only because the latter was convinced that the initial process of tutor selection would ensure that the correct vision would be transmitted. He was always convinced that the W.E.A./university form of workers' education would be a superior product that would simply crowd out the shoddy goods available from the Labour College movement. Both men knew the importance of individual leaders and teachers. For Ablett the task that confronted him was to create a cadre of men who would seek to give to the organized working class an understanding of their historic role to challenge and overthrow capitalism. For Lleufer Thomas it was to create a leadership influenced in the direction of a non-revolutionary, reformist progressivism.

2. 'TOWARDS CAPITALISM THEIR ATTITUDE IS UNCOMPROMISING'

August 1914 was the high summer of Labour College fortunes. The S.W.M.F. and the N.U.R. were committed to taking over the college and the Miners' Federation of south Wales was committed to establishing a coalfield-wide scheme of scholarships free from the vagaries of district support. An editorial in the August edition of the *Plebs* magazine, written by Ted Gill, was filled with hope and enthusiasm for what appeared to be an assured future for the college and the I.W.C.E. movement.

The euphoria was soon dispelled. The C.L.C. became a legal football for the two union hierarchies and their legal advisers. Union leaders, terrified that they would be hauled by a disgruntled member in front of the judiciary for misuse of union funds, were duly cautious about any new spending commitments.[25] There was also the not entirely unfounded suspicion that some of the union leaders were prevaricating in the hope that delays would see the demise of the Labour College. The railwaymen's leader, J. H. Thomas, was particularly suspect in this regard.[26] Even some of the south Wales miners' leaders not noted for their enthusiastic support of the college began to express disquiet at what appeared to be obstructionist tactics by elements on the N.U.R. executive.[27] It was not until June 1916 that the C.L.C. premises were formally acquired by both unions. Ablett was one of the first set of S.W.M.F. governors of the college, now formally renamed the Labour College, though still known popularly as the Central Labour College to distinguish it from the local classes and 'colleges'.[28]

Despite the enthusiasm and hope of August 1914, the Labour College had only clung to existence through subventions from the S.W.M.F. In the session 1913–14 there had been ten students at the college; by July 1915 there were only six in residence.[29] Simmering student discontent had been suppressed only by the desire to avoid the closure threat which would have followed any public outbursts. However, whatever the threats to its existence which emanated from the N.U.R. leadership, from student unrest, or foreclosure by the banks on its massive debts, they were as nothing compared with the exigencies of war which, by the summer of 1916, were encroaching on the C.L.C.

The first blow was the loss of an effective champion in Ted

[25] N.U.R./S.W.M.F., C.L.C. joint committee minutes, 14 Aug. 1914; N.L.S., Acc. 5120, C.L.C. correspondence, Box 2, fo. 1914; see also S.W.M.F. E.C. minutes, 24 Aug., 1, 29 Sept. 1914.

[26] J. Reynolds, assistant secretary of the C.L.C., to Ebby Edwards, c. February 1915: N.L.S., Acc. 5120, C.L.C. correspondence, Box 2, fo. 1915.

[27] See the statement by John Williams, miners' agent for the Merthyr area, accusing elements within the N.U.R. of deliberately delaying the settlement of the C.L.C. issue. Llais Llafur, 30 Jan. 1915; [Merthyr] Pioneer, 30 Jan., 20 Feb. 1915.

[28] S.W.M.F., E.C. minutes, 21 March 1916; Labour College, deed of Settlement, 26 June 1916.

[29] C.L.C. Board of Governors' minutes, 27 July 1914, 31 July 1915.

Gill, after Ablett the college's staunchest advocate. He left the coalfield in the autumn of 1914, breaking with I.W.C.E. principles, to take up an economics lecturing appointment with Manchester Education Committee. By the early months of 1915 he was back in the coalfield seeking to raise a company of miners to serve with the South Wales Borderers,[30] an effort which earned him a commission and later the Military Cross. By the summer of 1916, just as the ink was drying on the deed of settlement which transferred the Labour College to the miners and the railwaymen, the military authorities began to express an interest in the students and the younger, fitter members of the college staff; Craik and Reynolds were conscripted.[31] The Labour College closed its doors at the beginning of 1917 for the duration of hostilities and its long term future once again looked bleak.

With the college unable to retain either staff or students, its premises became a severe burden on the controlling unions' finances. Thomas Richards proposed, and the S.W.M.F. executive committee agreed to, the disposal of the Labour College buildings.[32] Although the Federation would maintain its commitment to re-establishing the college after the war, Labour College supporters realized that such a task would be made infinitely more difficult if the premises were sold. By early 1917 the Labour College class movement in the coalfield was a considerable force with class groups, it was claimed at the time, catering for up to 1,200 students, and the Richards plan gave them a focus for co-ordinated activity.[33] A vigorous campaign was conducted throughout the spring of 1917 and, at a S.W.M.F. special conference in May, the Richards plan was overwhelmingly rejected, being supported by only twelve delegates out of more than three hundred. It was a personal triumph for Ablett, who spoke against the executive committee proposal at the special conference; it guaranteed the Federation's commitment to reopening the college, but it also

[30] G.F.P., 4 Feb. 1915.

[31] S.W.M.F., E.C. minutes, 10 Feb. 1917. The N.U.R. and the Federation tried to secure exemption for Reynolds and Craik as trade union officials, but to no avail.

[32] S.W.M.F., E.C. minutes, 6 Jan., 31 Mar., 4 Apr. 1917.

[33] See the report of the conference of south Wales I.W.C.E. classes in February 1917, Plebs (March 1917); Message from Students and Teachers of C.L.C. Classes in South Wales (c. March 1917), N.L.S. Acc. 5120, Box 3.

reflected the phenonmenal rise of local I.W.C.E. classes as a force in the Federation, a force which was changing the atmosphere in the coalfield.[34]

In the first years of the war, Labour College classes declined. In 1914–15 only two classes were being run, one in the Rhondda with Ablett as tutor and one in Barry under A. J. Cook. The 1915–16 session saw a slow but steady recovery, particularly in the eastern part of the coalfield, under the energetic leadership of Sydney Jones, an ex-C.L.C. protégé of Ted Gill and the New Era Union.[35] By the summer of 1916 there were five classes operating in the Ebbw, Sirhowy and Rhymney Valleys. In July 1916 the representatives of these classes met at Pontllanfraith and established an organization called the Workers' Democratic Education League, a body which, initially, had no formal links with the Plebs League or the Labour College.[36] Its prime aim was the establishment of I.W.C.E. classes throughout the coalfield; it was also designed to promote the creation of a more aggressive stance by the Miners' Federation. Sydney Jones made no bones about the close link between the growth of classes and the development of a class-conscious, militant union organization. 'Education led to perfecting organization [sic]', argued Sydney Jones; the classes would 'destroy the old dogmas', and assist in 'removing the old organisation preparatory to founding a positive aggressive organisation based on objective class antagonism and prepared to wage the war to a successful conclusion'.[37] Thus the political and industrial militancy of the period, although having its roots in the strengthened bargaining position of organized labour and reinforced by hostility to the introduction of military conscription, was easily linked in the minds of supporters and opponents with the growth of I.W.C.E. classes.

Sydney Jones and another protégé of Ted Gill, Will Hewlett,[38] were keen to see further co-ordination of class work in

---

[34] S.W.M.F. Conference minutes, 1 May 1917; *Plebs* (June 1917).

[35] Sydney Jones became a lodge chairman and a Monmouthshire county councillor upon his return from the C.L.C. Later he became a miners' agent and member of the E.C. of the S.W.M.F. A powerful influence in the western valleys of Monmouthshire he was also something of a political mentor of Aneurin Bevan and Harold Finch. See M. Foot, *Aneurin Bevan, 1897–1945* (London, 1975), 34–7, and H. Finch, *Memoirs of a Bedwellty M.P.* (Newport, 1972), 21–2.

[36] *Plebs* (August 1916).

[37] [*Merthyr*] *Pioneer*, 21 July 1917.

the coalfield, but they ran up against a feeling, particularly strong in the Rhondda area, that such an organization might undermine the objective of making class work an integral part of trade union activity. This was to be a recurrent theme in the history of the I.W.C.E. movement, especially in south Wales. At a conference of the south Wales classes held in Cardiff in December 1916, these differences came out into the open when the Rhondda representatives pressed for the S.W.M.F. and the N.U.R. (and kindred organizations) to take over the classes in south Wales. A further resolution was passed renaming the W.D.E.L. the C.L.C. League, reinforcing the link with the college and a commitment to reopen it.[39] It was the C.L.C. League which in 1917 spearheaded the coalfield campaign against selling off the Labour College premises. The South Wales C.L.C. League also campaigned for the renaming of the Plebs League as the C.L.C. League at the Plebs annual conference in July 1917.[40] This proposal, backed by Mark Starr, A. J. Cook and W. H. Mainwaring, failed.

The phenomenal and spontaneous rise in the number of I.W.C.E. classes quickly outstripped the capacity of the movement to supply competent and experienced tutors. In January 1917 the *Plebs* magazine listed some seventeen classes in south Wales; by January 1918 the number had risen to forty. The result was that the quality of provision varied enormously. Will Coldrick, later a C.L.C. student, was introduced to the I.W.C.E. movement in these years. His memories of the early classes were that they were of a fairly rudimentary character. His first tutor, Will Hewlett, was 'no scholar but it was a case of those knowing little teaching those who knew less'.[41] At the end of 1916, John Evans, who had attended Ruskin College on a Rhondda No. 1 District scholarship at the same time as Ablett, delivered a series of lectures to full houses at the

[38] Hewlett did much to build up the Labour College class movement in south-east Wales as secretary of the W.D.E.L. and then the C.L.C. League. He joined the Communist Party on its formation and was killed in a railway accident whilst travelling to Moscow in 1921 as a delegate to the Communist International. *Plebs* (Oct. 1921).
[39] See the report on the south Wales Labour College class conference in the [*Merthyr*] *Pioneer*, 9 Dec. 1916; *Plebs* (Jan. 1917).
[40] Ibid. (Aug. 1917).
[41] Interview by author and David Egan, 24 Sept. 1973. Transcript held at the South Wales Miners' Library (S.W.M.L.), University College of Swansea.

Progressive Free Church in Nantyffyllon in the Llynfi Valley. The lectures were in fact based on transcripts made by Evans of Hird's lectures on the subject originally delivered when Evans was at Ruskin.[42] There were also, of course, great and charismatic tutors such as Ablett and Mark Starr.

Starr returned from the C.L.C. after its wartime closure to the Aberdare Valley just as the demand for classes exploded. Aberdare had been an isolated island of W.E.A. activity in the coalfield, with John Thomas safely fending off the occasional attack from Labour College supporters such as Wil John Edwards. The Merthyr *Pioneer*, the main organ of the I.L.P. in the eastern part of the coalfield, had been generally sympathetic to Thomas in his years as district secretary of the W.E.A. After 1916, however, the influence of the Labour College class movement in the area resulted in a change in tone and less positive coverage for the association.[43] With the banishment of Thomas to war work in the Swansea area, Edwards and Starr began to dominate workers' education in the Aberdare area. In regular, well-written and well-argued pieces in the *Pioneer*, Edwards and Starr portrayed the W.E.A. as an agency of social control, in which bright young men of the labour movement were seduced by the dreaming spires of the universities and eventually given pensionable jobs with the National Insurance Commission. Edwards wrote of how 'They develop ideas quite harmless to capitalism, and for ever they are lost to the Labour movement. How different are these respectable humbugs, with their grandmotherly notions of social development, to some of those young men who contribute so much to the Labour cause ... Towards capitalism their attitude is uncompromising ... Victimization stares them in the face but they keep up the fight ...These are the men our movement depends upon; theirs is the stuff that goes to make revolutions'.[44] There was a rather bitter tone about the pieces written by Edwards; Starr was less vitriolic about his former tutors and associates in the W.E.A. He

---

[42] [*Merthyr*] *Pioneer*, 30 Dec. 1916.

[43] See the series of letters on the relative merits of the W.E.A. and Labour College by Thomas and Edwards in the [*Merthyr*] *Pioneer*, 5, 12, 26 Feb., 4 Mar. 1916.

[44] [*Merthyr*] *Pioneer*, 13 May 1916. See also an earlier piece on the W.E.A. by Edwards in the *Pioneer*, 11 Mar. 1916.

wrote that it was not possible to judge the association by 'its local members or branches which have been "nobbled" by the Socialists ... Sooner or later—like an unorthodox minister in an orthodox chapel—the progressive elements will have to come out of the W.E.A. and take up the working-class stand-point.'[45]

By 1917 Starr and Edwards had established classes in Marxian economics and industrial history under the aegis of the Aberdare District of the S.W.M.F. at Aberaman and Mountain Ash.[46] The lectures in industrial history given by Starr were reprinted in the Merthyr *Pioneer* and became the basis of one of the most famous and successful of all Plebs text-books, *A Worker Looks at History.*[47] These classes were a model of well-organized and well-structured teaching, with a clear syllabus based on readily available texts. The problem of tutor shortage was also tackled by the creation of standard tests, whereby students who reached a certain level were deemed eligible to act as class leaders.

The preamble to the Aberdare District classes made it clear that the purpose of the scheme was to reveal to the working classes their mission to overthrow the existing economic order. To achieve this end, the workers needed knowledge of the forces at work in the capitalist system, knowledge which the governing classes were seeking to conceal, not least by supporting educational movements 'brazenly called "democratic" whose only purpose is to gull the workers through the channels of the Universities, the educational establishments of the ruling class'. The oblique reference to the W.E.A. was obviously necessary in John Thomas's old stamping ground. The links with the Labour College were stressed and the purpose of the classes made manifest: 'Like the College itself, these classes have for their object the training of men and women for the industrial, political, and

[45] Ibid., 29 July 1917.

[46] *Aberdare District Miners' Federation, Evening Classes, Commencing October, 1916* (Aberdare, 1916). A copy of this document is held in the Mark Starr collection of the Tamiment Library, New York University, Box 1, fo. 2. The classes were subsidized by the district committee by reimbursing the fees of those students who achieved a 75 per cent attendance rate. The fees were 1s. 6d. per subject, 2s. 6d. for two.

[47] [*Merthyr*] *Pioneer*, 4 Nov. 1916 to 12 May 1917. By 1930 over 20,000 copies of Starr's first edition of the book had been sold. A second edition, published in 1925, sold a further 10,000. J. P. M. Millar, *Education for Emancipation* (London, 1930), 31–2.

social work of organized Labour, and the creation of an intelligent rank and file'.[48]

The issue of class co-ordination in the coalfield resurfaced at a
conference of south Wales I.W.C.E. groups in May 1918. Ted
Williams, an ex-C.L.C. student, who had joined Starr and Edwards in the Aberdare District scheme, once again proposed
the creation of some kind of co-ordinating agency for the
Labour College classes in south Wales. Once again the idea
was opposed by those who felt that it would undermine the
demand that such work should be the direct reponsibility of
the unions.[49] Critics of this line argued that such a stance was
preventing the expansion of class work in those areas where
no trade union support was forthcoming. By 1917 the two
Rhondda districts, the Aberdare and the Dowlais Districts,
were supporting I.W.C.E. classes for their members. In fact
this area accounted for twenty-four of the forty south Wales
coalfield classes in a well-known list published in the *Plebs*
magazine in December 1917 and January 1918. Outside this
tight area, support was less forthcoming. The Rhymney Valley
District initially refused to give financial support on the
grounds that the teaching was atheistical.[50] Later, in September
1917, the Monmouthshire western valleys, and in the following
year the eastern valley miners, established classes supported out
of district funds.[51] Ten of the forty classes listed in December
1917 were in Monmouthshire; thus the vast bulk of the classes
of this period were being run in the eastern and central part of
the coalfield. Further west the class list becomes much smaller.
D. R. Owen and J. Dicks ran classes in Gwaun-Cae-Gurwen
and Garnant, and J. L. Rees ran a class in Clydach, in the
Swansea Valley. In south Wales outside the coalfield there
were only three classes, one in Barry, which had been running
since before the war, and two in Cardiff, both closely linked
with the N.U.R.

[48] Aberdare District Class List (1916), op. cit., 2.
[49] [*Merthyr*] *Pioneer*, 25 May 1918.
[50] *Plebs* (April 1917).
[51] Ibid. (Oct. 1917, Jan. 1919). George Daggar, ex-C.L.C. student, and W. J.
Saddler, a Ruskin College contemporary of Ablett and Gill (later vice-president and
general secretary of the S.W.M.F.), took the western valley classes. Arthur Jenkins
established some classes in the Pontypool area, with the financial support of eight local
S.W.M.F. lodges as early as March 1917. *Plebs* (Apr. 1917).

The great centre of I.W.C.E. activity remained the Rhondda, with eighteen classes listed in 1917.[52] It was the area with the longest tradition of Labour College classes and the area with the largest reservoir of ex-C.L.C. students on which to draw for tutors. Ablett, Cook, Maddocks, Mainwaring, D. W. Thomas, N. Thomas, E. J. Williams and Ted Williams could all contribute. Yet in many ways some of the most dynamic class work went on in the Aberdare Valley with Starr and Edwards. Many of the ex-C.L.C. students were becoming very active in the work of the Federation; Ablett, Cook and Mainwaring were very involved in the revival of the Unofficial Reform Committee, and this became the focal point of their activism. Ablett's main concern, as ever, was the residential college and its prompt reopening.

Mark Starr, in the Aberdare Valley, was far less active in union life, and the focus of his attention was class work. He was first and foremost an educationalist. A regular contributor to the *Plebs* magazine, he played a key role in converting the Merthyr *Pioneer* into an organ of the Labour College movement. This was an important development because the *Plebs* magazine had only a very limited circulation in south Wales.[53] Many of the reports from south Wales which appeared in the *Plebs* magazine were in fact reprinted from the Merthyr *Pioneer*.

Starr had also the most seminal mind in the south Wales I.W.C.E. movement as far as pedagogical matters were concerned. Few of the other leading tutors seem to have given much thought to the process of teaching. In October 1917 he laid down ground rules for the establishment of social science classes, a popular contemporary euphemism for I.W.C.E. classes, with an order of preference for the methods of tuition. The best was a course of lectures, funded by a union, and led by an ex-C.L.C. student, or at least someone who had completed the correspondence courses of the Labour College.

[52] The massive upsurge of interest in the Labour College classes in this period is well illustrated by the fact that the first resolution in support of district-sponsored classes was passed by the Rhondda No. 1 committee in November 1915 by 17 votes to 13. In October 1916 a similar resolution was passed by 25 votes to 3. Rhondda No. 1 minutes, 22 Nov. 1915, 23 Oct. 1916.
[53] *Plebs* (June 1918).

Next best was a class based on a C.L.C. correspondence course (similar to the Rhymney model mentioned above) with limited or no tutor support. Finally, there was collective perusal of a book with the text being read aloud in a group. This method was slow, but had one advantage in that individual development was easier to check compared with the large lecture group dominated by a well-known lecturer haranguing a 'mostly tongue-tied audience'. This article was also revealing about the structure and syllabuses of the 'Social Science classes'. Classes should commence with a session on the value and purpose of I.W.C.E.; this should then be followed up by a brief introduction to socialist thought, mostly using texts by the American Marxist intellectual Daniel de Leon and those published by the main British Marxist political organization of the period, the Socialist Labour Party (S.L.P.). Some texts by Marx and Engels, especially the *Communist Manifesto* and *Socialism, Utopian and Scientific*, were also regarded as suitable. The more substantial parts of the course, usually on economics or industrial history, would be based on Plebs texts such as Ablett's *Easy Outlines of Economics* and Starr's own work.[54]

Starr's experience of the difficulties involved in establishing effective class groups seems to have made him more willing to consider expedients which departed from the more fundamental principles of I.W.C.E. In November 1917 he even suggested that local authority classes could be used for the propagation of I.W.C.E., where control was in Labour hands, arguing that 'expediency and opportunism are only to be attacked where they are based on false principles.' Suitable premises would be made available, and any attempts by the government inspectorate to withdraw grant-aid would expose the true nature of the capitalist state and result in much beneficial publicity. He even suggested that I.W.C.E. supporters should infiltrate the W.E.A.: 'We need the courage and the brains to capture every possible avenue of education.'[55] His ideas were too advanced for most Plebs idealists, but in practice his strategy of what might be termed academic 'entryism' was adopted by many I.W.C.E. groups in south Wales in the inter-war years.

[54] Ibid. (Oct. 1917).
[55] Ibid. (Nov. 1917).

The massive and spontaneous expansion of classes which started in 1916 seems to have peaked some time in 1918. One factor which checked further expansion of the classes in the last stages of the war was the harassment and persecution of some of the leading tutors in the Labour College movement such as Cook and Mainwaring.[56] Starr was a victim of the notorious 'comb out' of miners hitherto protected from military service as being in a reserved occupation. Starr decided, like many others, to 'go on the run'. He was captured in the summer of 1918, and he used his court martial as a platform to denounce the war in an eloquent and defiant manner. He did not use ethical or religious arguments against fighting, but asserted that the war was the product of capitalist imperialism. After lecturing the court on these matters, he ended by stating that he did not want to 'blow heads off' but to put new ideas into them'. His only desire was 'to advance another cure for all war—the education of the workers'. The court responded to this homily by sending Starr to Wormwood Scrubs.[57]

The rapid expansion in the number of I.W.C.E. classes reflected a significant change in the influence of the movement in industrial south Wales. Marxian economics and history were now profound formative influences on a significant slice of the young activist element in the S.W.M.F., the N.U.R. and other unions. The exact number of students who attended Labour College classes in south Wales must remain a matter for speculation. There was no systematic collection of attendance figures, and the numbers quoted by supporters and opponents of the I.W.C.E. movement must be treated with caution because both sides had their own reasons to exaggerate them, and the figures quoted are often suspiciously rounded. In early 1916 it was estimated that some 300 students were attending C.L.C. classes. At the end of 1916 the W.E.A. increased this figure to 400. Lleufer Thomas, in his evidence to the Haldane Commission, increased this to 500, or roughly twenty-five per class. Evidence about actual individual class attendance is equally

[56] R. Page Arnot, *South Wales Miners: A History of the South Wales Miners' Federation, 1914–26* (Cardiff, 1975), 151.

[57] [*Merthyr*] *Pioneer*, 7 Sept. 1918. See also the interview by David Egan of D. J. Davies, who was captured with Mark Starr, 3 Nov. 1972. S.W.M.L., Swansea.

sketchy, but twenty-five seems to have been the figure for the
Aberdare area, perhaps a little higher in the Rhondda Valley.
By November 1917 *Welsh Outlook* calculated that some 1,200
students were being catered for in some forty classes in south
Wales.[58] Whilst these figures might inflate the numbers attending classes closely associated with the Labour College, those
recognized by the *Plebs* magazine, they take no account of the
vast number of informal groups or I.L.P. groups that ran
classes on I.W.C.E. lines. It also takes no account of the impact
of I.W.C.E. tuition transmitted through the pages of the
Merthyr *Pioneer*. At its height, in 1917–18, the Labour College
movement was without doubt the most formative influence in
the coalfield and did much to instil a deep antipathy towards
capitalism, which was to have a lasting effect on the development of organized labour in south Wales.

The war was probably as popular amongst the rank and file
workers of south Wales as it was in other parts of the United
Kingdom.[59] News of the defeat of James Winstone by the rabid
jingoist C. B. Stanton in Keir Hardie's old seat in Merthyr
Tydfil came on the same day that Edmund Stonelake was
about to deliver a lecture to a Penrhiwceiber W.E.A. class on
the subject of 'The power of democracy'. The irony of subject
and event was too cruel for him, and the talk was cancelled.[60]
Yet amongst a substantial section of the activist element the
war, from the outset, concentrated their minds on matters
political in a way that no previous event had done. The disen-
gagement of many young trade union activists from religion
prior to the war was even more pronounced after 1914, as
many of them contrasted the detachment of many preachers of
the gospel from the industrial strife of pre-war years with their
sudden enthusiasm for the prosecution of a very worldly conflict. The spectacle of ministers appearing on recruitment platforms, some in uniform, drove one young lay preacher called

---

[58] *Welsh Outlook* (July 1916, Nov. 1917); Haldane Commission, vol. III, minutes of
evidence, note to Q 12,170, 72; [*Merthyr*] *Pioneer*, 14 Oct. 1916. The figure of 1,200
seems to have come from the C.L.C. League's campaign leaflet against selling off of
the college premises.
[59] See A. Môr-O'Brien, 'Patriotism on trial: the strike of the south Wales miners, July
1915', *Welsh History Review*, 12, No. 1 (1984), 76–104, and 'Keir Hardie, C. B. Stanton,
and the First World War', *Llafur*, 4, No. 3 (1986).
[60] [*Merthyr*] *Pioneer*, 4 Dec. 1915.

Arthur Horner to denounce them: 'the followers of the Prince of Peace have deserted their Leader's counsel and live alone to serve the new found protector of the nation. The God who is worshipped as the creator of the greater God: Patriotism.'[61]

For those who were leaving the chapel there were many alternatives with which to fill the intellectual void. The First World War was remembered by many as a time when old ideas and attitudes were tested to destruction. Those who were approaching adulthood were particularly susceptible to the ferment of ideas that circulated amongst the working-class communities of south Wales. 'It was a period in which now the young men, or people that were prepared to shed old ideas, had opportunities of doing so.' For Dai Dan Evans, later a leader of the south Wales miners, the shortages and the 'dire methods' the authorities used to maintain control over the working class in the war period combined with the intellectual destabilization of the era to produce, 'a great dynamic period of thought in the working-class communities'.[62] Will Coldrick also remembered the war as a time of new ideas, particularly those which called into question the religious assumptions of ordinary people.[63] W. (Bill) Gregory recalled as a boy in Briton Ferry that the local I.L.P. branch functioned as a centre of opposition to the war. It also acted as a refuge for opponents of the war wishing to spread their ideas. 'Due to the accident of war all sorts of highly educated people moved through the area.'[64] The war fostered an almost insatiable demand for knowledge, for explanations of the changes that seemed to be engulfing communities in the era of total war.

The surge in demand for classes was also closely related in the minds of contemporaries to the industrial unrest which afflicted the region in the later war years. Whilst it is clear that the rise in the number of social science classes was a close concomitant of the industrial unrest, there was, in some quarters, a belief at the time that they were, in some way, a cause of the unrest.

[61] Ibid., 24 July 1915.
[62] Interview with D. D. Evans by Hywel Francis, 5 Dec. 1972, S.W.M.L., Swansea.
[63] Interview with W. Coldrick, loc. cit.
[64] Interview with W. H. (Bill) Gregory by the author and Hywel Francis, 23 Sept. 1973. After attending W.E.A. classes, Gregory obtained a scholarship to Cambridge and later became a research officer with the I.S.T.C. He subsequently became national organizing secretary of the W.E.A./W.E.T.U.C.

Whilst the bulk of the mining workforce in south Wales never became anti-war in a pacifist sense, after July 1915 their support for the war did not include acceptance of an industrial truce which would allow for profiteering by their employers. In April 1915 the south Wales miners gave formal notice that their wages agreement would terminate in three months' time and that industrial action would follow the failure to negotiate a satisfactory replacement. The prospect of an 'official' strike in the most important coalfield in the country alarmed the government and outraged the jingoist press. Despite having a Royal Proclamation issued against their contemplated action, two hundred thousand south Wales coalminers downed tools. Only the direct involvement of Lloyd George and massive concessions from the government and the employers induced them to return to work. The 1915 strike was a watershed. From the summer of 1915, the state was forced to intervene time after time in order to maintain industrial peace in the coalfield, eventually being forced to take over the running of the industry. These trends reinforced anti-capitalist sentiment in several distinct but related ways. First of all, by forcing the government to intervene, the miners grew in confidence, and ideas of the workers' control of industry no longer appeared outlandish to intelligent activists. Secondly, the exercise of coercive government power over workers seemed to underscore the Marxian message that the state was actually an agency of class oppression and not the neutral force it was assumed to be by many ethical and Fabian socialists. Finally, as one recent study has noted, the word 'profiteering' entered the language of class in the latter stages of the war. Capitalism was now seen by many workers as not only immoral but also unpatriotic. Calls for sacrifice by labour were not matched by signs of restraint by the owners and managers of capital.[65]

If these indigenous pressures did not help to support the anti-capitalist message of the I.W.C.E. classes and trigger a deep desire to understand the nature of the capitalist beast, external developments in the later war years certainly did. Events in

[65] The role of the concept of 'profiteering' in promoting the language and imagery of class conflict and the 'labour–capital dichotomy' in the later war years is examined in B. Waites, *A Class Society at War, England 1914–1918* (Leamington Spa, 1987), 55–74, 221–31.

Russia after the February revolution were a subject of intense interest in industrial south Wales, and they gave industrial unrest a more menacing aspect for the government and the ruling élites. The spectre of Bolshevism was to change the nature and tone of political debate for socialists and anti-socialists alike, for to the threat of internal anti-capitalist agitation was added a perceived threat of external subversion.

In an era of unprecedented change, when the very fabric of western civilization seemed to be disintegrating, the demand for explanation and understanding of these changes was great. For many young miners the classes in Marxian economics and history offered a ready-packaged set of ideas which gave meaning and coherence in a way that was not offered by any other available world view. The effect on some young workers had the quality of a religious conversion, an experience well illustrated by Starr after his first year at the C.L.C. The economics of Marx, the labour theory of value, the class struggle, the materialist conception of history, the 'mind clearing logic' of the German Marxist philosopher Dietzgen and the books of the American socialist publishers Kerr and Company were 'undiscovered continents of enlightenment'. He wrote of how he had been dissatisfied with the old ideas, 'perplexed' with current problems and 'lost in the longings of idealism amidst sordid surroundings'. His personal testament then explained how the C.L.C. had given 'point and purpose to my view of life'. The Labour College movement had given him a guiding thread through the 'tangled skein' of modern society. 'Light has shone in dark places. Contradictions are understood and reconciled. The new is seen evolving from the old; the solution is contained within the problem.'[66]

Mark Starr's experience was shared by many young activists in industrial south Wales in the latter stages of the war. It bred a confidence which was underpinned by a profound belief that the secrets of an inexorable historical process had been vouchsafed to them. With an explanation of the past and the present, they could predict the future, and it belonged to them. That is not to suggest that the C.L.C. classes developed in their students a uniform ideology or view about how the future was

[66] *Plebs* (August 1916).

going to be secured for the workers. A semi-syndicalistic perception, closely associated with the Rhondda classes and men like Ablett and A. J. Cook, was a powerful influence, and the later war years saw a flowering of ideas about workers' control of industry which derived great stimulus from the exercise of workers' power and the experience of state control of the railways and the mines. An old state socialist like George Barker, the scourge of the syndicalists before 1914, had asked in 1912, 'Is there any possibility of any man going out and persuading the people to take possession of the mines? He would be laughed at as a lunatic.'[67] By 1917 the climate had changed, and workers' control now seemed to be a real possibility. Barker could now assert, 'The industrial worker of the coming generation will be intellectually equipped, not for "Collective Bargaining" with his employer, but for taking over and controlling his own industry.'[68] Barker's views do not denote a wholehearted conversion to syndicalism; he remained, as did the bulk of south Wales activists, a state socialist and committed to the primacy of political over direct action. What he was saying was that the intellectual climate operating amongst the rising generation of activists had been transformed to the point where a naïve belief in the benefits of nationalization had been overtaken by a deeper understanding of the nature of the capitalist state.

Even amongst I.W.C.E. class tutors, simon-pure syndicalists were rare. Wil John Edwards estimated in 1918 that only six out of more than a hundred C.L.C. class activists 'disbelieved in some form of political action'.[69] Both Craik and Starr were critical of those who dismissed the necessity for workers to challenge the capitalists on the political battlefield.[70] There was a larger minority within the I.W.C.E. movement which was hostile to the parliamentarism of the I.L.P. and the Labour Party; some of these belonged to the—avowedly Marxist—Socialist Labour Party. In the western part of the coalfield D. R. Owen was a member, and in the east W. J. Edwards, Will

---

[67] K. O. Morgan, op. cit., 37.
[68] 'Foreword' to Mark Starr, *A Worker Looks at History* (Oxford, 1917).
[69] [*Merthyr*] *Pioneer*, 16 June 1918.
[70] *Plebs* (March 1917).

Hewlett and Ness Edwards.[71] However, this seems to have been fairly unusual; most C.L.C. tutors were either I.L.P. members or were active in the Unofficial Reform Committee, or they found involvement with the Federation sufficient engagement with the labour movement. The links between the classes and the U.R.C. are well known, and some writers have argued that the concept of 'encroaching control', which was the 'Next step' strategy, was popularized largely through the agency of the C.L.C. class movement.[72] But it would be a misconception simply to see the classes as an adjunct of the U.R.C.; the class movement was more than that. The Labour College movement had a clear sense of purpose, but that was never translated into a universally accepted vision of how the classes fitted into a strategy of revolutionary political change. Its ultimate objective was the overthrow of capitalism, but it did not have a programme for action. Wil John Edwards denied that the classes had anything to do with political or industrial action, but rather their function was to lay bare the economics of capitalist production and this 'eventually creates within the breast of every student the desire to abolish the rule of capital'. It was up to the student which branch of the labour movement he wished to join. Indeed, the exposure of the nature of capitalism was the key to change, for once the workers were acquainted with these fundamentals, 'Socialism will then follow as night follows day.'[73]

There was in such ideas the implication that any activism that was not underpinned by a grounding in Marxian economics and the materialist conception of history was doomed to failure, or was at best a wishy-washy reformism. There was also a strong whiff of determinism which suggested that political activity was little short of useless in the playing out of a historical drama in which the roles had already been written and, once the working class learned its lines, the denouement was bound to follow. Finally, once the scales had fallen from the eyes of many of the young activists in the classes, they tended to display an arrogant contempt for those who had not

[71] [*Merthyr*] *Pioneer*, 29 June 1918.
[72] M. G. Woodhouse, 'Mines for the nation or for the miners? Alternative perspectives on industrial democracy, 1919–1921', *Llafur*, 2, No. 3 (1978), 93.
[73] [*Merthyr*] *Pioneer*, 29 June 1918.

undergone a similar experience or who questioned the truth of the revelation. Many active in the I.L.P. in south Wales resented the credit being given to the Labour College classes for the rising socialist consciousness of the labour movement. From 1916 onwards, there was constant sniping at the Labour College classes from elements within the south Wales socialist movement who disliked what they saw as both its academic detachment and its ideological certainty. When a writer in *Welsh Outlook* ascribed the rising militancy of the S.W.M.F. to the influence of the C.L.C. classes, an anonymous contributor to the Merthyr *Pioneer* pointed out that the I.L.P. had been far more responsible than the C.L.C. for the shaping of Federation policy and leadership. It was the I.L.P. members who were 'not only the most intelligent but also the most active workers in the organization'. Whilst acknowledging the great influence of the 'old students of the Central Labour College', the author stated that 'it is quite certain that the I.L.P. has more to do with the shaping of Federation policy than any other body'.[74]

Conflict between the C.L.C. classes and the I.L.P. was complicated by the fact that many I.W.C.E. tutors were active members of the I.L.P. In 1917 Mark Starr and Ted Williams ran two very successful social science classes for the I.L.P. in Hardie's old power base in Merthyr. However, tensions between the less rigidly ideological I.L.P. members and the 'born-again' Marxians of the social science classes came to the surface in March 1918, when Emrys Hughes launched a fierce attack on the effect the classes were having on the local labour movement. Hughes's criticism was twofold: first of all, that the classes were divisive in that they suggested that only those whose fundamental principles were based on the C.L.C. version of Marxian economics and history were of any value to organized labour, and, second, that the classes dealt with subjects that were too detached from current issues and problems. There was, he felt, a tendency for the tutors and taught to adopt an arrogant and dismissive attitude towards non-believers and well-meaning doubters. For Hughes the labour

---

[74] Ibid., 29 July 1916. The article in *Welsh Outlook* (July 1916) was entitled 'The mind of the miner'.

movement should be inclusive and tolerant; the classes bred exclusiveness and intolerance. 'Socialist Philosophy has now progressed from the propaganda state, when rigid Marxians looked upon the W.E.A. and the Fabian Society as dastardly devices of a loathsome Capitalist Class, and the Fabians misunderstood the Marxians and looked upon them as Syndicalists and Anarchists.'[75] In a later article he pointed out that H. M. Hyndman was well acquainted with the materialist conception of history, whilst E. D. Morel was not, yet it was Morel and not Hyndman who understood better the imperialist nature of the European war. He also attacked what he felt was the irrelevance of much of what was taught, especially with regard to the study of history; only the 'necessities of the moment' were of value to the workers.[76] Hughes triggered a torrent of letters and articles, some in support of criticisms but most in defence of the Labour College classes. A regular theme from those backing Hughes was the intellectual rigidity of the products of the classes and the abstract nature of their studies. Henry Brockhouse, the national organizer of the I.L.P., waded into the dispute with several contributions which reinforced the Hughes critique. The C.L.C. supporters were 'pedantic, narrow doctrinaire young men, who, from the superior heights of their supposed economic wisdom, offer no programme of action'. They seemed to think that the world could be won for socialism by 'formulae', whilst in truth it could only be won by a programme for action. 'The Socialist who would compress his organization within the hide-bound covers of a musty theoretical programme is no Socialist. He is a fool, for "nothing is, all is becoming".'[77]

The telling criticisms of Hughes and Brockhouse did not prevent the steady growth in the influence and impact of the classes. So complete was the triumph of the Labour College perspective on workers' education in industrial south Wales by 1917 that even John Thomas, the exiled erstwhile district secretary of the W.E.A., was telling the Swansea Valley

---

[75] [*Merthyr*] *Pioneer*, 30 Mar. 1918.
[76] Ibid., 11 May 1918.
[77] Ibid., 29 June 1918; the debate filled the columns of the *Pioneer* from March until August 1918. That some older I.L.P. members found the atmosphere of the classes uncongenial is indicated in letters to the paper, 27 July 1918.

I.L.P. that the only form of education of value to the workers was in industrial history, economics and social and political evolution.[78] By the end of the war, many of the leading figures in the S.W.M.F. were closely associated with the Labour College movement, and from these leaders came new perceptions which shattered the static world view of many workers, the 'as it was in the beginning is now and ever shall be' mentality, as Starr called it.[79] One indication of the scale of the change is illustrated by the final ballot for the S.W.M.F. nominee for the secretaryship of the Miners' Federation of Great Britain held in November 1918, which was a close-fought contest between Frank Hodges and Noah Ablett, both closely associated with the I.W.C.E. movement.[80] Whilst only ever directly touching the lives of a fraction of the rank and file miners, the Labour College movement in the later war period did help to reinforce and consolidate a new ethos amongst the activist elements and the 'secondary leaders'. Lib-Labism gave up the ghost, and ethical and state socialism was forced to take on board a more rigorous critique of capitalism. By the end of the war, most young activists were operating on the assumption that their union was not simply engaged in a struggle for better pay and conditions, but actually engaged in a war against capitalism itself. The rhetoric of class conflict became as common as the biblical vocabulary of earlier years amongst union officials. The war did not, as one writer has noted, produce anything new in British socialist thought,[81] but it did have a profound effect on the development of socialism in Britain because it greatly accelerated the spread of socialist thought and activity. This was certainly the case in industrial south Wales. War also gave socialist ideas a credibility they might not otherwise have gained. The collectivist pressures of total war, combined with the enhanced bargaining position of organized labour, made schemes for workers' control seem plausible for the first time amongst significant numbers of workers. In south Wales the Labour College movement played

[78] Ibid., 7 Apr. 1917.
[79] Ibid., 13 Apr. 1918.
[80] R. Page Arnot, op. cit., 152. George Barker was third and Mardy Jones a poor fifth.
[81] J. M. Winter, *Socialism and the Challenge of War* (London, 1974), 270.

a pivotal role in this process by embedding this anti-capitalist consciousness deep in the minds of many activists. William Brace, the old Lib-Lab (Labour since 1908) M.P. and miners' leader, saw what was happening and marvelled at the change the war had wrought. 'The war', said Brace, 'has driven us at least twenty five years in advance of where we were in thought in 1914. The young men have thought deeply and, indeed, they are educated.'[82]

3. 'POLITICS AND ECONOMICS WILL PLAY A LARGER PART THAN EVER AFTER THE WAR IS OVER'

Misgivings about the impact of Labour College teaching soon spread beyond the ranks of the I.L.P. As before the outbreak of the war, the academic world took an interest, especially after the strike of July 1915, when it seemed that the miners behaved in a way which threatened the very survival of the nation. In September 1915 the first of two articles appeared in the *Economic Journal* which sought the underlying causes of the strike. Quickly disposing of press claims that German agents were behind the stoppage, the author moved on to the social context of the dispute. He cited overcrowding, bad housing and a cosmopolitan population thrown together in the narrow mining valleys to serve the labour needs of a single industry long afflicted by the 'guerilla warfare' of bad industrial relations. He saw 'syndicalism', now a term applied to all forms of militant socialism, as a symptom of a deeper social malaise, not a direct cause of the dispute. Only schemes to remedy the underlying social deprivation could cure the problem, and a major effort in the field of adult education would be an important element.[83]

Throughout 1915 and into 1916, *Welsh Outlook* and the circles it represented took a close interest in developments in the coalfield. The 'Mind of the miner' series emphasized the close link between anti-capitalist and anti-war propaganda. 'Opposition

---

[82] Quoted in M. W. Kirby, op. cit., 36; also quoted in A. R. Griffin, *The Miners of Nottingham* (London, 1962), 37.

[83] G. R. Carter, 'The coal strike in south Wales', *Economic Journal*, XXV, No. 99 (1915), and 'The sequel of the Welsh coal strike and its significance', ibid., No. 100 (1915).

to the Anglican church and to landlordism has made and kept
them [the miners] Radicals during past years; the growing real-
isation of the tyranny of capitalism is now converting them into
Socialists.'[84] The Haldane Commission also helped to focus
attention on the influence of the C.L.C. classes. It was the growing concern of government about the temper of the workforce in
industrial south Wales which triggered further interest in the
issue of workers' education. In August 1915 Lloyd George,
whilst addressing some Clydeside employers, asserted that
there was a strong link between the anti-capitalist doctrines
being fostered in south Wales and a strand of hostility to the
war effort.[85] But it was with the establishment of the Commission on Industrial Unrest in the summer of 1917 that interest
in the workers' education boomed for a period. The Commission
for Wales was chaired by Daniel Lleufer Thomas, with another
member of the Cardiff–Barry coterie, Edgar L. Chappell, as
secretary. The trade union representative was Vernon Hartshorn, by now regarded as a respectable and responsible labour
leader whose stature and credibility had grown considerably during the war. Not surprisingly, the report was to contain a good
deal about the way in which inadequate housing and educational provision contributed to social unrest.[86]

The evidence collected in the summer of 1917 reinforced the
conviction of Lleufer Thomas that the miners were in need of a
'balanced' form of adult education.[87] From mine owners and
managers came a litany of complaints about the corrosive influence of the Labour College classes. J. P. Kane, president of the
South Wales Colliery Managers' Association, estimated that
the militants numbered less than 10 per cent of the workforce,
but that their influence was disproportionate because of the inces-
sant anti-capitalist propaganda of the C.L.C. classes: 'The latter

[84] 'The mind of the miner, II', *Welsh Outlook* (August 1916).

[85] He stated that these ideas were being 'deliberately fermented by a man who is
spending his wealth in training people to instruct workmen in doctrines of this
kind'—possibly a reference to Davison. Quoted in C. J. Wrigley, *David Lloyd George
and the British Labour Movement* (London, 1976), 181. See also D. Hopkin, 'A. J. Cook
in 1916–18', *Llafur*, 2, No. 3 (1978).

[86] *Commission of Enquiry Into Industrial Unrest, Division 7 (Wales and Monmouthshire)*,
Cmnd. 8668 (London, 1917), 32–3.

[87] The evidence, collected by Edgar Chappell, is contained in his papers in the
National Library of Wales. At the time the author consulted them they were un-
catalogued.

[the C.L.C. classes] have this last few years grown considerably and unless it is dealt with in a prompt and efficient manner it may cause tremendous upheaval in a few years time.'[88] Kane advocated a major programme of university-type classes in economics and related matters specifically designed to counter the influence of the C.L.C. A mine manager from Morriston spoke of the great influence of the classes and of the anti-capitalist doctrine they preached. He argued that the products of such classes controlled the Federation by simply being more active than the ordinary union member.[89] The need for a systematic programme of education in economics and related matters was also advocated by a retired mine manager and mining engineer, W. Rees, from Llandybïe. He also argued that such provision was not only necessary to counter the teaching of the C.L.C. but also to allow the workers to participate fully in the post-war democracy and allow them to articulate their legitimate demands.[90]

This latter theme was to be an important feature of the commissioners' final report. Adult education was not seen simply as an antidote to Marxism. The attitudinal changes wrought in the mining workforce would be irreversible; once the war was ended, the last restraint on open conflict, patriotism, would disappear, and the forces of capital and labour would engage in mortal combat. Only significant concessions by capital could create the conditions necessary for the recreation of a working partnership with labour. This new partnership would, in the idealist language of the final report, be governed by 'a more human spirit, one in which economic and business considerations will be influenced and corrected, and it is hoped, will be eventually controlled by human and ethical considerations'.[91]

In line with the proto-corporatist spirit of the late war period, the commissioners advocated the creation of tripartite Standing Industrial Councils for each major industry, in which owners and workers would be represented by their respective organizations. There would be a closed shop for employers and

[88] 'Statement of J. P. Kane, President of the South Wales Colliery Managers' Association', 28 June 1917. N.L.W., E. Chappell papers, Box 4. Some of Kane's comments were reproduced, though unacknowledged, in the commission's report, 22.
[89] 'Evidence of D. L. Thomas, Manager of the Copper Pit, Morriston', Chappell papers, Box 4, loc. cit.
[90] Letter from W. Rees, Llandybïe, 23 June 1917, Chappell papers, Box 4, loc. cit.
[91] Unrest Commission, 28–9.

employees, and each group would be responsible for the discipline of its own members. Such bodies would succeed, however, only if there was a change in the mental disposition of both sides. To this end the commissioners advocated the establishment of a large-scale re-education programme, based on the universities, in which economics, history and citizenship would be taught in an impartial manner by 'recognized' authorities. The commissioners, only too aware that opposition to their schemes would come as much from the employers as from the trade unionists, also advocated a major programme of tuition in improved managerial techniques.[92]

The Unrest Commission gave Lleufer Thomas another platform for his social, political and reforming ideas. It allowed him to gather and deploy evidence in support of his demands for a massive expansion of university extra-mural work. He was always willing to build up and publicize the perceived threat from the Labour College movement, and to squeeze every ounce of political capital out of the I.W.C.E. classes to support his plans for adult education. Labour College supporters basked in the notoriety and used the Unrest Commission as further evidence that the W.E.A. and the universities were handmaidens of capitalism.[93] The danger for the W.E.A. was that, by building up the I.W.C.E. classes as an agency which was effective in transforming the world view of many young activists, it was actually serving the propaganda interests of the Labour College movement amongst those activists. The problem was compounded for the association by the fact that the Labour College classes started to expand just as the W.E.A. was going through a phase of organizational weakness.

The session 1915–16 saw virtually no class activity by the association in south Wales. From 1916 there was a slow recovery. In the summer of 1917 some additional funding from the national association allowed the district committee to appoint John Davidson as a full-time tutor/organizer. In the same year an Australian academic, B. H. Molesworth, was

---

[92] Ibid., *passim.* For a clear statement about the spirit behind the report, see Edgar Chappell's article, 'The struggle for industrial control', *Welsh Outlook* (November 1917).
[93] See J. F. Horrabin's editorial on the Unrest Commission in *Plebs* (September 1917).

appointed by the Cardiff joint committee to take classes in the Swansea area. Under these two men classes were established in several centres in south Wales. Seven full tutorial classes were established, significantly all on economics and economic history, in the Swansea tinplate area, the Vale of Glamorgan and in Cardiff. Other classes were established in Barry, Cymmer (Afan Valley), Bridgend, Fforest Fach, and Port Talbot. One-year classes were also established in Cardiff, Cwmavon and Newport. The W.E.A. also helped to organize a number of public lecture courses by leading local academics. For example, in Cardiff Professor Barbara Foxley gave talks on psychology, and in Newport Professor H. J. W. Hetherington spoke on 'The study of social institutions'. There were five such courses run in the session 1917–18.[94] It was a substantial programme, but it made little impact on the coalfield, and the total numbers catered for could not match the scale of operations of the Labour College movement at the same time. All the W.E.A.-organized courses catered for a total of some 265 students, perhaps a quarter of the number attending the various types of I.W.C.E. classes. Nor was the association getting at the young coalfield activists. The precise social composition of W.E.A. classes is not known, but there is some evidence from the records of the formal university tutorial classes. In the classes provided under the aegis of the Cardiff joint committee in 1917–18 there were 46 miners, 19 teachers, 18 clerks, 13 metal workers, 16 builders and 9 railwaymen. There was a miscellaneous category of 33 which covered non-employed persons, and a further 7 who were classed as managers.[95] The old problem of the classes being dominated by non-manual grades of worker and professional people was still very much in evidence. It was a problem well illustrated by the experience of a class on 'Land—laws and rent' at Llantwit Major in the Vale of Glamorgan, conducted by J. G. Smith, an economics lecturer at Cardiff. The W.E.A. branch secretary, Miss Jessie Trigg, wrote a letter of appreciation to John Davidson after he took over one class session at short notice when Smith was indisposed. Miss

[94] W.E.A. Welsh district council minutes, 28 July, 6 Oct. 1917; *W.E.A. Welsh District, Eleventh Annual Report, 1917–18*, 18–27.
[95] *Central Joint Advisory Committee on University Tutorial Classes, Eighth Annual Report, 1917–18*, 15.

Trigg took great pride in pointing out to Davidson that at the class 'you had the local Conservative Agent (the young farmer Mr. Rees). The local Liberal Agent (Mr. Morgan). Mr. Lloyd the tall gentleman is a farmer and a Liberal. The other two gentlemen were the Vicar of the Church of England and the Revd M. Morgan of the Nonconformists, so you see we certainly are mixed.' Smith later commented to Davidson that although the class was an academic success, it failed to reach the local labourers, who were put off by the presence of farmers and their families.[96] Thus, whilst the association was functioning in south Wales, it was in no way challenging the hegemony of the Labour College movement amongst the activist elements in the coalfield.

The later war period also witnessed another attempt by the W.E.A. to establish local branches of the organization. In practice these bodies were little more than secretarial bases for class groups which had little other purpose. In Cardiff, Barry and Penarth, however, the ruling élite on the district committee used the branches to promote their educational ideals. In Cardiff in the 1917–18 session, the district annual report records public talks and lectures on educational and public policy matters arranged for over thirty-six local organizations, from the Jewish Club to the I.L.P. One such public lecture was delivered by G. D. H. Cole on the subject of the 'Principles of industrial reconstruction'. One particular success of the branch formation policy occurred in Newport because it brought into the work of the association Lewis Webb, secretary of the trades council and leading labour figure in the area.[97]

Under the auspices of the Newport Trades Council, a meeting was organized in October 1917 to found a local W.E.A. branch. The meeting, addressed by the general secretary of the association, J. M. Mactavish, was also interesting because it reflected a sudden upsurge in enthusiasm for 'reconstruction'. A term originally used simply to mean a return to pre-war conditions, it was soon reinterpreted by those keen to promote social, economic and political reform to mean using the experi-

[96] Miss Jessie Trigg to J. Davidson, 8 Jan. 1918; note from Smith to Davidson, 17 Apr. 1918. Llantwit Major file, South Wales W.E.A. Records, Cardiff.

[97] Lewis Webb, J.P., was to become vice-chairman of the Welsh District of the association in 1919–25, and chairman of the reconstituted South Wales District from 1925 to 1935 and again from 1943 to 1951.

ence of war to build something better. By the summer of 1916, the term 'reconstruction' was on every politician's lips. Those associated with *Welsh Outlook* were at the forefront of the demand that something positive should come out of all the carnage and destruction. 'A country which is rightly prepared to spend £6M per day on warfare must be prepared to spend vastly more on the making of men and women capable of building the new world which must emerge if our victory is to be anything more than meaningless bubbles in the stream of time.'[98] By the summer of 1917 the W.E.A. was pressing very hard for commitments by the government to a major expansion in educational provision. Thus, when Mactavish delivered his address to the new Newport branch, the focus of his speech was on how labour might fail to secure major reforms when its bargaining position was strong because, 'In the mass they lacked the mental equipment which would enable them to control the social and economic processes which moulded, made or marred their lives.' The local newspaper was also enthusiastic about the W.E.A., not because it would enhance the demands of labour and the people but because 'Politics and economics will play a larger part than ever in our national life when the war is over.' Good government would depend on creating the right economic relations; 'we need an educated people to exercise through their mental and moral powers restraint and decision.'[99] From both perspectives within the broad boundaries of wartime progressivism the time was right to put pressure on government for change.

At the outset of the war, the W.E.A. district council had taken on board responsibility for defending public education against attempts to use the war as a pretext for cutbacks. In 1915 they campaigned against attempts to extend the use of child labour and also against what they felt was the tendency for local authorities to cut education first before other services. They also felt that the government should not pressurize male teachers for war service, because the loss of experienced teachers would blight the education of a whole generation of pupils. This was an issue which was also listed as a source of discontent by the S.W.M.F. submission to the 1917 Unrest Com-

[98] *Welsh Outlook* (January 1917).
[99] *South Wales Argus*, 8, 10 Oct. 1917.

mission, when they called on the government to 'bring back the trained teacher, reduce class sizes and raise his pay'.[100] Pressure from the association sometimes had the desired effect. The Penarth branch complained to the W.E.A. district council that schools were cutting back on the length of their lunch breaks to save money, which created severe difficulties for the provision of school meals. This issue was raised with the local education authority, and the original break times were restored.[101]

This generally defensive stance by the association changed in tone during 1916–17, and the Welsh district of the W.E.A. jumped enthusiastically on to the reconstructionist band-wagon. In July 1916 Lleufer Thomas stated that one of the prime functions of the Welsh W.E.A. was to ensure that there was already a strong public interest in education once the war was ended, when there would be severe pressure on public funds.[102] Enthusiasm for this task was reinforced in December 1916 by the appointment of H. A. L. Fisher to the post of President of the Board of Education. He succeeded Arthur Henderson who, as the first Labour man to hold the post, was a disappointment to educational reformers as he tended to accept the view that the pressures of war excluded the possibility of significant improvements in educational provision.[103] In its January 1917 issue, Welsh Outlook welcomed Fisher's appointment and suggested that the new minister should adopt the W.E.A.'s programme of reform. The association also had a direct line to the government through Tom Jones, the district treasurer, who went to work for Lloyd George in his embryonic cabinet secretariat. Jones seems to have been instrumental in Fisher's appointment, which many W.E.A. supporters took as evidence that the Lloyd George coalition was serious about improved educational provision.[104] The association now began to campaign with even greater enthusiasm for extensive reform. Some of the leading figures in the

[100] W.E.A. Welsh district council minutes, 20 Mar., 2 Oct. 1915.

[101] Ibid., 28 July 1917.

[102] Minutes of the annual general meeting of the Welsh District of the W.E.A., 1 July 1916.

[103] C. Wrigley, Arthur Henderson (Cardiff, 1990), 101–3.

[104] T. Jones, Whitehall Diaries, ed. R. K. Middlemass, vol. I (London, 1969), entry for 7 December 1916. Tom Jones remained as treasurer of the Welsh district of the association until Dec. 1917. Minutes of the W.E.A., Welsh district council, 7 Dec. 1917.

Welsh association, such as E. P. Hughes, Percy Watkins, and Stanley Watkins were also prominent members of the Welsh National Association for Reconstruction.[105] The highlight of the Welsh W.E.A. campaign to influence Fisher's legislation came in July 1917 with a conference on Educational Reconstruction held in Cardiff and addressed by the very personification of wartime progressivism, R. H. Tawney. In the previous November, Tawney, Thomas Jones and several other academics and administrators had handed Lloyd George a memorandum arguing that in order to prosecute the war to a successful conclusion, the labour movement would need to be won over by greater state intervention and a genuine commitment to extensive social reform.[106] It was a theme that Tawney repeated in *Welsh Outlook* in January 1917, where the dual struggle against Prussianism abroad and obscurantism at home was linked in a demand for social reform.[107] At the July conference Tawney emphasized how only education of the workers could create a truly democratic society.

The conference was a triumph for the W.E.A. Over 300 delegates attended, but the S.W.M.F. declined to participate, and Tom Richards and T. I. Mardy Jones both had to decline an offer to address the meeting.[108] Despite the fact that it was unable to gain the support of the leading trade union in the area, the association pressed on with its reconstructionist campaign. The Welsh W.E.A. was disappointed by Fisher's draft bill when it was published and stated that it did not do enough to 'inculcate the spirit of cooperative service for the communal welfare and provide systematic instruction in matters of civic and national concern'.[109] When Fisher visited Cardiff in the autumn of 1917, the Welsh district sought an interview and prepared a memorandum consisting of the views of members of the district committee on his bill; this memorandum contained demands for greater expenditure on adult education, better medical services for school children, an avoidance of a vocational bias in state education and fears about possible

[105] [*Merthyr*] *Pioneer*, 15 June 1918.
[106] Jones, *Diaries*, op. cit., 28 Sept., 16 Dec. 1916.
[107] See also Winter, op. cit., 169.
[108] S.W.D.N., 9 July 1917; S.W.M.F. E.C. minutes, 2 Apr. 1917.
[109] W.E.A. Welsh district council minutes, 15 Sept. 1917.

militarist values being inculcated by physical training in schools. The district committee failed to obtain an interview, and the high hopes of early 1917 were dashed when the government refused to proceed with Fisher's measure later the same month.[110] Disillusionment gradually replaced optimism when a new measure was published in the spring of 1918. The Welsh W.E.A. tried with very limited success to stir up organized labour in south Wales to oppose the watering down of Fisher's bill in respect of continuation classes and child labour.

For Lleufer Thomas the last years of the war were a period of great danger to his hopes of recreating in the industrial areas of south Wales an ideal of popular culture. The hold of Labour College teaching over certain influential sections of the miners' union was matched by the fear that the business community of south Wales was interested in education only in so far as it promoted its commercial well-being. Some, like T. E. Watson of the Cardiff Chamber of Trade, hoped to see the university actively countering the 'narrow and misguided teaching' of the Labour College, but were not prepared to countenance any concessions to the labour interest envisaged in the Unrest Commission's report.[111] Whereas Lleufer Thomas was convinced that a well-financed programme of tutorial classes, which addressed the great social and economic issues of the day in an 'impartial' manner, would in the long run expose the inadequacies of Marxian economics and history, Watson and his ilk wanted an all-out intellectual assault on the Labour College movement. Lleufer Thomas's vision of class harmony was based on an ethical vision of citizenship, a democratic society where the development of character was held in higher regard than money-getting, and service to the community was more important than self or sectional interest. These ideals still drove the leading figures in the association, despite the fact that the end of the war did not bring about that transformation which they had envisaged only a few years earlier.

[110] Minutes of the emergency W.E.A. Welsh district council meeting, 6 Oct. 1917; 'Proposed statement on the Education Bill to be submitted to the President of the Board of Education by the Welsh District of the W.E.A.', adopted by the Council, 6 Oct. 1917; *Western Mail*, 11 Oct. 1917.
[111] *Welsh Outlook* (Dec. 1917). See also the comments of the *Colliery Guardian*, 10 Aug. 1917.

Recent studies of the social and political impact of the war have tended to emphasize the absence of concrete evidence that it resulted in the emergence of a new class-consciousness amongst British workers. Older, fragmented patterns of behaviour were remarkably resilient, and the old jingoist and often xenophobic traits of the British worker easily obscured any tendency to think in clear class terms about his/her condition.[112] There is little evidence that the average south Wales worker, even among the miners, was any different. However, there are two points at which the experience of the 1914–18 war does seem to have qualified this picture, at least as far as the south Wales coalmining community is concerned. First of all, the language of class tended now to assume that there was an inherent conflict of interest between labour and capital. Secondly, the politics of the mining community had a built-in anti-capitalist bias after 1918, even if in practice this was confined to rhetoric. As both the language of class and the language of politics were to a large extent shaped and controlled by the leaders of thought in the community, the Labour College movement contributed to this significant attitudinal change. The problem for the W.E.A., with its belief in the fostering of civic harmony and the creation of an integrative, co-operative community, where the values of religion and Welsh nationality gave a spiritual underpinning to the social order, was that the attitudinal change amongst the leaders of opinion in the coalfield, on the side of capital as well as of labour, made such a development, in the literal sense, incredible.

---

[112] Waites, op. cit., 231–9; Tanner, op. cit., 384–442.

IV

TAKING SIDES: 1918–1929

1. 'THE HUNGRY SHEEP LOOK UP AND ARE NOT FED'

The hopes of social reformers in the later war years that a better society would be created out of the carnage of the war, and the confident militancy of the far left in the early post-war years when revolution was seen as not just inevitable but imminent, were soon to be shattered by the economic depression which afflicted the south Wales economy from 1921 almost until the outbreak of the Second World War. An essentially new phenomenon, large-scale structural unemployment, became an abiding feature of industrial south Wales. The staple industries of the region, which had seen almost unbroken expansion in the later years of the nineteenth century and in the Edwardian era, and virtual boom conditions during the war and immediate post-war years, were now plunged into almost perpetual recession. Over-committed to international trade, the industries of south Wales, especially the mining of steam coal, were peculiarly ill-suited to the new world trading situation. The consequences for industrial south Wales were long-term unemployment and emigration from the coalfield. The new economic situation was one for which neither orthodox nor Marxian economics had either a ready-made explanation or, more importantly for those afflicted by the economic blight, a solution. The remedies of the past, cutting factor costs for the orthodox or the socialization of the means of production, distribution and exchange for the Marxians, were still offered as the only answer to capitalism's crisis. It was the intractable nature of the problem, and the inability to see any obvious solution to this new crisis, which created in the politics of the period—increasingly polarized along discernible lines of social class—a tone of bitterness and conflict qualitatively different from that of pre-war years.

The bitterness was deepened by major industrial disputes and the spectre of Bolshevism. The decline of the Liberal

Party in industrial south Wales was swift, and it changed the
terms of political debate.[1] Social radicals now tended to see
the Labour Party as the only viable vehicle for reform, whilst
many of their former colleagues inside the Liberal Party
entered into anti-socialist alliances with their erstwhile Conservative enemies. In the ranks of organized labour the mood also
changed. The slump and the defeats of 1921 and 1926 led to a
brooding, bitter hostility to the capitalist system amongst the
activist elements. Yet, whilst the rhetoric of class war still
reverberated around the coalfield, and an overtly class conscious political party, Labour, gained an unparalleled ascendancy in both the parliamentary representation and local
government of industrial south Wales, the men (still mostly
men) elected to public office still tended to share the values of
public and community service which had characterized their
Liberal and Lib-Lab predecessors.[2] This element of continuity
reduced the significance of the change of party label, and put
into perspective the actual impact of the revolutionary socialist
ideas prevalent in the region's labour movement. But these
values were now conditioned by strong collectivist and anti-
capitalist instincts, which differentiated them from their progressive forerunners. In the long run, these traditions of
public and community service were to be features of the
south Wales labour movement which the W.E.A. was able to
exploit. In the context of the early 1920s, however, prospects
for the association were not too bright.

For the reconstructionists of the W.E.A., the immediate post-
war years were a great disappointment. Lleufer Thomas's fears
that the pressures for retrenchment in public expenditure
would soon eclipse any political commitment to expanded educational provision proved to be well-founded as the limited
reforms of Fisher's Act were subjected to the rigours of the
public expenditure cuts initiated by the Geddes committee,
commonly known as the 'Geddes axe'. In May 1922, Lleufer
Thomas chaired a mass meeting of Welsh educationalists,

[1] K. O. Morgan, 'Post-war reconstruction in Wales, 1918–1945', in J. Winter (ed.),
The Working Class in Modern British History (Cambridge, 1983), 87.
[2] For the elements of continuity in working-class political and industrial leadership in
south Wales, see P. Stead, 'Working-class leadership in south Wales, 1900–1920', *Welsh
History Review*, 6, No. 3 (June 1973).

organized by the Welsh W.E.A., to protest at the cuts in educational expenditure, and he denounced the 'immorality' of
making the children pay for the cost of the war.[3] Of equal concern to him was the polarization of south Wales society and
politics along class lines. Unemployment and the attendant
ills of emigration and victimization were not conducive to the
creation of the harmonious, integrative community so cherished
by leading figures in the south Wales W.E.A. Even the gentle,
introspective cultural nationalism promoted by them was being
overtaken by a less accommodating form of nationalism with
the creation of Plaid Cymru in 1925.[4]

The early post-war years were ones of extreme difficulty for
the W.E.A. The hopes of 1917–18 were overtaken by the cold
reality of January 1920. In that month *Welsh Outlook* commented, rather brutally, that in the twelve years of its existence in
south Wales the W.E.A. had made virtually no impact on the
area. Throughout this period the association struggled to survive a recurrent series of financial crises. Indeed, as in the
immediate pre-war years, it survived as an organization only
through the largesse of the Davies family of Llandinam. In
the years 1920–1 David Davies gave £500 and the Davies sis-
ters gave an unsecured loan of £300 to cover the salary of the
district secretary and office expenses. In 1922 the association
nearly collapsed again, when the district secretary's salary
was reported to be six months in arrears.[5] On that occasion it
was saved by the closure and sale of the East Moors Settlement, the funds raised being transferred to the Welsh District
of the W.E.A.[6] In 1927 another crisis was averted by a further
timely gift of £250 from the Davies family.[7] This dependence
on wealthy subscribers was used by Labour College supporters

---

[3] *W.E.A. for Wales, Fifteeenth Annual Report, 1921–22.* W.E.A., Wales, executive committee minutes, 11 Mar. 1922. The conference was funded by the N.U.T., and was
addressed by the Revd Herbert Morgan and E. P. Hughes.
    [4] A. Butt Philip, *The Welsh Question* (Cardiff, 1975), 13.
    [5] W.E.A. executive committee minutes, 27 July 1920; 'Final report by the Financial
Secretary' (E. W. Wimble), presented to the W.E.A. executive committee, 28 Apr.
1922.
    [6] W.E.A. for Wales, district council minutes, 9 June 1923; *W.E.A.for Wales, Sixteenth
Annual Report, 1922–23.*
    [7] *W.E.A., South Wales District, Twenty-first Annual Report, 1927–28.* Seventy per cent of
the (non-grant) district funds came from individual subscribers in this session; only 12
per cent came from unions and other affiliated bodies; the remainder came from local
branches and class groups.

to considerable effect when they accused the W.E.A. of being a handmaiden of capitalism. Certainly, in the context of south Wales the association does seem to have been unduly dependent on individual subscribers. Branch activity was negligible, and union and other affiliations relatively insignificant. This was partly due to the nature of the area, which had few large urban centres, and where John Thomas had found branch organization both difficult and unrewarding, but also it was due to a large extent to the personality of the district secretary, John Davies.

Appointed as organizing secretary in September 1919, John Davies soon developed a very personal style. Thomas Jones, in a candid posthumous assessment, wrote that he 'played the game but broke all the rules'.[8] Under Davies, the W.E.A. in south Wales became very much the creature of the district secretary. Lleufer Thomas resigned as chairman in 1919, the light of the 'Welsh ideal of popular culture' being carried by his successor, Percy Watkins. In 1925, Watkins left to take up an appointment in London, E. P. Hughes died, and the district was redivided into sections for north and south Wales. Thereafter, in Tom Jones's words, 'there was an executive of quite worthy and responsible figures, professors and the like, but they too were equally obedient to the nods of the genial dictator.'[9] Many of those who were active in the association in south Wales during his period of office found Davies to be both difficult and eccentric and his administrative style was not to the taste of the precise and the fastidious. Nevertheless, he kept the W.E.A. functioning in the crisis years of the early 1920s, and he was able to build up the work of the W.E.A. in the late twenties and early thirties, when it became an integral part of the 'social service' response to chronic structural unemployment in the region.

Davies personified the Lleufer Thomas ideal. From a mining family, he was Welsh-speaking, a devout Calvinistic Methodist to the end of his life, and also utterly committed to the labour movement. Apprenticed as a draper's assistant, he became

---

[8] From Davies's obituary, *Highway* (February 1938); reprinted in *John Davies* (Gregynog, privately printed and circulated, 1938), 12.
[9] Ibid.

active with the shop assistants' union and the I.L.P. He also worked as the west Wales reporter for *Llais Llafur* and as secretary of Swansea Trades and Labour Council. Declared unfit for war service, he subsequently worked for Seebohm Rowntree as a rural social investigator before being appointed as the west Wales organizer of the agricultural labourers' union.[10] His Welshness, his religious convictions, and his commitment to labour made up for his lack of formal qualifications. He was a wide and avid reader and a quick-witted operator in the academic and political circles in which he was compelled to move as a W.E.A. official. Appointed against some strong competition,[11] Davies piloted the association through some difficult times, not just financial ones but also through the organizational problems which flowed from being given formal recognition as an 'approved association' under the revised Board of Education regulations of 1924. A minor benefit which resulted from the first Labour government, the regulations, which made the W.E.A. responsible for running one-year and terminal courses, also tended to make it more of an adult education agency and less of a workers' education movement.[12] The enhanced status and additional funding brought further suspicions that the W.E.A. was losing its deeper political purpose in its zeal to emphasize its lack of partisanship. This was to lead to profound problems of identity when the state and organized labour clashed, as they did all too frequently in the 1920s. It also changed the nature of the W.E.A. as it became essentially a sub-contractor for the organization and supply of short courses for the Board of Education. The scale of the change is well illustrated by the growth in state grants for courses received by the South Wales district, which grew steadily from £128 in 1924–5 to £972 in 1929–30.[13]

[10] W.E.A. district council minutes, 20 Sept., 18 Oct. 1919. His father was one of eighty-one miners killed in the explosion at Mardy colliery in 1885, when John Davies was three years old. *John Davies*, op. cit., 24.

[11] The advertisement for the job brought in over 130 applications from all over the U.K. The shortlist included E. J. Hookway, district secretary for the north-west of England. Davies's main rival was David Thomas from Tal-y-sarn, Penygroes, north Wales, a close political associate of Silyn Roberts and a major figure in north Wales labour and I.L.P. politics. R. Merfyn Jones, *The North Wales Quarrymen, 1874–1922* (Cardiff, 1982), 320. See also C. Parry, 'Gwynedd politics, 1900–20', *Welsh History Review*, 6, No. 3 (June 1973), 316.

[12] Stocks, op. cit., 96.

[13] *W.E.A., South Wales District, 23rd Annual Report, 1929–30.*

The nature of the W.E.A. was also changed by its relationship with the expanding extra-mural provision of the university colleges. The campaign by Lleufer Thomas to promote the extra-mural dimension before the Haldane Commission had resulted in strong recommendations from the commission that this side of the university's work should receive particular support. It was a recommendation further endorsed by the final report of the Adult Education Committee of the Ministry of Reconstruction, published in 1919.[14] One of the reforms advocated by the Haldane Commission was the establishment of an extension board for the whole university to foster and co-ordinate extra-mural provision for all the constituent colleges. The result was a steady expansion of the number of grant-earning tutorial classes from twenty-four for the whole of Wales in the session 1918–19 to over ninety-seven by the end of 1923.[15] The W.E.A. had played a significant role in stimulating the demand for these classes, but there was still great disappointment in the ranks of the association that the great hopes and enthusiasm of the late war years and early post-war period were not realized, particularly in south Wales, where the expansion of class provision was nothing like as extensive as in the rural areas covered by Bangor and Aberystwyth. In south Wales the W.E.A. was constantly frustrated by the lack of commitment by Cardiff's university college. Unlike Bangor and Aberystwyth, where the new enthusiasm for extra-mural work was soon translated into action, the college authorities in Cardiff declined to assume financial responsibility for the classes held under the auspices of its joint committee until the session 1923–4. Up to that time the classes were provided only because of the willingness of the members of the joint committee to underwrite personally the committee's overdraft. What were perceived to be the apathy and indifference of Cardiff to extra-mural provision became notorious throughout the adult education world. In 1922 an anonymous, but obviously well-informed, writer attacked the failure of the college to meet the needs of an area which was one of the 'danger

[14] Haldane Commission, 'The extra mural student', *Final Report*, Cmnd. 8991, para. 129–35, 259–61, 273; Ministry of Reconstruction, *Final Report of the Adult Education Committee*, Cmnd. 321 (London,1919), 373–8.
[15] B. B. Thomas, op. cit. (1940), 24.

zones' in the industrial life of Britain. The author referred to the existence of an 'active and advanced body' among the workers who rejected the university and all its works, and had established their own provision under the Labour College movement; it was a matter of regret that Cardiff did not 'seize eagerly the chance of extending its teaching to the working population, and bridging the gulf of prejudice which tends to separate the so-called educated from the so-called "working classes"'.[16] Matters were made worse in south Wales by the continued jurisdictional rivalry which prevented Glamorgan County Council from co-operating fully with the W.E.A. and the joint committees of the university colleges. Glamorgan made its own arrangements for non-vocational class provision and made no direct contribution to the work or the funds of the W.E.A.—a source of annoyance to W.E.A. supporters until after the Second World War. The author of the February 1922 survey of adult education provision in Wales hoped that the W.E.A. would facilitate the coming together of the various educational and other agencies in a society marked by deepening divisions. 'Sectionalism and distrust' were the hallmark of the current situation. The churches distrusted labour and labour the churches; the local education authorities and the University of Wales 'quarrelled' over their responsibilities; the socialists distrusted the nationalists and vice versa, and meanwhile 'the hungry sheep look up and are not fed'.[17]

Cardiff's failure was seen by some to reflect a more profound lack of vision in the University of Wales. Alfred Zimmern, a close ally of R. H. Tawney and Thomas Jones, one of the men behind the Oxford report and, between 1919 and 1921, the holder of the newly created chair in international politics at Aberystwyth, was convinced that the educational establishment in Wales had abandoned the ideals of those who wished to weave the university into the very fabric of Welsh life for an 'English mess of pottage'.[18] Whilst at Aberystwyth, he became a close friend of John Davies and attended many W.E.A. classes in south Wales. The experience made him

[16] 'Adult education in Wales', *Bulletin of the World Association for Adult Education*, No. 7 (February 1922).
[17] Ibid.
[18] A. Zimmern, *My Impressions of Wales* (London, 1922), 32.

particularly withering in his criticism of the failure of the
university to confront the challenge of industrial south Wales:

> That the University should mean so little to the coalfield,
> that it should even display, on occasion, a deliberate prefer-
> ence for the unlettered, if titled, capitalist over the zealous
> and lettered proletarian is surely an ironical comment on
> the meaning of the word University, and would be a bitter
> disappointment to those who dreamed dreams at its founda-
> tion.

Denying that he was either a communist or a socialist, he did,
however, understand the attitude of the editors of the *Plebs*
magazine and their followers. He contrasted the earnestness
and intellectual integrity of these proletarian seekers after
truth with the faint hearts of the University and the 'still
fainter hearts in the churches'.[19]

Pressure from the newly established university-wide extension board, combined with more generous provision of funds
from the Board of Education, did result in Cardiff expanding
its provision after 1924. Swansea's new university college, a
product of the Haldane Commission, displayed rather more
enthusiasm than Cardiff for extra-mural work. In part this
was due to the missionary mentality which often drives a new
institution, and partly because in a period of financial restraint
extra-mural work carried on in borrowed premises and requir-
ing limited administrative back-up was easier to establish than
full-time internal courses where growth would inevitably be
slow. A further factor was the establishment of the Workers'
Educational Trade Union Committee (W.E.T.U.C.), which
was able, from 1920, to support a full-time tutor, Dr Illtyd
David, in the Swansea area; from the outset he worked closely
with the new college. [20]

Aberystwyth had the inestimable advantage of having an
endowment which permitted the appointment of a director of
extra-mural studies.[21] The man appointed to this post, which

[19] Ibid., 38.
[20] 'University College Swansea, adult education in the area of the college' (n.d.,
c. 1939), 1–3. This document appears to have been prepared as part of a survey by the
University of Wales, Extension Board; supplied to the author by W. Gregory, Croydon.
[21] B. B. Thomas, op.cit., 25.

he held for the next twenty years, was the Revd Herbert Morgan, very much a man in tune with the socially conscious Nonconformism advocated by Lleufer Thomas. Morgan, who worked closely with Lleufer Thomas in the creation of the Welsh School of Social Service, stood as a Labour candidate in 1918. His appointment as head of extra-mural studies at Aberystwyth was perhaps one of the greatest successes for the 'Welsh ideal of popular culture'. He also shared with Lleufer Thomas a concern for the quality of leadership being developed in the ranks of organized labour. The temptation of modern trade union leaders was, he argued, not to 'capitulate to the suavity of the employer, but to pander to the men for the sake of popularity'. For Morgan the chief mission of the churches and the university was to provide an education which could help to develop leaders selected not for their 'loquacity and pushfulness' but because of their 'real wisdom'. Morgan asked why a 'professedly democratic university' should not train labour leaders as well as teachers and preachers.[22]

The challenge which the new atmosphere posed was something which exercised (Sir) Henry Jones in his twilight years. Addressing the National Eisteddfod at Corwen in 1919, he argued that the churches could find a new relevance for themselves only by meeting more fully the demand for adult education. It was an idea taken up with some enthusiasm by the Welsh W.E.A.,[23] and throughout the 1920s there were periodic attempts to bring the churches of Wales more fully into the adult education movement, by and large with limited success. There were ministers who felt that the churches ought to encourage their young members to attend tutorial classes for fear that otherwise they might be lost to the churches, and the adult education movement would become totally secularized, to their mutual disadvantage.[24] There was a steady growth in the number of ordained ministers who became class tutors, reflecting, perhaps, both a relative decline in

---

[22] H. Morgan, *The Social Task in Wales* (London, 1919), 78–80.
[23] W.E.A. for Wales, district council minutes, 18 Oct. 1919.
[24] John Lewis, 'The university, the W.E.A. and the Church' (n.d., *c.* 1921), miscellaneous memoranda, W.E.A. Records, Cardiff. Lewis was the minister of a Congregational church in Cardiff.

clerical incomes and status and a greater willingness to engage in more secular forms of tuition. This may have been one of the long-term consequences of the influence of the neo-Hegelian and 'new theology' ideas propagated before 1914.[25] John Davies felt that his fellow Nonconformists had failed to rise to the challenge offered by the social and economic crises which afflicted industrial south Wales.[26]

The 'Welsh ideal of popular culture' had sought to harness socially conscious religion with cultural nationalism in order to produce a new sense of community and common purpose in industrial south Wales. Religion failed to respond fully to the challenge and Welsh nationalism took a direction which put it at odds with the internationalist rhetoric and the anti-capitalist ethos that permeated the leadership of labour in south Wales. One of the by-products of the collapse of popular liberalism in industrial south Wales was the divorce of Welsh cultural nationalism from the political life of organized labour. The apparent lack of interest of the new breed of nationalist in social and economic questions irritated many of those who associated with the W.E.A. They were baffled by those whose chief anxiety was not 'that a hundred men own all the collieries in South Wales, but that the language of Dafydd ap Gwilym may cease to be known in the valleys where he sang'.[27] They were also concerned at what appeared to be an almost incestuous intellectual narrowness: 'Let them go amongst the intelligent miners of South Wales, let them turn among the students who attend the lectures of the London W.E.A.,' suggested *Welsh Outlook*.[28] The redivision in 1925 of the Welsh District into separate districts for the north and south finally ended the hopes of Mansbridge and Lleufer Thomas that cultural nationalism could assist the W.E.A. in its construction of a new sense of purpose. Silyn Roberts, a member of the Cardiff–Barry coterie, was appointed as the new district secretary for the north Wales district of the W.E.A.

---

[25] In 1917–18 there were no ministers of religion tutoring W.E.A. or university tutorial classes. By 1929–30, of the seventy-five one-year or terminal classes in the district, twenty-seven were taken by ordained ministers. Information taken from the District annual reports.
[26] Ruby Davies, 'Memories', in *John Davies* (Gregynog, 1938), 8–10.
[27] 'Adult education in Wales'.
[28] *Welsh Outlook* (July 1926).

By the late 1920s the nature of the W.E.A. in south Wales had changed from that of a vehicle for an attempt by a small group of middle-class educationalists to assert an intellectual hegemony over the region's working classes, to, in the main, an agency for the supply of liberal, non-vocational adult education classes. The dominant group within the association in south Wales had been frustrated by a lack of enthusiasm for their essentially extra-mural perception of higher education amongst the authorities in the constituent colleges of the University of Wales. Above all, they were frustrated by the polarization of south Wales society, the widening gulfs between social groups. The uncompromising stances of both employers and employed, forcing everyone to 'take sides', were utterly alien to the philosophy which guided most of the leading lights within the W.E.A. in south Wales. 'The appeal of class had outstripped the call of community—or of nationality in Wales and Scotland.'[29] When the pride and the defiance had been all but knocked out of the communities of industrial south Wales, by the breaking of strikes, by victimization, emigration and, above all, by chronic unemployment, the outlook of Lleufer Thomas and the Cardiff–Barry coterie seemed to take on a new relevance and become a guiding influence in the W.E.A.'s new role within the 'social service' response to the 'problem' of south Wales.

2. 'Y BOLSHIES YW Y GORRAH!'

John Thomas, formerly the organizing secretary of the W.E.A. for Wales, visited the newly reopened Labour College in the spring of 1920 to view a production of Shaw's *The Shewing up of Blanco Posnet*, put on by the staff and the student body. Thomas was impressed by the production, but also by the spirit of the college, which exuded a confident, not to say insolent, militancy as exemplified by the suitably amended Welsh rugby chant ('The Bolshies are the best') quoted above, which, Thomas reported, had become the 'now famous Labour College yell'.[30] At a time when the capitalist system

[29] K. O. Morgan, *Consensus and Disunity, The Lloyd George Coalition Government, 1918–1922* (Oxford, 1979), 297.
[30] *Plebs* (May 1920).

seemed on the edge of a precipice which required only a class-conscious, organized working class to hurl it into the abyss of history, the Labour College cry heard by Thomas warmed his heart and reinforced his conviction that the final struggle with capitalism was at hand. The Russian revolution and the substantial gains made by organized labour during the war and the immediate post-war period seemed to indicate that ultimate victory was assured. Yet by the end of that decade the Labour College had closed, John Thomas was regretting his enthusiasm for the revolutionary posturing of the immediate post-war years, and crisis-ridden capitalism still showed no sign of giving up the ghost.

By 1920 Thomas had moved a long way from the ideals of Mackenzie and Lleufer Thomas. While compelled to work at a farm on the outskirts of Swansea, Thomas maintained his links with the anti-war elements in the I.L.P., and as a lecturer and speaker he built up contacts with socialist elements in the west of the coalfield. He was elected full-time lodge secretary and checkweigher at the Diamond colliery in Ystradgynlais and then, in a remarkable testimony to the way that being a popular workers' education tutor had become a route into a career as a union official, in 1920 Thomas was elected as miners' agent for the anthracite district of the S.W.M.F.[31] His reputation as a firebrand, on the most advanced wing of the I.L.P., had been reinforced by the publication, in 1919, of an I.L.P. pamphlet entitled *The Economics of Coal*. In this 'class-conscious analysis of the coal industry', Thomas described how the miners' 'vague feelings' that they were being exploited had grown, 'thanks to studious members', into 'an intellectual conviction' that 'at bottom the coalfield but reflects the ceaseless struggle of the proletarian forces with the property-owning classes, characteristic of the stage of economic development known as Capitalism'.[32]

John Thomas's political development mirrored the experience of the coalfield. The miners, having forced the government to take control of the industry in 1916, sought the

[31] Interview with John Thomas, Apr. 1972; Neath W.E.A., op. cit. He defeated James Griffiths for this post; Griffiths replaced Thomas when he resigned from the miners' agent's post in 1925.

[32] J. Thomas, *The Economics of Coal* (London, 1919), 3.

consolidation of their new-found strength by the nationalization of the industry and the enforcement of a closed shop as
far as union membership was concerned. In the heady atmosphere of 1918–20 it looked as if the ambitions of the miners'
federation were about to be achieved as the government con-
ceded a Royal Commission (the Sankey Commission) to inves-
tigate the organization of the industry. The rejection, after
much delay, by the government of the majority recommendation of the Sankey Commission, namely, that the coal industry
should be nationalized, ended the hopes of the miners that the
gains of the war and post-war period could be consolidated.
The mines were de-controlled on 24 March 1921. The owners
immediately embarked on an industry-wide programme of
wage cutting, and by 1 April 1921 the miners were 'locked
out'. The ability of the miners' union to resist the owners was
weakened by the arrival of large scale unemployment in the
industry, and the failure by their partners in the 'triple alliance' (the railwaymen and the transport workers) to back
them with sympathetic strike action. From 15 April 1921,
'Black Friday', the miners were on their own, and by the end
of June they were forced back to work on the owners'
terms.[33] The shattering defeat of the miners in 1921, the
'betrayal' of Frank Hodges, general secretary of the
M.F.G.B., who, it was felt by many on the left in the miners'
union, had connived with those who wished to force the
owners' terms on the miners, brought bitterness and disillusionment into the ranks of the activists. It led many of them, like
John Thomas, to re-evaluate their position. Hodges, the most
successful of the products of the C.L.C., had written an enthusiastic introduction to Thomas's 1919 pamphlet, but the experience of 1921 drove Thomas to see the need for a more extensive
and intensive campaign when lodges would be turned into
'lecture rooms and classes, centres of discussion and planning
about the next phases of the struggle, to win the control of
their industry for the workers'.[34] By the end of 1921 he was flirt-
ing with the Communist Party and sniping at his old employers

---

[33] For a detailed account of the S.W.M.F. and the 1921 lock-out, see Page Arnot, op.
cit., 201–21. On the issue of the government and de-control, see Kirby, op. cit., 48–65.
[34] J. Thomas, *The Miners' Conflict with the Mineowners* (London, 1921), 68.

in the W.E.A. and the reformist policies of the M.F.G.B. leader-ship.[35] He continued to support the most advanced elements within the S.W.M.F. executive committee, Cook, Ablett, S. O. Davies, and Ted Williams, well into 1924. Yet, despite his fellow-travelling with the Communist Party and his support for S.W.M.F. affiliation to the Red International of Labour Unions,[36] Thomas still kept his links with orthodox adult edu-cation, conducting an extra-mural economics class for Aberyst-wyth from 1922 to 1925. A taste of the reality of class conflict in the violent industrial dispute which convulsed the anthracite district in the summer of 1925 proved too much for Thomas, and he returned to academic life as a tutor for the Oxford extra-mural delegacy in Tawney's old stamping-ground in the Potteries.[37] James Griffiths, a product of the C.L.C. but a far less mercurial personality than John Thomas, became the new miners' agent and commenced his distinguished career in the British labour movement.

Few south Wales miners were as fortunate as John Thomas; most could not opt out of the class struggle. Unemployment and, if they were activists, victimization became all-too-real experiences which made the confident militancy of the immedi-ate post-war years soon seem a distant memory. One long-term victim of the new atmosphere was the Labour College itself. Reopened in October 1919 at a gathering presided over by its most ardent enthusiast, Noah Ablett, the college seemed set to produce a cadre of class-conscious leaders and teachers which, Ablett believed, would pilot the labour movement and the organized working class to a new socialist order.[38] Indeed, in the early years of its second incarnation the Labour College did produce a 'golden' crop of Labour leaders, of whom Nye Bevan, Jim Griffiths, Ness Edwards, and Bryn Roberts were but the most notable Welsh examples. Ablett's hope that the college would expand as more unions affiliated

---

[35] See Thomas's article 'The present and future prospects for the south Wales miners', *Communist Review* (January 1922).

[36] R. Page Arnot, op. cit., 245–7. Thomas wrote an article in support of affiliation to the R.I.L.U. in the August 1923 edition of *The Colliery Workers' Magazine*. Arthur Jenkins wrote an article critical of the 'Red International' in the same edition.

[37] Interview, Apr. 1972. On the anthracite disturbances of 1925, see H. Francis, 'The anthracite strike and the disturbances of 1925', *Llafur*, 1, No. 2 (May 1973).

[38] *Plebs* (October 1919).

and offered scholarships was shattered by the collapse of the post-war boom and the advent of chronic unemployment, when most unions could not consider such expenditure. South Wales miners remained the largest single group within the student body;[39] and very soon the old afflictions of internal disorder and poor financial management returned to dog the college. Within a few years, far from expanding on the basis of new affiliations, it was locked once again into a struggle for survival. By the summer of 1924 Mark Starr was writing that the students were not returning to their places of work 'with a new view of life but disgruntled and angry'.[40] The college, he argued, was no longer a source of strength to the labour movement.

The precise reasons for the Labour College's failure and eventual closure have been the subject of some debate amongst those who have sought to chronicle the history of the Labour College movement. W. W. Craik, a former principal, in his history of the college published in the mid-1960s, pointed an accusing finger at the National Council of Labour Colleges (N.C.L.C.), the body which co-ordinated the provincial class movement, which, he argued, was a rival for the resources of the trade union movement.[41] J. P. M. Millar, the eternal general secretary of the N.C.L.C., denied culpability and instead blamed the closure on the hostility to the college of some leading figures inside the N.U.R. and also the disruptive influence of active communists among the student body, which compounded the very real internal problems of the college.[42] The role of the Communist Party and internal disorders have also been cited by other commentators as being the key factors in the college's decline and fall.[43]

Student discontent soon re-emerged as an abiding characteristic of Labour College life. The student body was very carefully

---

[39] There were twelve two-year S.W.M.F. scholarships available at the Labour College on the basis of eight in one year, four the next. So that after the first year there were always twelve Federation students in residence. S.W.M.F., E.C. minutes, 3 Feb. 1919. Some of the districts provided other scholarships, but these were less secure.

[40] *Plebs* (July 1924).

[41] Craik, op. cit., 153.

[42] Millar, op. cit., 91.

[43] See, for example, Macintyre, *op. cit.*, 83–5; C. Tsuzuki, 'Anglo-Marxism and working-class education', in J. Winter, op. cit., 192–7; G. D. H. Cole and R. Postgate, *The Common People, 1746–1946* (London, 1966), 560.

selected by its supporting unions. The S.W.M.F., now funding twelve scholarships at the college, laid down strict rules about who could apply, imposed equally rigorous guidelines on methods of examination, and also required formal commitments from candidates that they would place their services at the disposal of the labour movement on the termination of their studies.[44] Thus, in practice, many of the successful candidates were men of mature age, some married, all well versed in trade union activity and effective in articulating grievances, and, as in the case of James Griffiths, already very adept at essay writing and other essential academic skills.[45] Such men bridled at the college discipline and resented being treated as irresponsible adolescents who had to be indoors at a certain time and who had their extra-curricular activities heavily circumscribed. Bryn Roberts and Jim Griffiths campaigned for latch-keys; Aneurin Bevan tended simply to ignore the rules.[46]

Student criticism took a more serious turn with the next cohort. D. J. Williams, from the anthracite district, and Ned Evans and Frank Collins, both from the Rhondda, complained about the quality and relevance of the teaching and demanded student representation on the governing body of the college. The campaign resulted in the expulsion of Evans and Collins, with Williams leaving of his own accord.[47] In 1923 trouble erupted again when the student body, led by Len Finch, an N.U.R. scholar from Barry, made far-reaching criticisms of the teaching. They attacked the economics syllabus and the tutor and vice-principal, W. H. Mainwaring. The teaching, they complained, was confined to a thirty-five-lecture course on Marx's *Capital*, to the exclusion of any study of more modern writers; thus students were leaving utterly unacquainted

[44] S.W.M.F., E.C. minutes, 6 Dec. 1920. There were over 200 applications for the first eight S.W.M.F. places at the C.L.C. *Plebs* (June 1919).

[45] Interview, 20 Nov. 1972; Griffiths started to attend a W.E.A./university tutorial class before the war and attended 'White House' and Labour College classes well before he took the entrance examination. J. Griffiths, *Pages From Memory* (London, 1969), 20–6.

[46] J. Griffiths and B. Roberts to W. W. Craik, 2 Oct. 1920, N.L.S., Acc. 5120, Box 2, fo. 1920. Interview with J. Griffiths, 20 Nov. 1920; Foot, op. cit., 38.

[47] Labour College, Board of Governors' minutes, 25 Nov. 1921, N.L.S., Acc. 6889, Item 5; Thomas Richards to W. W. Craik, 22 Nov. 1921, N.L.S. Acc. 5120, Box 2, fo. 1921. Evans and Collins tried to gain the support of their district committee, but with no more success than George Daggar had with the Western Valley miners in 1913. Rhondda No. 1. minutes, 28 Nov., 12 Dec. 1921, 9 Jan. 1922.

'with the modern view of the subject'. Finch advocated a broader course of study, along with some practical training in book-keeping and statistics, a curriculum geared to making the college a true 'labour' college.[48] Irritation with the obsession of the Labour College movement generally with Marx's *Capital* was growing in this period amongst many activists. D. J. Williams, having left the Labour College, secured a scholarship to Ruskin College, and in 1924 published his study of modern capitalist organization, *Capitalist Combination in the Coal Industry*. In the same year he launched, in a letter to the *Plebs*, a vituperative attack on what he called the leaders of thought in south Wales, presumably Ablett et al., who regarded the first ten chapters of *Capital* as the alpha and omega of education. Williams argued that it was necessary to study capitalism as it was in the 1920s, not 'from the pages of the sages of the nineteenth century'.[49]

When attempts to reform the curriculum were rebuffed, many students decided to find enlightenment beyond the formal teaching at the college. Idris Cox, S.W.M.F. student at the C.L.C. from 1923 to 1925, felt that 'although you might not have learned a great deal from the lectures you had the spare time and books for study.'[50] Others went outside the college. Glyn Evans (S.W.M.F. student, 1922–4) and W. H. Williams (S.W.M.F. student, 1923–5) spent much of their time working for the Labour Research Department, learning (they felt) much more about modern capitalism than they could have done from the teaching at the Labour College.

The internal conflicts were further complicated by the attempts of the Communist Party of Great Britain (C.P.G.B.) to assert some kind of control over the teaching of Marxism in Britain.[51] This led to divisions within the college between communist and non-communist students, which resulted in

---

[48] Labour College students' manifesto, 24 July 1923, N.L.S., Acc. 5120, Box 2, fo. 1923. There had been a committee of inquiry led by Arthur Jenkins earlier in the year and this gave the college a clean bill of health. 'Report of enquiry by A. Jenkins and W. T. A. Foot', 18 May 1923, N.L.S. Acc. 5120, Box 2, fo. 1923.

[49] *Plebs* (December 1924). D. J. Williams became M.P. for Neath, 1945–64.

[50] Interview with Idris Cox by Hywel Francis, 9 June 1973, S.W.M.L., Swansea.

[51] Macintyre, op. cit., 85; J. Klugman, *History of the Communist Party of Great Britain*, vol. I. (London, 1968), 335; R. Challinor, *The Origins of British Bolshevism* (London, 1977), 272–3.

stories appearing in the press to the effect that 'differences of opinion were settled by fisticuffs. More than once over tea-table discussions a student, to clinch an argument with another obstinate Bolshevik, dashed a hot cup of tea into the other's face.'[52] Whatever the truth of this assertion, there can be little doubt that communist students in the college (around half the student body were C.P.G.B. members by early 1926) did confront their non-communist colleagues with the claim that 'one cannot be a Marxist and remain outside the Communist Party'.[53] In the aftermath of the General Strike, these tensions became even more pronounced, and in the process many of the communist students began to display a rather crude class-conscious philistinism in which the ideas of the small group of middle-class intellectuals who dominated the Plebs League were derided. Idris Cox, at the time a communist student at the C.L.C., was particularly scathing: 'What do the masses care for art? What are they clamouring for—Art or bread and cheese?'[54]

Gradually, the attitude of the C.P.G.B. leadership towards the Labour College movement in general became more hostile, to the point where in the summer of 1929 the *Sunday Worker* (the official organ of the C.P.G.B.) took undisguised pleasure in the final closure of the C.L.C., stating that the teaching of Marxism should henceforth be under the 'direction and control of auspices which are avowedly Marxian in theory and practice'.[55] Sectarian certainty was now added to ideological dogmatism as one of the less appealing, and self-defeating, by-products of the 'success' of the Labour College movement.

The Labour College could probably have survived the hostility of the C.P.G.B., but the activities of communist students within it gave the college a reputation as a hotbed of Bolshevik subversion. In 1928 the involvement of Labour College students in an unofficial dispute at a London clothing factory and an attempt to establish a communist-led breakaway

---

[52] *Daily Dispatch*, 16 Jan. 1929.
[53] *Anvil*, 2, No. 1 (Jan. 1926). The *Anvil* was the Labour College students' magazine.
[54] Ibid. See also criticism of the role of C.P.G.B. students in the Labour College, by J. A. Sparks in *Railway Review*, 22 July 1927.
[55] *Sunday Worker*, 4 Aug. 1929.

union in the clothing industry triggered a backlash from the orthodox trade union movement.[56] The college authorities started a belated purge of those students connected with the Communist Party. The result was the expulsion of seven communist students, including three from south Wales, one of whom, George Thomas, was secretary of the students' house committee.[57] The affair convinced many right-wing trade unionists that the college was breeding nothing but communist agitators who were a 'plague to every decent trade union official'.[58] The college's reputation certainly deterred some unions, for example, the Yorkshire miners,[59] from establishing scholarships, and there always existed an element in the N.U.R. hierarchy that was hostile. It was certainly not helpful that on one occasion the college was found to be the centre of an unofficial railway strike committee.[60] By early 1929 the patience of some south Wales miners' leaders had been tried beyond endurance, and the London correspondent of a Newcastle newspaper had it on good authority that the S.W.M.F. in the end decided to withdraw support because it was tired of 'paying out to teach "Reds" the art of vilifying and undermining officials'.[61] On the other hand, the expulsions were felt to be unfair by many rank and file members of the S.W.M.F. and may have weakened grass roots support for maintaining the college.

However, the role of the Communist Party in the decline of the C.L.C. has also to be seen in the wider context of the terrible defeats inflicted on the miners' union in the 1920s. These defeats came close to bankrupting the Federation, and in

[56] This was part and parcel of the Communist Party's 'new line' which, on Comintern instructions, sought a break with non-C.P. elements wihin the labour movement. L. J. Macfarlane, *The British Communist Party* (London, 1966), 256.

[57] The man singled out as the ringleader was George Thomas from Treherbert in the Rhondda. Six other C.P. students were expelled, including two from south Wales, D. A. Latcham and Alun Thomas. Statement by E. G. Thomas to the Labour College Board of Governors, 3 Jan. 1929; T. Richards to E. G. Thomas, Apr. 1929; J. M. Williams, secretary of the Bute Merthyr lodge, to T. Ashcroft, 1 Jan. 1929. George Thomas papers, University College of Swansea Library. See also *Western Mail*, 13 Dec. 1928; *Sunday Worker*, 23 Dec. 1928; *South Wales Echo*, 29 Dec. 1928.

[58] *Daily Dispatch*, 16 Jan. 1929.

[59] R. G. Neville, 'The Yorkshire miners and education', *Journal of Educational Administration and History*, VIII, No. 2 (July 1976).

[60] F. Moxley, 'Railwaymen and working-class education', in P. S. Bagwell, *The Railwaymen, A History of the National Union of Railwaymen* (London, 1963), 685.

[61] *Newcastle Chronicle*, 16 Jan. 1929.

these circumstances all expenditure had to be looked at carefully, both in terms of its general value to the members and also to ensure that it was being handled effectively. The Labour College failed to match up to either requirement. Its failure to attract additional support meant that from an early stage it was in financial difficulties. But matters were made much worse by a shocking series of financial scandals involving embezzlement of funds by college staff. In January 1923 the college secretary, George Sims, absconded with some college money. In January 1925, the principal, W. W. Craik, disappeared along with college funds. The following year, W. T. A. Foot, the new secretary, was jailed for six months for misappropriation of the scholarship fees paid by the Monmouthshire Western Valley Miners' District.[62] It was a catalogue of peculation which would have tried the patience of any sponsoring body, but at a time when the miners and their organization were fighting for their very existence, it is a testimony to the fund of goodwill in the coalfield towards the C.L.C. that the S.W.M.F. did not abandon the college. Former C.L.C. students on the S.W.M.F. executive committee, such as Jim Griffiths and Ted Williams, were, however, finding it progressively harder to defend the institution. Ted Williams had no doubt that these events made the continued support of the south Wales miners' union for the college very problematic: 'I will fight all the way for I.W.C.E. but there is little hope to get them all to my point of view after our sad experiences at the College.'[63] For Ablett, by this time increasingly dependent on alcohol, the problems of the Labour College only served to deepen his sense of despair at the way his hopes for revolutionary change had been dashed. The cruellest blow came in 1926, when the Federation, in an attempt to get a grip on the Labour College removed him as chairman of the college governors. It was a decision which caused Jim Griffiths to reflect on the sad consequences of Ablett's weaknesses: 'I am sorry for Ablett as I think he felt it acutely but he has become

[62] Craik to Board of Governors, 20 July 1923, N.L.S. Acc. 5120, Box 2, fo. 1923; Labour College, Board of Governors' minutes, 21 Feb. 1925, 25 June 1926; *Daily Herald*, 11 Aug. 1926.
[63] E. J. Williams to J. P. M. Millar, 26 Jan. 1927, N.L.S. Acc. 5120, Box 2, fo. 1927.

useless . . . had there been a *sober* man at the head of the college governors its recent history might have been different.'[64]

The fate of the college was also intimately bound up with a power struggle inside the Labour College movement that was focused on the N.C.L.C. and its energetic and autocratic general secretary. Millar and some of his supporters tended to feel that the C.L.C. was a drain on resources which could be more efficiently deployed in the provincial class movement.[65] In so far as they felt the college had a useful purpose, it would be as a training centre for local class tutors.[66] This was an idea which cut directly across Ablett's vision of an I.W.C.E. movement woven seamlessly into the trade union movement. The result was an abiding hostility between the N.C.L.C. and some of the S.W.M.F. supporters of the Labour College. When, in 1925, the T.U.C. offered to take over the Labour College as part of a scheme to rationalize workers' education the idea met with support from the S.W.M.F. but was actually opposed by Millar and the N.C.L.C.,[67] who feared that this would divert scarce union resources away from the N.C.L.C. By allying with some right-wing union leaders, Millar sabotaged the T.U.C. scheme at its Bournemouth congress in 1926, and, in the process, created a tenacious and irreconcilable enemy in Will Mainwaring. Mainwaring was by now miners' agent for the Rhondda and the S.W.M.F.'s leading representative among the college governors. He was also rapidly losing his former reputation as a Marxist firebrand. Mainwaring loathed both Millar and the N.C.L.C. with its 'curious mixture of W.E.A., anarchic and communist ideas'.[68] He was particularly embittered by the way that Millar's allies at Bournemouth had used the opportunity to attack the Labour College as élitist and uneconomical, echoing the opinions of earlier critics of

---

[64] J. Griffiths to J. P. M. Millar, 9 Nov. 1926, N.L.S. Acc. 5120, Box 2, fo. 1926.
[65] J. H. Roberts, 'The N.C.L.C.: an experiment in workers' education' (University of Edinburgh M.Sc. thesis, 1970), 88, 112.
[66] N.C.L.C., executive committee minutes, vol. 1, 9 June 1924; N.L.S. Acc. 5120.
[67] Millar to W. H. Mainwaring, 7 Apr. 1925, N.L.S. Acc. 5120, Box 2, fo. 1925. Initially, Mainwaring seems to have been sympathetic to Millar's plans. For the background to the T.U.C. scheme, see A. J. Corfield, *Epoch in Workers' Education* (London, 1969), 42–55.
[68] Mainwaring to Millar, 29 Nov. 1926, N.L.S. Acc. 5120, Box 2, fo. 1926.

the C.L.C. When the N.C.L.C. offered to take over the college, Mainwaring made it plain that he would not tolerate such a development, and his opposition proved decisive.[69] It was a clash of personalities which proved fatal for the Labour College, for although Mainwaring's anger with Millar and the N.C.L.C. was understandable, the N.C.L.C. scheme was probably the only way whereby the Labour College could have survived.

However much the Communist Party, the N.C.L.C. and the weaknesses of individuals contributed to the closure of the Labour College, its ultimate demise was due to the wider crisis that was afflicting the British economy in general and the south Wales coal industry in particular. One of the most unpleasant side-effects of the economic crisis was the emergence of victimization of union activists and its concomitant, emigration from the coalfield. This had always been a problem: T. I. Mardy Jones encountered difficulties in obtaining work after he came back from Ruskin College, and Frank Hodges, when miners' agent for the Garw, found that students who attended his classes were subject to discrimination by colliery managements. During the war, A. J. Cook and Ted Williams received a taste of what was to become common for the later products of the Labour College.[70] With the collapse of the post-war boom and the advent of chronic structural unemployment, managements were much more willing to single out Labour College men for special treatment. The trend was discerned from the early 1920s. Frank Phippen returned to his native Rhondda only to discover that the owners of the pit where he had previously worked refused to guarantee his reinstatement.[71] His plight, and that of all other returning students of the college, was made worse by the fact that under existing regulations they did not qualify for unemployment benefit. The situation worsened in 1921: 'Go and ask Lenin for a job', was one mine manager's piece of careers guidance offered to D. J. Davies when he requested his old place.[72] Davies did not act on the manager's suggestion, but neither did

[69] Mainwaring to Millar, 14 Jan. 1927, N.L.S. Acc. 5120, Box 2, fo. 1927.
[70] *Plebs* (June 1913); S.W.M.F., E.C. minutes, 30 Oct., 11 Dec. 1915.
[71] Rhondda No. 1. minutes, 14 Nov. 1921.
[72] Craik, op. cit., 174. See also the interview with D. J. Davies, held at the S.W.M.L., Swansea.

he return to the coal industry. Nye Bevan was not treated as a pro-
digal son by the Tredegar Iron and Coal Company upon his
return to the Sirhowy Valley.[73] By 1923, Glyn Evans, a communist student from Garnant, was writing to *Plebs* in his capacity as
secretary of the C.L.C. students' house committee, stating that
half the returning students could not find employment. In 1924
he complained that union officials were often reluctant to press
the claims of ex-students when so many men were on the dole.
Evans pointed out that the function of the Labour College
would be undermined if this trend were not challenged: 'The
student must have economic security if his work is to be successful.'[74] Even if the union did succeed in securing a place, the management would often contrive to isolate the ex-student from other
workers in the pit.[75]

In earlier days the problem of victimization would be offset
by giving the student a paid post with the union. The job of
checkweighman, which was in the gift of the rank and file
miners, was always a popular option because it kept the activists in direct touch with the membership. Indeed, the existence of these posts has led some writers to suggest that the
issue of victimization was less acute for the miners than it was
for the railmen.[76] This is not the case. There was not an inexhaustible supply of such jobs; indeed, as the pits closed and
the membership of the Federation dropped, the number of
paid positions also declined. W. H. Williams, a student of the
1923–5 generation, summed up the problem thus: 'In the
first stage after the war and the students returned to South
Wales, they became Miners' Agents and so on ... But with
my lot all the jobs were taken up.'[77]

---

[73] Foot, op. cit., 46–7.

[74] *Plebs* (Oct. 1923, Apr. 1924). See also the letter from Eden and Cedar Paul, June
1924. Evans was lucky in the anthracite district where the union was able to enforce a
'seniority rule'; he did secure a place in his old pit.

[75] Interview with Idris Cox, loc. cit. Cox secured a place only after the direct intervention of Vernon Hartshorn on his behalf. He was, however, deliberately assigned a
poor and isolated place to work.

[76] Millar, op. cit., 92. It is repeated in M. Cohen, 'The Labour College between the
wars', in B. Simon (ed.), *The Search for Enlightenment: The Working Class and Adult Education in the Twentieth Century* (London, 1990), 108.

[77] Interview with W. H. Williams, by author and Hywel Francis, 21 Nov. 1972
(S.W.M.L., Swansea); Williams was unable to secure work in his old pit near Pontypool, and he left the industry and the region.

The result of the victimization was to destroy the central purpose of the Labour College. Products of the college were denied the opportunity to serve the union which had sent them, as the rules of the Federation denied them membership if they took up any form of paid employment outside the industry. Many were thus forced out of the Federation in a desperate search for a living. In 1924, Jack Bailey, a victimized ex-student from Mountain Ash, wrote of one S.W.M.F. district where three ex-C.L.C. students were working as a tram conductor, a council navvy and an insurance agent.[78] Many were forced to leave south Wales as part of the general exodus from the coalfield to the better prospects of the Midlands and south-east of England.

By the end of 1926 some candidates from the coalfield, like George Thomas, were applying to go to the college to escape victimization. It is not difficult to imagine the effect on morale amongst the student body of attending a college which seemed to ensure them exclusion from the very movement they aimed to serve, and would even deny them a place in the dole queue. Few of those who attended the college in its last years made much impact on the S.W.M.F.; some, like Morgan Phillips, gave service to the wider labour movement. Ironically, one beneficiary was the N.C.L.C., which found it had a large pool of talent from the ranks of ex-S.W.M.F. Labour College students, on which it could draw for tutors and organizers. But this is not what Ablett intended. His ideal of a teaching leadership for the labour movement was frustrated by the victimization and the emigration. It was also frustrated by the sectarian divide which was opening between those who belonged to the older pre-Leninist Marxian traditions, which stressed the need to decentralize power and decision-making to the rank and file, and the Communist Party with its rigid organizational structures and its stress on centralized power, decision-making and ideological discipline. The result was that the college became a focal point for frustrated ideals and ambitions; the confident, insolent militancy, which John Thomas experienced in 1920, had by the end of the decade turned into a generalized antipathy to anyone or any-

---

[78] *Plebs* (July 1924). Bailey himself left the coalfield to become an organizer with the Bradford Co-operative Society.

thing which did not fit into the clockwork views of the world that were being expounded there. In the end, even its most ardent supporters on the S.W.M.F. executive committee found it impossible to save the Labour College, and Ablett's dream came under the auctioneer's hammer.

In seeking to assess the significance of the Labour College there is a danger of judgement being clouded by the sheer eminence of some of the products of the institution. It simply cannot be assumed that these men would not have achieved such prominence without a stay at the college. The fact is that they were pre-selected by their colleagues, already marked out for office. It is difficult to believe that Nye Bevan's career would have been seriously derailed if he had missed the chance of a sojourn at Penywern Road, and Arthur Horner's development was little impaired by his decision not to seek a scholarship. The value of the college lay not so much in its teaching, which was often of doubtful quality, but in the experience of the wider world: the political and cultural life of London, the endless debates and the ability to read without the pressure of having to earn a living at one of the most arduous and dangerous activities known to man.[79] The Labour College accordingly left an indelible mark on the leadership of the south Wales miners and, through them, on the political life of industrial south Wales. It gave a collegial quality to the miners' leadership; they were from the same school, shared the same world view and similar value systems, reinforced by two years at the C.L.C. By 1927 eleven ex-Labour College products sat on the S.W.M.F. executive committee, and elections for office in the union became popularity contests amongst them. By 1940 seven Labour College 'old boys' sat in the Commons representing south Wales constituencies; looked at in that light, Ablett's vision of a cadre of teachers and leaders was a success.[80] But the

---

[79] Interviews with W. H. Williams, Idris Cox and J. Griffiths, loc. cit.; see also J. Griffiths, op. cit., 25–6.

[80] S.W.M.F. E.C. members included: N. Ablett (not strictly a C.L.C. 'graduate'), W. Coldrick, G. Daggar, D. L. Davies, J. Griffiths, A. Jenkins, S. Jones, W. H. Mainwaring, B. Roberts, W. J. Saddler (a Ruskin College 'striker') and E. J. Williams. Arthur Horner and S. O. Davies, closely associated with the Labour College movement, were also on the E.C.. M.P.s included A. Bevan (Ebbw Vale), G. Daggar (Abertillery), N. Edwards (Caerphilly), J. Griffiths (Llanelli), A. Jenkins (Pontypool), W. H. Mainwaring (Rhondda East), E. J. Williams (Ogmore).

tragedy for Ablett and perhaps for the labour movement was that neither he nor his college could cope with the changing industrial and political atmosphere. The closure of the Labour College is more poignant because it occurred just as its critics, on the right and the left, were realizing the value of residential workers' education. From the late 1920s the C.P.G.B. began to send its brightest young members to Moscow and the Lenin School, and, from 1927, Coleg Harlech started to recruit able students from the W.E.A. classes of south Wales.

3. 'MANY DIFFICULT PROBLEMS AND STRUGGLES CONFRONT THE WORKER AT HOME AND ABROAD'

Thus opened the concluding paragraph of Mark Starr's second edition of *A Worker Looks at History*, published in 1925. Nothing perhaps better illustrates the change in the atmosphere within the ranks of organized labour activists since the era of revolutionary hope at the end of the war, when Mark Starr concluded the first edition of his book with the confident statement that 'in every country Capitalism begets its gravediggers'. In place of the certainty of emancipation, there was now the complaint that a deadweight of apathy and ignorance and the 'miseducation of capitalism and national prejudices' would prevent the international workers' revolt against capitalism. Starr's 1925 conclusion presaged a defeat for organized labour, and for the miners in particular, far more devastating and traumatic than that of 1921. The failure of the General Strike of May 1926 was more bitter because it showed the potential of working-class solidarity, but it also illustrated the power of the state when confronted with a challenge to its authority.[81] Through the summer and autumn of 1926, the miners endured a lock-out, and by early December, their ability to carry on the fight broken by poverty and the prospect of an even bleaker winter, they had returned to work on the

---

[81] M. Starr, *A Worker Looks at History* (London, 1925), 132. For the impact of the General Strike and lock-out in south Wales see the collection of essays and recollections in *Llafur*, 2, No. 2 (Spring 1977). For the impact of the strike and lock-out on the S.W.M.F., see H. Francis and D. Smith, *The Fed: A History of the South Wales Miners in the Twentieth Century* (London, 1980), 52–107.

owners' terms. The era of revolutionary posturing was finally over.

The advent of chronic unemployment and the defeat of the miners in 1921 and 1926 may have ended the era of revolutionary posturing, but it altered the tone rather than the substance of debate about workers' education. As the immediate threat of revolutionary change faded, the transformation of Labour into a party of government restimulated the debate triggered by its electoral success in 1906. Frank Hodges, speaking to the T.U.C. at its Cardiff Congress in 1921, feared that unless the rise of Labour to political power were based on an educated democracy, the social discontent that brought Labour to power would soon breed disillusionment and despair if the party failed to match the very high expectations of the people. The need to educate workers to be more than agitators and propagandists, to train them to meet the challenges of government, Hodges argued, was equally vital if the rise of Labour to power was to be permanent. The need for the unions to enhance and co-ordinate their educational provision was thus essential.[82] Hodges was speaking to an assembly where the stock of the unions most imbued with the semi-revolutionary spirit of the years before Black Friday, those of the miners and railmen, was falling and the initiative was passing back to union 'bosses', whose perception of their role owed little to Marxism and more to an updated Labourism, albeit one articulated with a socialist vocabulary. The inter-war years saw the rise to prominence of union leaders such as Walter Citrine and Arthur Pugh: men who had decided that policies of total war with capitalism were too dangerous to the long-term interests of organized labour.

Pugh was the national secretary of the recently amalgamated Iron and Steel Trades Confederation (I.S.T.C.), one of the most tightly organized unions in the country. He had brought together a disparate group of often hostile regional and sectional organizations into one large entity. He was a typical product of the old Steel Smelters' union which, under John Hodge, had laid great emphasis on professionalism in union

[82] *Report of the Proceedings at the Fifty-Third Trades Union Congress, 1921* (London, 1921), 363–4.

organization; apart from being one of the first unions to send officials to Ruskin College, it was also one of the first to establish a statistical department and employ a full-time lawyer.[83] Little affected by the semi-revolutionary ideas of the later stages of the war, the steelworkers' union was dominated by an ethos of pragmatic Labourism in which disputes were avoided, if at all possible, and collaborative industrial relations were not seen as a class betrayal. Pugh rejected the principles of 'independent' working-class education in so far as it excluded the use of public funds and institutions. 'Millions per year are granted from the Treasury to equip the experts who run capitalist industries ... we claim that the trade-union movement also requires its trained expert advocates, administrators and leaders.'[84] The I.S.T.C. was a union which had also always associated with Ruskin College and the W.E.A. when it engaged with workers' education. Thus, when Pugh decided that the newly amalgamated union needed a programme of education, he quickly responded to an approach from the W.E.A. national secretary, J. M. MacTavish. The result was the creation of the Workers' Education Trade Union Committee (W.E.T.U.C.), a body which was designed to act as an agency for the supply of workers' education to subscribing unions, with participating unions paying for the service its members actually received from the committee; in straitened times this made the scheme attractive to many unions. The scheme, which came into effect in the autumn of 1919, also ensured that, although it rested on the educational expertise of the W.E.A., effective control remained in the hands of the affiliated and participating unions; hence the creation of a separate agency actually to administer the scheme.[85]

The opportunity, at long last, of creating close relations with the trade unions was seized enthusiastically by the national leaders of the W.E.A., in particular by MacTavish. In south Wales two co-ordinating committees, with John Davies as secretary, were established coterminously with the two I.S.T.C. districts (Nos. 5 and 6) for the east and west of the region. For the

---

[83] See the entry on John Hodge in the *D.L.B.*, vol. III.
[84] Quoted in Corfield, op. cit., 15.
[85] Ibid., 8. See also Pugh's article, 'The Trades Union Congress and the workers' educational movement', *The Labour Magazine* (Oct. 1925).

important iron and steel smelting area around Swansea, it was
decided that a full-time organizing tutor's post was necessary
and MacTavish thought he knew the very man for the job,
none other than John Thomas. MacTavish visited Thomas in
the early months of 1920 and, despite the fact that Thomas
had moved far to the left, persuaded him to put his name forward for the W.E.T.U.C. post.[86] There was some reluctance
on the part of the district committee of the south Wales
W.E.A. to accept this idea, and although MacTavish and
John Davies, both of whom seem to have been happy to
indulge Thomas's revolutionary ideas, railroaded the
nomination through the W.E.T.U.C. area committee, it was
not fully endorsed by the W.E.A. district executive committee.[87] Indeed, there seems to have been some lack of
enthusiasm at W.E.A. district level to the entire W.E.T.U.C.
concept, which gave a lot of power to supporting unions, but
the national association ignored these qualms and pressed
hard for rapid implementation. MacTavish's cavalier machina-
tions, which sought to exploit Thomas's undoubted popularity
with the labour movement in the Swansea area, were frustrated
by the latter's election as miners' agent for the anthracite
district.

The vacancy was filled in September 1920 by Illtyd David.
Unlike Thomas and Davies, Illtyd David had few direct links
with organized labour but was very much in tune with the educational outlook of the dominant group in the Welsh W.E.A. As
a sixth-form student at Barry Grammar School, he had lodged
at the home of the headmaster, Edgar Jones, and there had
become well acquainted with members of the Cardiff–Barry
coterie, Tom Jones, Percy Watkins and E. P. Hughes. Whilst
a student at Cambridge, he met R. H. Tawney and, through
his good offices, David was invited to act as a tutor for the
Oxford Extension Summer Schools, and thus was soon steeped
in the ethos of educational progressivism.[88] Whilst David's

[86] Interview with Thomas, Apr. 1972: Thomas, a teetotaller, was much struck with
MacTavish's capacity to consume Scotch whisky.
[87] W.E.T.U.C., Division No. 6 minutes, 29 Mar. 1920; W.E.A. for Wales, executive
committee minutes, 30 Mar. 1920. MacTavish always regarded himself as a man of
the left who acknowledged Marxian influences on his political development. Corfield, op. cit., 24–5.
[88] Interview with Dr Illtyd David, 16 May 1972.

appointment may have pleased the leading lights of the association in south Wales, it was not, in many ways, a very happy choice. Although sympathetic to the labour movement, David was committed to the detached analysis of social and economic problems, and he found it difficult to cope with trade unionists who demanded an uncritical commitment to the cause of the workers. 'They expected the tutor to rationalize their opposition to Capitalism. I felt it was expected of me as a tutor of the W.E.T.U.C to be really sympathetic to the working-class movement.'[89] As a means of financially underpinning the organizer's post in south west Wales, Illtyd David was expected to take some tutorial classes for the University College of Swansea. Here David was much more at home, and he encountered difficulties with some members of the W.E.T.U.C. district committee, who regarded this work as a diversion from the main purpose of the scheme, which was the provision of shorter and more elementary courses geared to the needs of union members.[90] Tensions continued throughout the decade and were relieved only in the early 1930s, when David was appointed to the extra-mural staff of the University College of Swansea.

David's difficulties illustrated another problem which the W.E.T.U.C. threw into stark relief, namely, the issue of political partisanship. Although close involvement with the trade unions was not of itself partisan political activity, the affiliation of most of the supporting unions to the Labour Party, and the serious clashes between organized labour and the state in the 1920s, obviously made the position of the W.E.A. a sensitive one. It was made more difficult because the Labour College movement would seize on the financial subventions of wealthy capitalists, or any apparent lack of enthusiasm by the W.E.A. for the cause of labour, to support their case. The result was that the W.E.A. felt obliged to press its districts to ensure that the association was seen to be taking sides in the contest

[89] Ibid.
[90] In 1924 an attempt was made to get David to drop his extra-mural work. This was blocked by the national W.E.T.U.C. W.E.T.U.C. Division No. 2 minutes, 7 June 1924. In 1922 the W.E.T.U.C. was redivided and west Glamorgan and the rest of west Wales became Division No. 2.

between capital and labour. This issue became even more sensitive after 1924 when the W.E.A. was a 'responsible body' for state grant-aid. The crunch came with the General Strike. The W.E.A. nationally decided that it had to display support for the labour movement in general and that it could not therefore stand aside in the conflict. When the strike was over, the national W.E.A. collected reports from its districts to amass evidence to refute any Labour College allegations about its role—especially as much prominence had been given in the popular press to the strike-breaking activities of many university undergraduates. Naturally the report from south Wales was particularly important, and John Davies provided evidence that the association in south Wales took an active part, with Davies acting as minute secretary for the Cardiff strike committee and using the W.E.A. office Gestetner duplicator to produce the local strike bulletin. These actions, Davies felt, ensured that the association was seen 'taking sides.' But Davies also did not disguise his despair at the outcome of the strike: 'the surrender has become "unconditional" in effect on the part of the workers', and it had further polarized opinion. The split personality of a movement that tried to be both non-partisan and committed to the labour movement, that wished to see organized labour accepted as a positive element in society, is displayed throughout Davies's report. 'Neutrals for the first two days became antagonists before the end of the week. Persons willing to consider the claims of the Labour Party and to vote Labour were antagonized as the days lengthened into a week.'[91]

Despite the failure of the General Strike, the W.E.T.U.C. remained an important area of work for the association in south Wales. The I.S.T.C. had, by the mid-1920s, been joined by two large newly amalgamated general unions, the Transport and General Workers Union (T.G.W.U.) and the National Union of General and Municipal Workers (N.U.G.M.W.), both of which were well represented in south Wales, especially in the Swansea area, where component elements of both unions, such as the Dockers' Union and the

---

[91] John Davies to J. MacTavish, 20 May 1926, original document supplied to the author by W. Gregory, Croydon.

Gas Workers, had long traditions of effective existence.[92] The organizational burden which fell on Illtyd David's shoulders became too much; there were, in 1928, 126 branches of the I.S.T.C. in the Swansea and south-west Wales area, and he asked to be relieved of the organizer's role. His long-standing differences with the W.E.T.U.C.'s west Wales committee were reflected in demands from them to appoint someone as an organizer who was 'experienced in trade union matters' and who had 'the confidence of the workers'.[93] Funds for such an appointment were not forthcoming in the late 1920s, and Illtyd David's job in this period was maintained only by grants from an educational charity, the Cassell Trust. At the depths of the slump in 1931, the post was abandoned when the I.S.T.C. withdrew financial support.[94] Trade unions in the late twenties and early thirties did not have the resources to sustain, let alone expand, their educational work, and so the W.E.A., whilst maintaining its links with the unions through the W.E.T.U.C., looked increasingly to other sources of money to gain access to the working class.

Whilst most of the struggle for union support between the W.E.T.U.C. and the N.C.L.C. took place at a national level, in south Wales the great prize of the S.W.M.F. eluded both bodies. The W.E.A./W.E.T.U.C. does not seem to have campaigned directly for the affiliation of the S.W.M.F., but did try the tactic of applying for funds from the Miners' Welfare Fund, which would have required the agreement of the S.W.M.F. executive committee; these, not surprisingly, were denied.[95] It was the N.C.L.C. which made the most sustained effort to win the affiliation and establish a scheme for the S.W.M.F. In many ways, the history of the N.C.L.C. in south Wales in the inter-war years was shaped by its desire to win over the Federation.

Established in 1921 in reponse to the creation of the W.E.T.U.C., the N.C.L.C. was initially supposed to be little

[92] See L. J. Williams, 'The new unionism in south Wales', *Welsh History Review*, 1, No. 1 (1963).

[93] W.E.T.U.C., Division No. 2 minutes, 13 Oct. 1928. A similar resolution had been sent to the national W.E.T.U.C. in Dec. 1924.

[94] Ibid., 12 Dec. 1931.

[95] South Wales, W.E.A. executive committee minutes, 3 Feb. 1926; S.W.M.F. E.C. minutes, 4 Mar. 1926.

more than a co-ordinating, rather than a supplying, body. J. P. M. Millar soon began to centralize control over the I.W.C.E. movement within the N.C.L.C., meeting resistance in some areas such as his native Scotland,[96] and also from the cradle of the movement in south Wales. Ablett seems to have decided from the outset to have nothing to do with an organization which cut across his idea of how unions should educate their members.[97] He clung to the belief that the Federation would, through its education committee, establish a co-ordinating body for the various district class schemes which were established in the later war period. The Rhondda No. 1 District proposed such a scheme in the summer of 1920; but events overtook the proposal and thereafter the parlous financial state of the Federation, which had to concentrate its resources on the Labour College, prevented any progress.[98] Many district class schemes collapsed during the 1921 lock-out and were only partially restored thereafter. In early 1922 there were district-sponsored classes running in Aberdare, Abertillery, Ammanford, Blackwood, Blaina, Gorseinon and Tredegar.[99] These schemes rested on the vagaries of district funding and were often the first activity to be jettisoned when membership and finances declined. The most elaborate scheme was functioning in the Rhondda District which, from 1920, could afford to employ a full-time tutor, D. R. Owen, and sustain ten classes. But even here the depression took its toll, and Owen's services had to be dispensed with in 1924.[100] They kept a class scheme functioning throughout the 1920s, initially refusing to entertain the idea of affiliating to the N.C.L.C. The Rhondda remained the focal point of hostility to Millar and his organization, Mainwaring as miners' agent maintaining his vendetta but also sustaining Ablett's principles long after

[96] Roberts, op. cit., 111–33.

[97] Speaking on Ablett's behalf at the foundation conference of the N.C.L.C., an N.U.R. governor of the Labour College, by the name of Charleton, stated that the Labour College existed 'to train miners and railwaymen—not tutors'. Minutes of the Class Co-ordination Conference held at Yardley, Birmingham, 8–9 Oct. 1921. N.C.L.C. E.C. minutes, vol. 1, loc. cit.

[98] S.W.M.F. E.C. minutes, 5 Nov. 1920.

[99] Plebs (Jan. 1922).

[100] Rhondda No. 1 minutes, 20 Sept. 1920, 3 Oct. 1924.

common sense dictated compromise.[101] The dire consequences of economic decline forced even the Rhondda District to approach the N.C.L.C. in 1928, but by that stage the district was so impoverished that it could not afford to fund even a very basic scheme, and in the following year, just as the Labour College closed its doors, the Rhondda No. 1 District suspended its educational work.

In 1923 the N.C.L.C. appointed as full-time organizer for south Wales (which became Division 4 of the organization), W. J. Owen, an ex-Labour College student from Blaina. One of his first tasks was to approach the S.W.M.F. to try to secure affiliation of the S.W.M.F. education committee, only to discover that it had gone into 'suspended animation'; and further approaches over the next few years were no more successful.[102] The continued existence of the district schemes was one factor. Another was the effect of industrial disputes. Ness Edwards, writing in 1920, felt that I.W.C.E. classwork could play a crucial role in countering 'strike weariness' and reinforcing commitment by illustrating the contradictions of capitalism.[103] Experience was very different, and classes took second place to practical measures for survival—such as soup kitchens, boot repairing and picket duty. Class activity actually declined during disputes, revived in the bitter aftermath, but then turned down again as the resource base of the miners' union suffered the long-term consequences of defeat.[104] Personalities also played a role. By 1927 Millar had no doubt that there was a strong anti-N.C.L.C. lobby within the S.W.M.F. focused on Will Mainwaring, but also including Ablett and possibly George Daggar, W. J. Saddler and D. J. Williams.[105]

Without the affiliation of the S.W.M.F., the N.C.L.C. in south Wales did run classes for its affiliates, the building

---

[101] G. Hicks to J. P. M. Millar, 13 Jan. 1927, N.L.S. Acc. 5120, Box 2, fo. 1927. In 1928 Millar told his executive committee that Mainwaring's district was the focal point of hostility to the N.C.L.C. within the Federation. N.C.L.C. E.C. minutes, 7 Jan. 1928, vol. 1, N.L.S. Acc. 5120. See also Millar, op. cit., 99.
[102] N.C.L.C. E.C. minutes, 18 June 1923, vol. 1, loc. cit.; S.W.M.F. E.C. minutes, 30 June, 5 July 1924, 24 Mar. 1925; *Plebs* (August 1924).
[103] Ibid. (Dec. 1920).
[104] Ibid. (Sept. 1922, Nov. 1923, Jan. 1924).
[105] List of supporters and opponents of the N.C.L.C. on S.W.M.F. E.C., N.L.S. Acc. 5120, Box 2, fo. 1927.

workers, the shop workers and the engineers. Also, occasionally, S.W.M.F. districts would briefly affiliate; in 1927, for example, the Maesteg, Ogmore and Afan Valleys districts arranged schemes with the N.C.L.C.[106] In the early 1920s the south Wales district of the N.U.R. ran classes in economics and history tutored by Mark Starr. In 1925 an attempt by south Wales branches of the N.U.R. to establish a scheme with the N.C.L.C. was blocked by the railwaymen's national executive committee.[107] Beyond the classes arranged for affiliated unions, the south Wales (No. 4 Division) of the N.C.L.C. was run on the basis of volunteers paying their own way. Much thus depended on the quality and commitment of local Labour College secretaries and unpaid tutors. In Cardiff the Labour College secretary, Alan Pope, was able to build up quite a healthy set of classes between 1923 and 1926, with the active support of the trades council and individual N.U.R. branches. By 1925 even local T.G.W.U. branches were supporting the local Labour College, despite the union's national affiliation to the W.E.T.U.C. However, the General Strike seems to have wiped out Pope's work, and the Cardiff Labour College collapsed. It was revived in 1929, but on a much lower scale of activity, based on a shop assistants' union group and the Penarth branch of the I.L.P.[108] The vulnerability of the N.C.L.C. to the effects of local economic difficulty is even more starkly illustrated by what happened in the Rhondda. When the local miners' district was forced to pull out of educational work, the N.C.L.C. was able to establish a local Labour College on the basis of volunteer tutors and in the 1927–8 session some twenty classes were organized. By the following year the effects of the depression and the victimization of tutors, which so often resulted in their enforced emigration from the area, meant that the local 'college' was able to run only eight classes.[109] Similarly, in 1927 the Swansea Valley Trades and Labour Council was able to employ the legendary Nun Nicholas on a full-time basis to organize N.C.L.C. classes in

[106] *Plebs* (September 1927).
[107] Moxley, op. cit., 685–6.
[108] *Cardiff Trades and Labour Yearbook* (Cardiff, 1925), 58; *Plebs* (Mar. 1929).
[109] Ibid. (Dec. 1927, Jan. 1929).

the area. But by the summer of 1929 this scheme had also collapsed.[110]

By the end of the 1920s, the battle between the N.C.L.C. and the W.E.A./W.E.T.U.C. for the support of the unions in Britain and south Wales had settled into stalemate as the unions struggled with declining membership and rising unemployment. However, whilst the W.E.A. could look to state and charitable trust funds to allow it to adapt to the new circumstances obtaining in industrial south Wales, the commitment of the N.C.L.C. to full independence in such matters meant that it was unable to overcome the organizational difficulties created by the collapse of union finances, and the W.E.A. type of workers' education began, slowly, to win the battle against I.W.C.E.

It is difficult to quantify the impact of workers' education, but there is evidence that by the end of the decade the I.W.C.E. movement was in slow but steady decline, at least in the coalfield. The peak was reached in the autumn of 1926, during the later stages of the coal dispute, when nearly two thousand students attended some sixty-five I.W.C.E. classes in south Wales. By 1930 just over a thousand students were attending forty-one classes; probably about three-quarters were miners. Bearing in mind the organizational and financial difficulties which confronted the Labour College movement in these years, it is an impressive figure and suggests that the I.W.C.E. movement still remained a force in the coalfield.[111]

Strict comparisons between the W.E.A. and the N.C.L.C. are difficult; class attendance figures are suspect for all organizations, as there were pressures on tutors to inflate the numbers, and the number of classes is probably a better guide to organizational health and buoyancy. In 1927, over five hundred students were attending thirty-one short and terminal W.E.A. classes (the nearest equivalent to the standard twelve-week N.C.L.C. course) in south Wales. By 1929 over one thousand

---

[110] *Plebs* (July 1929). The N.C.L.C. even relaxed its rule on not paying tutors in order to secure Nicholas's services, N.C.L.C. E.C. minutes, 8 Apr. 1927, vol. 1, loc. cit.

[111] These figures are based on the quarterly divisional returns contained in the N.C.L.C. minute books held in the National Library of Scotland, Acc. 5120.

students were attending fifty-four such classes.[112] Whilst the
W.E.A. and university-type courses did attract many middle-
class and white-collar grades, such as teachers, in 1929 over
80 per cent were manual workers, and at least 20 per cent
were miners.[113] Whilst the S.W.M.F. may have been hostile
to the W.E.A. and its university allies, a significant number
of its members were happy to attend classes supplied by the
agencies of orthodox workers' education. In the session 1929–
30 a total of 561 south Wales miners attended W.E.A. classes,
whilst 379 were reported as attending classes supplied by the
extra-mural departments which covered the coalfield.[114] The
extent to which the W.E.A. was able to penetrate the bastions
of I.W.C.E. teaching by the late 1920s is illustrated by the fact
that in the 1929–30 session the N.C.L.C. was able to run six
class groups in the Rhondda Valley, while the W.E.A. and
the Cardiff extra-mural department were able to run fourteen.[115] In the end, superior financial and organizational
strength could overwhelm even the most profound commitment to a particular view of workers' education.

4. 'A FEELING OF DISQUIET'

During the 1920s the nature of the relationship between the
W.E.A. and the state became problematic, especially during
the difficult middle years of the decade, when there was considerable tension and frequently an inability to reconcile the
W.E.A.'s non-partisanship in political matters, which was
necessary to secure state funding, with its desire to construct
and consolidate links with organized labour. This came to the
fore in 1925 with the T.U.C. scheme to rationalize and co-ordinate
workers' education. Pressure from the N.C.L.C. secured the inclusion of a clause which would commit the T.U.C. to provide education which would, *inter alia*, 'assist the working class movement
in its efforts for social and industrial emancipation'.[116] The

---

[112] B. B. Thomas, op. cit., table III, 111.
[113] *W.E.A., South Wales District, 23rd Annual Report, 1929–30.*
[114] Ibid.
[115] Ibid.; *Plebs* (January 1930).
[116] R. Fieldhouse, 'Voluntaryism and the state in adult education: the W.E.A. and
the 1925 T.U.C. education scheme', *History of Education*, 10. No. 1 (1981), 47.

N.C.L.C. proclaimed that this committed all participating bodies to a programme of anti-capitalist education.

The response of the leadership of the W.E.A. and the agencies of state provision indicated considerable disquiet over the implications of this clause. The W.E.A. leadership, however, tended to see the clause as a 'rhetorical flourish', necessary to win the confidence of the trade union movement.[117] The agencies of the state, the Board of Education and the local authorities, on the other hand, tended to see the clause as committing state funds to partisan political purposes. In the end, for reasons already stated, the scheme was never implemented, but it exposed two trends of thought in the ranks of orthodox adult and higher education. There was what might be termed the 'progressive' stance, which believed that concessions to labour were necessary to prevent workers' education drifting away from influence and control by orthodox educationalists, and what might be termed the 'Tory' stance, which opposed any concessions which might be seen as support for anti-capitalist propaganda.

This debate had its echoes in south Wales. Lleufer Thomas had realized that the strong anti-capitalist ethos of the era was something which could not be ignored, but that to fail to respond to it, or actively to campaign against it, would be fatal and would leave the field open to I.W.C.E. He clung to the belief that the values of university education would ultimately triumph over the narrow dogmatism of the Labour College movement. That is not to say that there was not disquiet amongst Welsh educationalists about the strategy. In 1918 R. T. Jenkins, in an attack on the very idea that education should have an objective beyond the development of a 'burning passion for knowledge', expressed his distrust of the 'mission theory of education' and feared the perversion of study for dubious and probably unachievable ends.[118] Lleufer Thomas and his followers, however, were willing to indulge the Labour movement in its anti-capitalist mood and, as reflected in the semi-corporatist ideas which came out of the Unrest Commission, press government and industry to concede elements

[117] Ibid., 49.
[118] See his 'Syndicalist education', *Welsh Outlook* (Apr. 1918).

of control to the institutions of organized labour. Under MacTavish and John Davies, the W.E.A./W.E.T.U.C. were even more willing to be seen as 'taking sides', though they went further than many of the Cardiff–Barry coterie would have wished. The need to win the confidence of organized labour remained paramount for many on the 'progressive' wing of the debate. Lord Haldane, the advocate of a more 'democratic' Welsh university, regularly chided the university authorities in the early 1920s for their laggardly attitude and their distrust of 'the democracy'.[119] He was convinced that if the University went to the people, 'the relations between Capital and Labour will be peaceably adjusted, and adjusted without friction, because people will take a larger view and see things as a whole instead of from the side of class only.'[120] Haldane's optimism soon gave way to a growing anxiety among 'progressive' opinion in south Wales about the tendency of a growing section of workers to take 'unconstitutional action'. At this time what some elements of 'progressive' opinion regarded as the underlying purpose of workers' education was stated overtly. Echoing Robert Lowe, the mouthpiece of the remaining elements of south Wales popular liberalism, the *South Wales News*, declared in 1925, 'We must educate our masters of the new democracy if we would strengthen the bulwarks against revolution, and ensure the ordered progress of our national life.' In this regard, argued the *News*, the W.E.A. had already 'proved its worth'. For 'there is no menace to a State so formidable as the ignorance of its people.'[121]

If the voice of south Wales Liberalism was happy with the W.E.A.'s activities, the voice of south Wales Conservatism, the *Western Mail*, most certainly was not. Embodying the 'Tory' critique, it was suspicious of all forms of workers' education, and throughout the 1925–6 period attacked the W.E.A. as a Labour or socialist organization; some critics on the right

---

[119] 'The university and adult education', substance of an address by the Rt. Hon. Lord Haldane, at the University College of South Wales and Monmouthshire, Saturday, 28 April 1923. South Wales W.E.A. Records, Cardiff.
[120] Viscount Haldane of Cloan, *The University and the Welsh Democracy* (Oxford,1922), 15.
[121] *South Wales News*, 6 July 1925.

even saw its classes as 'nurseries of bolshevism'.[122] This was a source of difficulty for the association, but it reflected its impossible position in such a polarized atmosphere. It also reflected a long-standing hostility by the Cardiff business community towards the semi-corporatist ideas of the Cardiff–Barry coterie. It was this element which desired a more overt pro-capitalist ethos in university education, and which had earlier opposed Tom Jones's appointment as principal of Cardiff University College, because of his too close association with the ideas of the Unrest Commission and concessions to organized labour.[123]

The accusation that the W.E.A. classes were 'nurseries of bolshevism' was, of course, denied by the association's friends. In the aftermath of the General Strike, the need to re-establish the credibility of the W.E.A. as an non-partisan agency in south Wales was acute. In the summer of 1926 the senior H.M.I. for Wales, W. J. Williams, addressed the A.G.M. of the south Wales W.E.A. In a well-publicized speech, he acknowledged that there was abroad a 'feeling of disquiet' about the conduct of University extra-mural and W.E.A. classes. 'Criticism of the social order must inevitably arise in the course of the study of such subjects as Economics, Sociology and History,' but, Williams contended, in the context of W.E.A./extra-mural classes this was conducted on 'university lines' where 'the temper of impartial judgement, and the quest for truth are predominant factors'. If some of the class members were 'precipitate and unorthodox in their thinking', then these were precisely the students who should be welcomed to help them shed 'preconceived opinions'.[124] This line, that it was precisely the most radical and extreme students that needed to be attracted to the classes, was one often repeated by W.E.A. supporters and was also a recurrent theme in H.M.I. reports on classes where there were suspicions about the nature and content of the education; it was argued that should support be withdrawn, such men would seek tuition

---

[122] Stead, op. cit. (1977), 31. Earlier in the post-war period, the W.E.A. was even suspected of revolutionary purpose by Basil Thompson and the Home Office Directorate of Intelligence. Morgan, op. cit. (1979), 53.

[123] *South Wales Echo*, 31 Jan. 1918; see also the Jones *Diaries*, op. cit., vol. I, 46, 52.

[124] *South Wales Argus*, 19 July 1926.

from the Labour College movement, beyond their influence and control. The reports always exuded confidence that classes conducted under W.E.A./university control were safe from the danger of becoming simply 'nurseries of bolshevism'. There was less confidence about local authority evening classes in Labour areas in south Wales, where evidence of left-wing, anti-capitalist teaching was stronger, but even here the H.M.I. tended to be fairly sanguine about their impact.[125]

In fact, the fears of the *Western Mail* and the section of south Wales opinion it represented were not entirely without foundation. The W.E.A. and its supporters tended to play down the extent of Marxist and left-wing influence within the orthodox adult education movement in south Wales, when in truth the W.E.A. was an important agency for the transmission of Labour and even Marxian ideas. Writing in 1922, John Thomas explained how even anti-Marxian tutors, feeling obliged by the interest of the students to examine the ideas of Marx in the hope of being able to refute them, had been, by the presence of able students already 'soaked in Marxism', forced to concede the validity of Marxian concepts. Thus, the class group, possibly even the tutor, was won over to Marxist ideas.[126] Conversion of the tutor may not have been necessary. There were active in the W.E.A./W.E.T.U.C. classes in south Wales in the 1920s teachers who had little time for 'liberal' educational values and saw the classes as the means of winning workers to the anti-capitalist cause. W. A. Hewlett, a leading figure in the I.S.T.C. in the Swansea–Neath area, made no secret of his left-wing ideas or of his belief that the classes were for the emancipation of the workers from capitalism. In some areas, such as Briton Ferry, the W.E.A./ W.E.T.U.C. classes, and not the N.C.L.C., were the main agencies for the transmission of Marxian economics and history.[127] Nun Nicholas, one of the most charismatic of the

---

[125] These reports can be found in the Public Record Office, Board of Education Files, Ed/25/593. See also B. Simon, 'The search for hegemony, 1920–26' in Simon (ed.), op. cit., 52–7.

[126] J. Thomas, 'The economic doctrines of Karl Marx and their influence on the industrial areas of south Wales, particularly among the miners', essay submitted to the Ammanford National Eisteddfod, 1922, S.W.M.L., Swansea.

[127] Interview with Illtyd David and W. Gregory.

Marxist lecturers produced by south Wales, tutored the first series of W.E.T.U.C. one-year classes on 'Industrial history' at Pontardawe.[128] The Swansea area W.E.T.U.C. also started to develop short, elementary classes and Saturday schools on topics very similar to those of the N.C.L.C. In the session 1926–7 there were day schools on such topics as 'Karl Marx and economic determinism', 'Capitalism and its alternative','The General Strike in history and theory'.[129] Within the W.E.T.U.C. in south Wales there was also a strong rank and file lobby for closer links with the Labour College movement, and on one occasion some Gorseinon I.S.T.C. branches requested the services of W. W. Craik as a weekend school lecturer, which was blocked by the regional W.E.T.U.C. [130]

The students and tutors engaged in workers' education cared little for the squabbling between the W.E.A. and the I.W.C.E. movement; most were happy to get access to a tutor and a venue. It was always the quality of the tutor that mattered, not the agency supplying the teaching. There is considerable evidence that many young activists in the inter-war years adopted the strategy of 'academic entryism' advocated by Mark Starr in 1917. Although the N.C.L.C. never sought direct financial aid from the state or its local authorities, evening classes in economics and industrial history, using Labour College and Plebs textbooks, were established under local authority auspices in Carmarthenshire and Glamorgan. In the Carmarthenshire case the H.M.I.s became concerned as the classes grew from four in 1921 to twelve in 1925. In a minor *cause célèbre*, the local H.M.I., in the aftermath of the anthracite troubles of 1925, demanded the withdrawal of local authority support unless the classes adopted a broader syllabus and a wider range of texts; ideally, they should become W.E.A. or extra-mural classes with properly qualified tutors. One of the tutors affected, Jim Griffiths, the newly elected agent for the anthracite district, wrote to the *Plebs* magazine about the affair and provided Millar with propaganda evidence that the W.E.A. was clearly only a lackey of the capital-

---

[128] W.E.T.U.C. Division No. 6, minutes, 30 Oct. 1920, 22 Apr. 1922.
[129] W.E.T.U.C. Division No. 2, minutes, 30 June 1927.
[130] Ibid., 21 June 1924, 6 June 1925.

ist state—a development predicted by Mark Starr nearly ten
years earlier.[131] Similar classes were run in Glamorgan with
Nun Nicholas as tutor; and they were also scrutinized by the
relevant H.M.I., but without serious consequences. There
was always the suspicion, and it was certainly rumoured, that
some tutors were using two sets of notes, one for the students
and one for the inspectors. Oral testimony supports this
belief. Len Jeffries, a communist activist from Monmouthshire, recalled attending an evening class led by a local history
teacher. The class was advertised as being on a fairly orthodox
topic, but in fact he lectured on Leninism. He arranged with
the students that they should tell any visiting inspector that
the tuition was indeed on the subject advertised. Will Paynter
also recalled that Communist Party lecturers working for the
W.E.A. in south Wales would often use two sets of notes.[132]

One of the factors which eased the consciences of Marxist and
communist tutors when they used the orthodox agencies of
workers' education was that, unlike the N.C.L.C., they were
paid. Archie Lush, close friend of, and election agent for,
Aneurin Bevan, often lectured for both the W.E.A. and the
N.C.L.C. in the inter-war years, 'The only argument between
the W.E.A. [and the N.C.L.C.] being that you were paid'.[133]
This was an important consideration; Millar realized that the
N.C.L.C. could never survive except on the basis of volunteer, unpaid tutors. This created problems in south Wales,
where there was a tradition of employing full-time tutors for
S.W.M.F. district classes. According to D. J. Davies, an ally
of W. J. Owen in his battle to secure an N.C.L.C. scheme
with the Federation, this was one of the reasons for resistance
to the establishment of such a scheme.[134] Indeed, in south
Wales, the N.C.L.C. had regularly to waive the non-payment
rule, when local Labour College class schemes were established;[135] this was a source of distress to Millar well into the

[131] *Plebs* (November 1926); interview with James Griffiths; *Education for Emancipation*
(London, 1931), 10.
[132] Interviews with Len Jeffries and Will Paynter (S.W.M.L., Swansea).
[133] Interview with (Sir) Archie Lush (S.W.M.L., Swansea).
[134] Interview with D. J. Davies (S.W.M.L., Swansea).
[135] N.C.L.C. E.C., minutes, vol. 2, loc. cit., 18 Sept. 1926. In the session 1925–6, eight
tutors in the Rhondda were being paid, Idris Cox was being paid in connection with the
Maesteg and Aberavon miners' districts, and there were two paid tutors in Ogmore
Vale and in the Swansea and Cardiff Labour colleges—all to Millar's chagrin.

next decade. Yet, in a coalfield racked with unemployment and victimization, this was often a vital source of income for tutors maintaining a precarious existence and determined to spread their mission and their message.

It is, of course, impossible to quantify the extent to which W.E.A. and extra-mural classes were transmitting Marxian ideas—probably not as much as the *Western Mail* claimed but far more than the W.E.A. leadership would admit. That there was a strong pro-Labour element in much of the teaching cannot be denied. Even *Welsh Outlook* admitted that this could be a problem. 'There is always the danger that the W.E.A. should become just a branch of the Labour Party; and its classes, intentionally or unintentionally, the incubation chambers of local Labour leaders.'[136] The author of this observation felt that the heavy emphasis on economics as a subject in W.E.A. classes explained the strongly pro-Labour attitudes to be found in them. Lleufer Thomas had hoped that the domination of economics and economic history would fade as the movement grew and matured. Philosophy, English and Welsh literature would liberalize the workers' outlook and make them more amenable to a view of the world which sought harmony in social and industrial relations. The change was slower than Lleufer Thomas had hoped, and in the session 1921–2 well over half of all joint committee classes were in economics or industrial history.[137] But by the end of the decade just over a quarter of W.E.A. terminal and one-year classes in south Wales were still on economics or industrial history. The change in the university tutorial classes was more dramatic by 1929–30; of the twenty-two tutorial classes put on by the Swansea joint committee in 1929–30, only four were in economics and industrial history; there were three in psychology, an increasingly popular subject in the inter-war years, and two in philosophy; and music, literature and international relations all now had their place.[138] It could be argued that

---

[136] *Welsh Outlook* (December 1926).

[137] *University of Wales Extension Board, Second Annual Report, 1922–23.* The report regretted the continued preponderance of economics as a class topic but felt that this was inevitable as 'Economics is the subject that stands closest and in most intimate relation to the life of the working class student.'

[138] *South Wales W.E.A., 23rd Annual Report, 1929–30.*

the 'progressive' strategy worked, as students were able to work out their feelings of hostility and bitterness towards the capitalist system in the class groups; their minds either rebelled against the half-formed, semi-revolutionary ideas of the immediate post-war years, or needed the harder edge of engagement with a Party, the Communist party, with a programme for, and a concrete example of, a real revolutionary change. Either way, the revolutionaries were isolated, and reformism and ameliorative political activity reasserted themselves as the routes to be followed by most south Wales Labour politicians and union leaders—something which might not have occurred if ideas critical of capitalist society had been rigorously excluded from the classes of the W.E.A.

The intellectual underpinnings of the teaching within the Labour College movement have come under close and critical scrutiny in recent years. These studies have tended to focus on two major aspects of the teaching: the economic and the philosophical interpretations presented to students. In the area of economics teaching, one writer has echoed the criticism of many contemporaries in south Wales that Labour College tutors 'treated Marxist economics as a final and complete system whose applicability to current events could be taken for granted'.[139] Ablett's *Easy Outlines of Economics*, based on a series of lectures originally published before the war, embodied the essence of Labour College economics teaching. It was essentially an attempt to present, in a form which would be understood by the average, elementary school-educated worker, the main analytical concepts developed in the first sections of *Capital*. Great emphasis was laid on the concept of surplus value, which was expropriated from the worker and also on the labour theory of value which ascribed to the worker the responsibility for the creation of all wealth. This emphasis was necessary in Ablett's eyes to counter the Marshallian ideas to be found in W.E.A. classes, which argued that value was given to a commodity by its marginal utility to a consumer.[140] Marshallian economics also ascribed a pivotal role to the entrepreneur as a factor in the production of wealth.

---

[139] Macintyre, op. cit., 151.
[140] Ablett (1919), op. cit., 24ff.

Essentially an updating of classical economic thought, Marshallian economics did provide scope for amelioration of the condition of the workers through social reform and a more ordered labour market.[141] The problem was that whilst countering the theory of marginal utility was the intention, Ablett's book encouraged the view that in the first ten chapters of Marx could be found a comprehensive description of capitalism which needed no updating or amendment in the light of modern circumstance. It took on the quality of Holy Writ and the ability to understand the obscure concepts was, many contemporary critics thought, too often more important than the ability to apply the knowledge.

A slightly different set of issues arose with regard to the attempts by British working-class Marxists to provide themselves with a sound philosophical foundation upon which their economic and historical view of the world could be based. The answer was to be found in the writings of Joseph Dietzgen. He was a genuinely working-class disciple of Marx, which made him even more attractive to worker-students, but his work is today seen as a deeply flawed and abstruse attempt to adapt the Hegelian dialectic to the materialist interpretation of existence to be found in Marx's economic and historical analyses.[142] The question of the role of the human mind in historical development was answered by Dietzgen's materialist dialectic. At a time when south Wales Marxists were struggling to displace a religious and idealist view of the world, Dietzgen gave them a 'proletarian philosophy' which also, in a potted version developed by Craik and called the 'Science of understanding', taught them that thinking was simply a physical activity of the brain and that dialectical thinking was achieved by understanding the processes by which the brain absorbed, analysed and interpreted information. In south Wales, Dietzgen's ideas, popularized by lecturers such as Nun

---

[141] A good example of the type of economics taught in W.E.A./W.E.T.U.C. classes in the early 1920s can be found in a lecture and booklist, prepared by W. Marwick, in the *Journal of the Iron and Steel Confederation* (Sept. 1920), 318–20. The main texts were Marshallian: Clay's *Economics for the General Reader* and Chapman's *Political Economy*. Marx's theories were mentioned, but it is clear that the theory of marginal utility is assumed to be correct. On the other hand, collectivist solutions to social/industrial problems are also highlighted, with Guild Socialism to the fore.

[142] Ree, op. cit., 23–37; Macintyre, op. cit., 129–40.

Nicholas, helped many young activists to break with the thought patterns they had learned in school, work and chapel, and adopt a new view of the world and their place in it. Despite the rejection of Dietzgenism by many middle-class intellectuals in the Labour College movement, and its displacement in the later 1930s by the concept of dialectical materialism as the philosophical basis of Marxism-Leninism, it remained a formative force in the coalfield throughout the inter-war years and assisted in the process of 'conceptual rupture' which reordered the outlook of many working-class leaders in industrial south Wales.[143] Nun Nicholas remained a loyal disciple and continued to use his 'theory of understanding' to help them break with the mental habits of the past. He evolved a quite extraordinary teaching method, which involved the brutal putting down of any sloppy thinking or use of ambiguous language by a student, combined with the liberal use of four-letter expletives. For many young activists in the west of the coalfield the experience was a revelation; for others the method caused them to doubt the validity of the message and the seriousness of the messenger. There was also a deterministic edge to much of Nicholas's teaching, which could either cause students to become fully involved in the unfolding of an inexorable historical process or produce a kind of 'professional' Marxist student, well-read but with little inclination to get fully involved in the struggle as the victory of the workers was, historically, certain.[144] This had been a source of criticism of the Labour College movement from I.L.P. activists in the war years; it was to be reiterated by communist activists in the inter-war years.

The trend away from economics and industrial history discernible in the classes of the W.E.A. is also detectable in the classes of the Labour College movement in south Wales. As the prospects of imminent revolution faded, so interest in the wider world developed, perhaps in order to explain the ability of a crisis-ridden capitalist system to adapt and survive. In 1920 nine out of ten classes run by the Rhondda No. 1 District were

[143] See Gwyn A. Williams's 'Bibliographical note' to his 'Locating a Welsh working class', in D. Smith (ed.), op. cit., 42–3.

[144] Interviews with W. Gregory, J. Evans (Abercrâf), and D. D. Evans; transcripts all held at the S.W.M.L., Swansea. Interview with Amos Moules, Nov. 1973.

on economics or industrial history. In the session 1930–1, in the south Wales division of the N.C.L.C. only just over a third were on these topics, the largest single group being called 'modern problems', with greater emphasis on international relations and current affairs.[145]

One of the consequences of the hold of Marxian and revolutionary ideas in the coalfield was a deep interest in what H. A. L. Fisher called the tendency of miners to be 'prone to the acceptance of contracted doctrines in enthusiastic form'.[146] The mind of the miner, and of the south Wales miner in particular, became, once again as it had been in 1912 and 1915, a source of speculation by academic observers. Baffled by the state of chronic strife which beset the industry, they soon settled on the hold that 'extreme' ideas had on the activist element. One writer, Dr J. A. Bowie, actually sought the explanation in the labour process: 'The miner undermines and undercuts day by day, and it is a fact beyond dispute that above ground he frequently employs his time in the same way on the constitution of his industry.' This ineluctable process could be countered only by a programme of education in the 'realities' of economic life, combined with employee share-ownership schemes.[147] It was a strategy which was also favoured by another writer, J. H. Miall, following a visit to the Rhondda during the 1926 stoppage. He felt that the miners' hostility to private ownership sprang from deep misunderstandings about the economics of coal and certain myths regarding the way that coal company profit figures were manipulated to justify wage-cutting by the employers. Again, share ownership and education were seen as the solution.[148] By 1929 W. Haydn Davies was able to state, with some justification, that 'the Welsh miner has a world-wide reputation for his extreme revolutionary views.' He also saw

[145] Rhondda No. 1. District minutes, 25 Oct. 1920. The figures for 1930–1 are taken from tables to be found in N.C.L.C., E.C. minute books, vol. 7, 124.

[146] H. A. L. Fisher, *A History of Europe*, vol. I (London, 1935), 212. Fisher commenced his great work in 1926. Fisher is drawing an analogy with the theocratic excesses of Cluniac monasticism.

[147] J. A. Bowie, 'The miners' mind', *English Review* (Feb. 1925); see also the reply to Bowie by A. E. Ritchie in the *English Review* (Apr. 1925), which is even more hostile to the miners.

[148] J. H. Miall, 'Talks with miners in the Rhondda Valley', *Fortnightly Review*, 20 Sept. 1926.

the nature of the miners' working life as fostering their revolutionary attitudes; the dangers which bred mutual dependence,
the lack of a sense of property, the communal life of the valley
pit villages and the general inter-dependence and uniformity of
work experience are seen to explain their willingness to commit
themselves and their Federation to 'the abolition of capitalism'.
He cited also the Federation's upkeep of a 'college at which
Marxian ideas are disseminated' and its help 'in the conduct
of classes which propagate independent working-class education' as adding to its revolutionary reputation and explaining
why the 'South Wales miner should be considered notorious'.
This article, which only reiterated viewpoints that could be
heard at any time in middle-class and educated circles in Britain in the 1920s, is worthy of note because it was prompted by a
report from the Industrial Transference Board which stated
that it was difficult to secure jobs for unemployed Welsh
miners because of their reputation for militancy, unrest and disturbance.[149] By the end of the decade it was unemployment
which was to breed in the hearts and minds of many miners
an abiding hatred of capitalism, but unlike the later war and
early post-war years, this festering hatred was developing
away from the point of production where there were no
obvious weapons at hand to challenge the system.

---

[149] W. Haydn Davies, 'The south Wales miner', *Welsh Outlook* (Feb. 1929), though
the ability of former Welsh miners to obtain jobs in the rising industries of the
Midlands and south-east of England does not appear to have been much affected by
this 'revolutionary' reputation.

V

SOUTH WALES AND THE 'NEW LEISURE'

1. The Welsh ideal of popular culture revived

Between 1929 and 1935 chronic structural unemployment in industrial south Wales was reinforced by the severest cyclical depression of modern times. In 1930 south Wales had the worst rate of unemployment of all the British regions, with over a quarter of the insured population registered as out of work.[1] The coalfield began to suffer a demographic haemorrhage as over a quarter of a million people left for better prospects in the Midlands and south-east of England.[2] Left behind in the valley communities were large numbers of men in a state of idleness for very long periods of time: entire villages where the majority of the adult male population was on the dole or public assistance. As unemployment was no longer a passing phase but a way of life, the workers of south Wales gradually became less of a revolutionary menace and more of a social problem.

Despite the pressures to leave the Valleys, there were also reasons to stay: family ties, the costs of removal, and the dole itself, though never really adequate, was enough to stave off actual starvation. The net result was that by the early 1930s south Wales was coming to terms with the fact that it was a chronically depressed area; hopes that a revival in the staple industries would soak up the jobless had long since died, and instead the coalfields tended to be seen as areas of economic and spiritual dereliction, made up of communities broken by the trauma of unemployment; incapable, without assistance, of breaking out of the apathy, poverty and hopelessness engendered by the slump. The great institutional bastion of working-class industrial, political and intellectual independence in the coalfield, the S.W.M.F., was enfeebled by a decline in member-

---

[1] W. Beveridge, *Full Employment in a Free Society* (London, 1944), 61.
[2] C. L. Mowat, *Britain Between the Wars* (London, 1955), 226.

ship, from 200,000 in 1920 to 63,000 by 1933.[3] Locked in a struggle against an owners-sponsored 'non-political' union, with a chronic non-unionist problem and sectarian divisions fostered by the growth of the Communist Party within its ranks, its internal problems left something of a leadership vacuum in the valley communities. In political terms the era of the 'slump' saw the consolidation of the Labour Party as the dominant political force in industrial south Wales. Virtually eliminated in the rest of the United Kingdom in the general election of 1931, Labour held its ground in the coalfield and, throughout the era of heavy unemployment, actually strengthened its grip on the local government of industrial south Wales. Local Labour councillors struggled to defend their ravaged communities, and tried to protect and even improve their local services such as education, often against the indifference, and sometimes the hostility, of central government. There was to be a challenge to Labour from the far left, in the shape of the Communist Party, for control of the organized labour movement, but in both the political and the industrial spheres, the Labour Party was to maintain its hegemony in south Wales.[4]

None the less, despite the fact that the Labour Party had control of the local authorities and the parliamentary seats, the economic crisis in industrial south Wales did create openings which the ideas and ideals of the social service missionaries could penetrate. They came initially in the immediate aftermath of the General Strike, usually driven by a socially conscious religious out-look. Often Quakers, a significant number of them educated women, this new type of missionary became, by the end of the decade, an integral part of what might be termed the 'social service' response to heavy unemployment in industrial south Wales.

The old hub of I.W.C.E. activity, mid-Rhondda, became the place where they settled first and established what was to be but

---

[3] J. Davies, 'Time to spare in Wales', in *Wales and the New Leisure* (Llandysul, 1935), 7. The euphemism 'the new leisure' (to describe unemployment) enjoyed, mercifully, only a brief vogue amongst social service workers.

[4] For an overview of the establishment of the 'Labour ascendancy' in south Wales in the inter-war years, see K. O. Morgan, op. cit., 272–303.

the first of many valley 'settlements'. The Maes-yr-Haf settlement in Trealaw, under the guidance of William and Emma
Noble, became the model, soon to be followed by others, such
as Hilda Jennings in Brynmawr and John Dennithorne in
Merthyr. By 1937 there were nine full settlements functioning
in the eastern part of the coalfield, the area most badly affected
by unemployment.[5] Although the settlements' function was
primarily educational, they had a broader social purpose
which incorporated practical training in such skills as wood-
working, handicrafts and allotment keeping. The staff resided
in the communities they served, and functioned as case workers and investigators of the populations there. From such work
flowed studies of the communities, such as Hilda Jennings's
study of Brynmawr.[6] The south Wales proletariat once again
became sociological specimens to be probed, analysed and dis-
sected so that, it was hoped, solutions could be found and
applied. It was an eminently respectable movement which,
under the aegis of the National Council of Social Service
(N.C.S.S.), enjoyed royal patronage. Funds were provided by
worthy institutions such as banks, public schools, churches
and Oxbridge colleges with some, but not much, from the
state. Linked with local authority provision, various 'distress committees' sprang up across industrial south Wales so that there
were in the region, by the summer of 1934, schemes to mitigate
the worst impact of unemployment in over ninety-three towns
and villages, supervised by more than 193 different committees.[7]

   That one of the motives of those involved in these schemes of
amelioration was to prevent the unemployed from venting their
frustration in protest and unrest was scarcely denied by those
active in the voluntary social service movement. Margaret
Gardner stated that tutors expert in economic and industrial
problems should meet and gain the confidence of unemployed
men so that their energies, 'at present dangerously concentrated upon the problem of how to redress their own grie-

---

[5] P. E. Watkins, *Educational Settlements in South Wales and Monmouthshire* (Cardiff, 1940),
2–4. See also J. Elfed Davies, 'Educational settlements in south Wales with special
reference to the Merthyr Tydfil Settlement', *Transactions of the Honourable Society of
Cymmrodorion* (1971).
   [6] H. Jennings, *Brynmawr* (London, 1934).
   [7] J. Davies, op. cit., 7.

vances', could be redirected towards community service.[8] After
Magdalen Morgan had delivered a course of lectures to some
unemployed men and their families at Cefn Coed (near
Merthyr), she was pleased to report that the local vicar spoke
of the lectures as a boon because they took the people's minds
'off their troubles and gave them a sense of escape'.[9] By 1930
John Davies was arguing that the era of 'Proletcult', a term
Labour College supporters used to describe their attempt to
create an alternative working-class culture, was over in industrial south Wales, as working men went back to their old
anchorages in music, literature and a socially conscious religious awareness.[10] He grossly underestimated the resilience of
the I.W.C.E. movement, but even in the Rhondda, in 1931,
the decline in attendances at N.C.L.C. classes was being
ascribed to the activities of 'the Quakers'.[11]

The interest of the old Cardiff–Barry coterie was soon aroused
in this new movement, containing as it did a strong practical
link between social service and religious commitment. *Welsh
Outlook* followed its development with great interest and support. In a very revealing editorial marking the death of two
great south Wales miners' leaders, Tom Richards and A. J.
Cook, one writer noted that Cook had moved to the right in
his later years, seeing the need for policies of conciliation and
compromise; 'the transformation of an extremist into a moder-
ate by a series of strikes is an expensive educational curriculum.'[12] The discovery of a cheaper one was a task the
writer commended to the university and the Welsh Council
of Social Service. The one dimension of the old ideal which
was not so apparent in the new movement was the sense of
Welshness, the rural cultural ideal of the literate Welsh peasan-
try, now perceived to be vital in the stricken coalfield communities. Percy Watkins saw it as essential to reinject this sense of

---

[8] M. Gardner, 'An impression of the conference', in *Distressed Areas of South Wales and Monmouthshire* (Newtown, 1932), 32.

[9] Quoted in 'Joint Committee for the Promotion of Educational Facilities in the South Wales and Monmouthshire Coalfields' (*c.*1930), 3. South Wales W.E.A. Records, Cardiff.

[10] Ibid., 9.

[11] *Plebs* (Feb. 1931).

[12] *Welsh Outlook* (Dec. 1931); though he flirted with Oswald Mosley's New Party, the extent of Cook's drift to the right may have been exaggerated by contemporary observers. See P. Davies, op. cit. 182–5.

Welsh nationality into the social service response to make it a movement with a 'rightful place in our national life and to give our national life its rightful place in the movement'.[13] To Watkins, chronic unemployment was destroying the cultural fabric of south Wales society and undermining the objective of creating an educated democracy; it struck at the very heart of the ideal of popular culture. It was the combination of sustained idleness with poverty which he characterized as being the most disturbing feature of the 'new leisure'.[14] Horrified by the long-term social and spiritual impact of this enduring blight on industrial south Wales, Watkins relinquished his senior civil servant's post at the Board of Education in London in 1932 and returned to south Wales as secretary to the Welsh Department of the National Council of Social Service. This body sought to co-ordinate and control the educational work of the major providers such as the W.E.A. and the National Council of Music, with the burgeoning and varied occupational activities, such as allotments, physical training and handicrafts, provided by the scores of unemployed clubs and groups that were springing into existence alongside the educational settlements. He collaborated closely with Thomas Jones, who left his job with the Cabinet Secretariat in 1930 to become secretary of the Pilgrim Trust.[15] By the early thirties two leading personalities in the old Cardiff–Barry circle were presiding over influential agencies as part of the voluntary social service response to unemployment in south Wales. The link with the Davies family of Llandinam was also strong, their home at Gregynog becoming a regular conference centre for social work agencies in south Wales.[16] The need to graft a sense of distinct Welsh identity was frequently stressed at this time, especially in the context of the adult education element of the social service response. The need to 'refine' the intellectual sensibilities of the (now idle) working class of the region was also an

[13] *Cambria* (Summer 1930).
[14] See Sir Percy E. Watkins, 'Adult education and the new leisure in Wales', in *Wales and the New Leisure*, op. cit., 45–51.
[15] P. E. Watkins, *Adult Education Among the Unemployed of South Wales* (London, 1935), 10–11. This is a pamphlet originally republished from an article in *The Yearbook of Education, 1935*; Stead (1977), op. cit., 62.
[16] The first of these was held in Jan. 1932. See *Distressed Areas of South Wales and Monmouthshire* (Newtown, 1932), the published report of the conference.

old theme which found a new lease of life in the years of the slump. Addressing the annual meeting of the south Wales W.E.A. in 1933, the warden of the Merthyr Settlement, Gwilym James, argued that, particularly in Welsh adult education, there was a need for a greater emphasis on subjects— especially literature—which appealed to the imagination and the emotions, rather than those, such as economics and psychology, which he asserted required considerable intellectual energy before even the most basic understanding of the discipline was acquired. The development of taste and refined sensibility was more important than the creation of 'crude thinking', which too often led to 'crude uncritical action'.[17]

John Davies and the south Wales W.E.A. soon saw, in the funds being made available through the various agencies for adult educational provision in the distressed areas of the region, opportunities to gain access to the coalfield in a way which had not been possible in the early 1920s. On the initiative of H.M.I., W. J. Williams, a Joint Committee for the Promotion of Educational Facilities in the South Wales and Monmouthshire Coalfield was created in the spring of 1929. The domination of the W.E.A. was assured when John Davies became the committee's secretary and its headquarters the W.E.A. office in Cardiff. It acted as an agency for the distribution of charitable funds from the U.K. Carnegie Trust for fostering educational provision in depressed areas, and co-ordinated other voluntary bodies with an interest in adult education, such as the Y.M.C.A. and the National Council of Music, as well as the educational settlements and those local authorities which were willing to co-operate.[18] At the centre of this network was John Davies. Under this committee additional funds for class work allowed a steady expansion in the number of full-time tutors. Originally, this benefited the extra-mural departments, with several tutors being appointed in south Wales, notably D. E. Evans for the Cardiff joint committee; he worked closely with the association.[19] The additional funds also allowed the south Wales W.E.A. to move to better

[17] *Welsh Outlook* (Feb. 1933).
[18] P. E. Watkins, op. cit. (1935), 6–7.
[19] *South Wales, W.E.A., 24th Annual Report, 1930–31.*

premises and improve secretarial assistance. They further allowed it to appoint a full-time organizer in the Swansea area, which more than compensated for the loss of Illtyd David after the collapse of the local W.E.T.U.C. scheme in 1931. Appointed in November 1931, Mansel Grenfell, the W.E.A. organizer for Swansea and west Wales, proved to be an energetic and dedicated worker for the W.E.A. cause, and the Swansea area, already a strong base for the W.E.T.U.C., soon became a W.E.A. stronghold in south Wales.[20]

In February 1934 the joint committee joined with the newly formed Welsh department of the National Council of Social Service to form the education committee of the South Wales and Monmouthshire Council of Social Service. This was able to administer state funds channelled through the N.C.S.S. and also funds to the educational settlements made available by the Special Areas Act of that year.[21] The steady growth of classes required further organizational assistance, and in 1935 G. H. Jones was appointed as organizer for south-east Wales, with special responsibility for the establishment and development of local branches of the W.E.A., a perennial problem for the association in south Wales. Further appointments were made possible in 1936, and area tutor/organizers were appointed for the Maesteg, Rhondda, Pontypridd, Ebbw Vale and Bridgend areas. Two other tutor/organizers were appointed in 1938 for the Neath/Dulais and Caerphilly areas.[22] Thus by the outbreak of war in 1939, the W.E.A. had eight full-time staff in addition to the district secretary. Whilst this expansion was able to consolidate the hold of the W.E.A. on adult educational provision in south Wales, it was a development which was not without its costs. John Davies's very personal style had been useful in saving the association in south Wales in the early 1920s, when he had to inveigle money out of wealthy benefactors whilst at the same time stressing his commitment to organized labour. In the words of Thomas Jones, 'no one quite knew what was happening or how.' By the late thirties this style was no match for the

[20] *South Wales, W.E.A., 30th Annual Report, 1936–37.*
[21] P. E. Watkins, op. cit., 12.
[22] *South Wales, W.E.A., 31st Annual Report, 1937–38.* Six part-time area organizers were also appointed in 1936–7.

scale of administration required, and an organizational subcommittee, which did not include the district secretary, was
established in 1936 to deal with an accumulation of administrative problems left unresolved by Davies.[23] In December
1937 Davies died after a short illness. He left a district of the
W.E.A. which had expanded from a situation in 1919 when,
in the whole of Wales, there were twenty-two tutorial and
pioneer classes to one in which, on his death in south Wales
alone there were over 320 classes of all types, nearly two
hundred of them run directly by the association. The south
Wales district had the highest class membership rate of any
W.E.A. district in the U.K. and the highest proportion of
manual workers attending its classes.[24] This was no mean
achievement for a man with only an elementary education
and no formal qualifications. He maintained his links with
the Labour and Co-operative movement, and remained until
his death an ethical socialist.[25] Yet in the process of the huge
expansion of the W.E.A., he was aware that something was
being lost; the vision was becoming clouded by the trend
towards being simply a provider or supplier of classes. In that
sense the W.E.A. in south Wales had become an organization
and not a movement; it represented a set of nebulous ideals
which were made even more vague as its links with the labour
movement atrophied and funds flowed in from state and semi-
official agencies.

The attempts to graft on to the educational dimension of the
social service response to unemployment the Welsh ideal of
popular culture were not really successful. *Welsh Outlook*, the
main organ of the ideals of the Cardiff–Barry coterie, folded
in 1934. In 1930 the south Wales district established a regular
journal of 'adult education and social service in Wales'. Under
the editorship of D. E. Evans, and entitled *Cambria*, it ran for

---

[23] *South Wales, W.E.A., 30th Annual Report, 1936–37*; T. Jones on John Davies, *Highway*
(February 1928). John Davies's inadequacies as an administrator were notorious by this
time. Interview with Len Williams (Neath), 21 May 1974. Williams became a very prominent member of the association, serving on the national executive committee of the
W.E.A. for many years; Illtyd David found Davies impossible to work with. Interview,
op. cit.
[24] *South Wales, W.E.A., 31st Annual Report, 1937–38.*
[25] Ruby Davies, 'Memories', in *John Davies* (Gregynog, 1938), 6–7. Ruby Davies (née
Part) was a women's organizer with the Workers' Union and was Labour candidate for
the Wells constituency. She married John in February 1929.

several issues, with enthusiastic articles exuding the ethos which sought to give coherence to the movement: a collective sense of purpose beyond simply keeping the unemployed occupied and diverted from paths of unrest and disturbance.[26] Yet this journal folded after only a few years. Whilst the costs of production and the paucity of advertising revenue were the immediate causes of the failure of such ventures, ultimately it reflected a change in the leadership of the workers' education movement itself. There were, in fact, two quite contradictory trends: an individualist drift in the perceptions of the adult educationalists, and a strong collectivist mentality amongst the students. There was a development away from regarding the workers' education movement as primarily geared to the workers as a class, or to their community rather than the individual. The Mansbridgean ideal of raising the intellectual and cultural level of an entire social class, not selecting individuals to enable them to rise to a new social group, was still something clung to by older members of the Cardiff–Barry circle. It was very apparent in the ideas which fired Thomas Jones to establish Coleg Harlech as a workers' college: not as a labour college, but as an institution which would bring together students from different occupations and areas of Wales to try to instil in them the ideals of service and citizenship, which they could then take back to the communities whence they came. 'It was of the essence of democracy that they should have intelligent citizens and the maximum number of effective individuals in their midst.'[27] To Jones the function of Coleg Harlech was not to raise students out of their social class but to take them away from the pressures of 'economic circumstance and the narrowness of their homes, be put in a decent place for twelve months and given a good time intellectually'.[28] Returning to their communities, they would then reflect the values and ideals they had acquired at Harlech for the betterment of that locality. Yet the warden of Coleg Harlech, Ben Bowen Thomas, whilst not breaking with the Mansbridgean ideal completely, reflected

---

[26] The title of the journal was originally to be *Citizen*, but this proposal was blocked by an objection from a similarly entitled journal in the west of England. *Cambria* (Spring 1930).

[27] *Western Mail*, 5 Sept. 1927.

[28] *Montgomeryshire Express*, 5 Jan. 1935.

the views of a new generation of adult educationalists who saw their mission in less collectivist and more individual context. 'Ultimately,' Thomas argued, 'the duty of the adult education-alists lies neither towards the industrial worker group nor towards his locality but to the man himself.'[29] He stressed that adult workers responded as diverse individuals to educational opportunities; some did use them as a chance to break out of the working class and enter the professions. For Thomas this was as valid a function for workers' education as the creation of labour leaders, or to populate the Valleys with well-read and well-meaning citizens who could be a 'desirable influence on their community'.[30]

In fact, Thomas was simply reflecting a long-term trend. From the early 1920s, funds were made available from various charitable bodies, such as the Cassell Trust and the Miners' Welfare Fund, to enable working-class students from tutorial classes to gain access to full-time study at universities. At first, the national W.E.A. sought to control this break with Mans-bridgean ideals by trying to relate the grants of money to some commitment on the part of the students that they would return, after completion of their studies, to serve their community or trade union.[31] The anxiety to prevent the classes simply becom-ing a way of 'getting on' was, however, countered by those who felt that no such hurdles should be placed in the way of students, and that ability alone should determine the award of scholarships.[32] By 1927 the annual reports of the South Wales district of the association started to boast of the numbers of students the W.E.A. had assisted to gain access to higher education.[33] Yet even in the late 1930s there were those in the association who were ambivalent about the W.E.A. simply being a 'second chance' or 'opportunity' agency. Typical was a

[29] B. B. Thomas, 'Adult education and the industrial worker' (substance of an address to the World Conference on Adult Education, Cambridge, Aug. 1929), reprinted in *Welsh Outlook* (Oct. 1929).
[30] B. B. Thomas, 'Notes of an address to the Coleg Harlech Consultative Conference in Cardiff, 24 May 1930', W.E.A. records, Cardiff.
[31] 'Workers Educational Association, provision of scholarships for tutorial class students' (1924), South Wales, W.E.A. records, Cardiff.
[32] Memorandum by Professor W. J. Roberts and the Cardiff joint committee secre-taries in reply to the above (n.d.) Joint Committee memoranda, W.E.A. records, Car-diff.
[33] In 1926–7 sixteen students from south Wales tutorial classes gained scholarships for places in higher education. *W.E.A., South Wales, 20th Annual Report, 1926–27.*

report of a talk by D. E. Evans to a Cardiff businessmen's club in which he recalled the case of a Monmouthshire steel worker who, it was discovered, had taught himself Latin and Esperanto, and was on one occasion found by a visiting tutor to be translating Virgil whilst he nursed his infant child. Through the association he was sent to Coleg Harlech, then on to university, where he subsequently joined the academic staff. Whilst Evans held up this prodigy as an example of the practical benefits that individuals could gain from the work of the W.E.A., he was impelled to add that the aim of adult education was not to 'take people out of their original social circle but to raise the whole tone and standard of a locality'.[34]

Evans, who took over the district secretaryship temporarily in 1938 following the death of John Davies, was also concerned that the W.E.A. in south Wales was losing its links with the labour movement, and in the process losing its sense of purpose. Ernest Green, the general secretary of the W.E.A., shared these anxieties and foresaw long-term problems for the association if these links were lost: 'we have to watch the maintenance of working-class contacts in South Wales. We shall need those when inflated money grants and unemployed settlements have ceased to exist.'[35] It was an anxiety born not just from practical financial concern but a reflection of the need to keep in touch with sentiment amongst the activist elements within organized labour.

Whilst the trend of thought amongst many educationalists seemed to be moving away from viewing the workers as a mass, and seeing their plight as individuals as the prime area for educational concern, the workers themselves still believed that workers' education, though necessary to raise the sights and the consciousness of the indidivdual, could only be really justified if it produced concrete action to improve the conditions of their fellow workers and their families. There was a growth of collectivist idealism at the same time as there was a

---

[34] *Western Mail*, 9 Feb. 1938. There were also those who felt the scholarships and Coleg Harlech were denuding the valley communities of their most able members and leaving behind, in the words of one anonymous commentator, only 'an alien residue', *South Wales Post*, 29 July 1936.
[35] Ernest Green to D. E. Evans, 18 March 1938. Miscellaneous correspondence, W.E.A. records, Cardiff.

shift of emphasis to the individual. D. H. Thomas, a miner from Capel Hendre who attended Coleg Harlech in 1930–1, stated that whilst merely observing the operation of the capitalist system should convert anyone to the need for collective action, it was necessary to go to Coleg Harlech to be 'equipped with the necessary knowledge that will enable us to transform society into the social order we require'. Simple class-consciousness would not be enough; it had to be informed, not 'a thin veneer over a colossal mass of ignorance. Such class conceit can be our doom and not our salvation.'[36] There remained a feeling, however, that Coleg Harlech and the W.E.A. generally were not producing the leaders or the leadership for which the working class was looking. The economic crisis which afflicted south Wales continued to undermine the hopes of those who looked to Coleg Harlech to provide leadership within the blighted communities. The tenth annual report of the college stated clearly that it was disappointed by the way that the most able students helped to 'swell the abnormal migration. These were men from whom we had hoped much in Local Government, Trade Unionism and social work.'[37] However, some former students felt that the blame should be laid not only at the door of emigration. Addressing the Coleg Harlech Old Students' Association in 1939, D. H. Davies, a former student and now a local councillor, attacked the unwillingness of many former students to take up political work. By that time, only twelve had entered local government, none was a county councillor or an M.P. 'We must bury the past and start afresh in the pursuit of collective happiness in political service. A modern tendency is a wider interest and an ever-increasing extension of Government intervention in human affairs.'[38]

Yet despite this drift of opinion in favour of a more collectivist view of the purpose of adult education, the state-supported voluntaryism of the era also bred within the social service response a powerful sense of mission to the benighted masses, which on occasion tipped over the edge into a patronizing dismissal of the values of collective action. Hilda Jennings was dismissive about the class-based loyalties of the miners' union

[36] *Cambria* (Winter 1931).
[37] Quoted in *W.E.A., South Wales, 30th Annual Report, 1936–37*.
[38] *Highway*, South Wales Supplement (Feb. 1939).

and of local party politics, which she saw as being at odds with
the development of a healthy community based on a multi-
plicity of mutual interests. Ultimately, the workers would have
to choose between 'two loyalties, that of the Cooperative Community based on cooperative industry and that of class and
sectional warfare'.[39] It was an attitude which fed the suspicions
of many in the local labour movement that the whole social
service movement was directed at breaking the power of organized labour. In July 1933, the chairman of the Monmouthshire
Federation of Trades and Labour Councils expressed his fear
that the local social service schemes would be used to 'break
up all wage rates and trade union conditions'.[40] None the
less, the unemployed clubs and the settlements did provide
some respite and support for the jobless of the valley communities. In the circumstances, it was difficult for the local
labour movement to shun a movement about which they felt
considerable unease. Local trade unionists and local Labour
councillors made use of the social service agencies, and through
this point of contact the W.E.A. was able to build up a new
relationship with the working-class activists of the coalfield.
In the process, they gained an influence over workers' education
in south Wales which the I.W.C.E. movement was never able to
counteract.

Closely associated with some social service schemes were
religious missions to the economically blighted areas of the coalfield, where communal forms of religious activity were fostered,
such as that of R. J. Barker in mid-Rhondda. They sought to
attract unemployed men and women back to the Christian
faith. These groups tended to adopt a more aggressively anti-
Marxian stance. R. J. Barker, a Methodist preacher, used the
settlements and the unemployed clubs to gain access to the
south Wales working class. From his multi-denominational
centre at the Community House in Trealaw, Barker arranged
lectures which were designed to 'counteract the materialist
teaching of economics etc., with teaching that was definitely
Christian'.[41]

[39] Jennings, op. cit., 82–3, 215.
[40] Lewis Blackwood, quoted in S. G. Jones, *Workers at Play: A Social and Economic History of Leisure, 1918–1939* (London, 1986), 125.
[41] R. J. Barker, *Christ in the Valley of Unemployment* (London, 1936), 84.

The W.E.A. in south Wales continued to avoid ideological conflicts, and the tutors and lecturers were drawn from a wide spectrum of opinion, ranging from members of the Communist Party to Roman Catholic priests. The sources from which the tutors came were quite diverse, though by the mid-1930s the largest single occupational group, almost a third of the total, was ministers of religion. The next largest group was school teachers, constituting about a fifth of the total.[42] Almost all were graduates or had received some form of higher education, and few seem to have had high political profiles. Yet this did not prevent the W.E.A. from being seen as either an agency whose work would 'make it more difficult for Communist agitators to harangue the crowds to the detriment of the workers' cause'[43] or allegedly designed 'mainly for the purpose of supporting the Socialist cause'.[44]

The mid-1930s saw a flowering of life amongst the branches of the association in a district with a notoriously low number of local branches. Neither John Thomas nor John Davies had regarded branch formation as a priority, and power had drifted firmly into the hands of the district secretary by the early 1930s.[45] In 1935 one of the new full-time organizers, G. H. Jones, was given the specific task of fostering new branches, and he does seem to have had an effect. In 1930 there was scarcely a functioning branch in the whole region; by 1937 there were eighteen, some, such as Swansea, with quite large memberships.[46] There had been sporadic attempts to create a branch in Swansea before Grenfell's arrival but only when he came was there sustained success. Mansel Grenfell, the full-time organizer, used the branch to promote his vision of what the W.E.A. should be, a vigorous campaigning but nevertheless eminently respectable organization for promoting education amongst the working people of the town. Through the W.E.T.U.C., he enlisted the support of the

[42] Welsh Department, Board of Education, *Education in Wales, Memorandum No. 5, Report on Adult Education in Wales, 1936* (London, 1937), table 12, p. 40.

[43] *Cambrian News*, 18 Aug. 1936.

[44] *Pontypool Free Press*, 6 Aug. 1937.

[45] Thomas Jones, in his remarkably candid obituary of John Davies, wrote of how the national W.E.A. had constantly chivvied Davies to increase the number of local branches but to little effect. *Highway* (February 1938).

[46] W.E.A., *South Wales 23rd Annual Report, 1929–30*; W.E.A., *South Wales 30th Annual Report, 1936–37*. In 1937 the Swansea branch had 113 indvidual members.

unions and local labour leaders; he also attracted the extra-mural tutors from the University College of Swansea, and some of the professors also became active members.[47] He enlisted the aid of the local N.U.T. by organizing public rallies against education cuts.[48] To attract middle-class support he put on lively popular lectures on topics of general interest such as radio broadcasting, the rise of Hitler, and psychiatry. With an eye to useful publicity, he secured the services of the novelist Richard Griffiths for a lecture on his own work.[49] He was an active member of the mayor of Swansea's Unemployed Welfare Council; his most important venture was with the unemployed and focused on the establishment of holiday schools for the employed and unemployed in the Gower peninsula. In 1934 he established a permanent base at Fellowship House, Langland, on the Gower coast. He encouraged involvement in the scheme by the myriad voluntary groups in his area, from the Girl Guides to the Left Book Club.[50] When charitable funds to support unemployed summer school students dried up in the mid-1930s, he developed a scheme whereby employed students subsidized unemployed students. Despite acquiring some charitable funding, the scheme never quite worked financially; the last summer school was held at Fellowship House in 1938.[51]

Under Grenfell, the Swansea branch became a lively focus of activity and debate at a time when south Wales in general was slowly recovering from the social and psychological traumas of the slump. Yet occasionally there were signs that the association at branch level displayed the limitations of the W.E.A. at district level: it was still dominated by the professional and educated middle classes. Something of a correspondence on this matter developed in the Swansea local press in 1935, when a working-class member of a W.E.A. class complained that well-educated 'superior persons' were 'dominating the class when discussion ensues'.[52] Another correspondent argued that the W.E.A. was

[47] Swansea, W.E.A. branch committee minutes, 19 Nov. 1931.
[48] Ibid., 7, 29 Sept. 1932.
[49] South Wales Post, 24 Oct. 1935; Herald of Wales, 23 Nov. 1935.
[50] Mansell Grenfell, 'Holiday school's great record', South Wales Post, 24 July 1937.
[51] W.E.A., South Wales, 32nd Annual Report, 1938–39. Earlier annual reports contain details on the holiday school and the various funding schemes which Grenfell used to keep it going.

under the control of the 'Haves' and not the 'Have nots', and consequently the education supplied was not relevant to the needs of working people, employed or otherwise.[53] The association locally and regionally could show that class memberships were overwhelmingly working-class in composition; almost half were unemployed. Teachers made up only five per cent of the students, and other professionals a mere two per cent, but the domination was not numerical but intellectual and psychological.[54] Branch officers were often teachers and were fully involved in the local social service response to unemployment; in Pontypool the creation of the local education settlement was regarded as the culmination of the activities of the teacher-dominated branch.[55] Elsewhere branch activity was irrelevant to the success of the association's work. In Briton Ferry, which did not have a separate branch, the W.E.A. classes keyed, successfully, into a long-standing tradition of working-class political education, which rested on an independent Marxian tradition associated with the local I.L.P. It was a tradition which revelled in debate and loathed the mind-closing antics and fear of the unauthorized which characterized the development of the Communist Party, but it was equally reluctant to be simply an adjunct of social service patronage.[56] The branches were thus too often a collection of small coteries which succeeded if they met a genuine local need, but they remained a less vital element of W.E.A. work in south Wales than in other regions of the U.K.

In 1938 D. T. Guy took over as district secretary. In many ways he embodied the experience of the association in the 1930s. A coalminer from Penclawdd, he attended W.E.A. classes, from where he gained a scholarship to Coleg Harlech and then to Aberystwyth, where he graduated in economics. After working briefly at the Merthyr educational settlement, he was appointed as district secretary of the south Wales W.E.A.[57] Acutely aware of the needs and aspirations of the south Wales working class, he was also under no illusions about

[52] *South Wales Post*, 14 Oct. 1935.
[53] Ibid., 18 Oct., 21, 24 Oct. 1935.
[54] Figures taken from *W.E.A. South Wales, 30th Annual Report, 1936–37*.
[55] *Pontypool Free Press*, 11 June, 24 Sept. 1937.
[56] Interview with W. Gregory, 23 Nov. 1972.
[57] Biographical details from *Highway*, South Wales Supplement, Nov. 1938; interviews, 15 Oct. 1971, 6 Mar. 1972.

the limitations of voluntaryism and philanthropy. He knew that ultimately the W.E.A. existed to equip working people with the knowledge and the confidence to assert themselves and convert aspirations into effective political action. By the late 1930s there was evidence that a subtle but profound change was taking place in the outlook of the working-class activists in south Wales; they were looking once again to the state, not for handouts, but for a new social order.

2. 'A GENERAL ATMOSPHERE OF WANTING ACTION'

For the W.E.A., the unemployment crisis which afflicted south Wales in the early 1930s opened up opportunities and provided resources which would not otherwise have been available, and these shaped its fairly rapid expansion. For the N.C.L.C., the slump exacerbated problems which had blighted its development throughout the previous decade. Locked into the strategy of independence, the Labour College movement depended on union financial support, and in south Wales that was sparse. The S.W.M.F. was in a parlous condition, with large numbers of its members unemployed or migrating from the coalfield. Most of the other unions in south Wales with large memberships were also weakened or affiliated to the rival W.E.T.U.C. The net result was that in 1930 the south Wales division of the N.C.L.C. had the fourth smallest number of affiliated union members of all the twelve divisions in the U.K.[58] The closure of the Labour College and the collapse of the small number of schemes which individual districts of the Federation had devised with the N.C.L.C. meant that by 1930 there was no organizational link at all between the S.W.M.F. and the Labour College movement. Only the creation of a Federation-wide scheme with the N.C.L.C. could revive the movement in the coalfield and the rest of south Wales. Following the closure of the C.L.C., the Federation had agreed, in principle, that the money raised from the sale of the college premises should be used for a local class scheme to be organized with the N.C.L.C. The dead hand of the law

[58] N.C.L.C., E.C. minutes, 25 Aug. 1930, vol.2, loc. cit.

soon descended when the Federation's lawyers ruled that such monies could be used only for the purchase of property for educational purposes.[59] Fear of litigation caused the issue to fade into the background as more pressing matters dominated the minds of Federation leaders. The creation of a scheme with the S.W.M.F., however, remained the prime objective of the local N.C.L.C. organizer. In 1930, W. J. Owen left south Wales to become a Labour Party agent in Leicester; he was replaced as divisional organizer by another ex-C.L.C. student, Len Williams, an ex-N.U.R. scholar from Birkenhead.[60] He brought new energy and excitement to the post, and his class reports in the *Plebs* magazine were full of enthusiasm and optimism. They disguised a dire situation. In 1931 Williams had his salary cut by £26 per annum and divisional funds were raided to support the national organization.[61] Nevertheless, he never wavered in his determination to rebuild the Labour College movement in south Wales, and he tramped the length and breadth of the region selling the N.C.L.C. to any audience or organization that would listen. When, in 1932, the Neath branch of the I.L.P. debated whether it should affiliate to the newly formed local branch of the W.E.A., as some of its members wished, or join the N.C.L.C., it was the advocacy of Williams that not only caused them to decide to affiliate to the N.C.L.C., but to establish a class scheme as well.[62]

Williams acquired in these years an effective ally in Ness Edwards, ex-C.L.C. student and full-time secretary of the Penallta lodge.[63] Unlike many ex-C.L.C. men active in the Federation, Ness Edwards maintained good relations with J. P. M. Millar and the N.C.L.C. Together, Williams and Edwards co-ordinated a campaign to secure a coalfield-wide joint S.W.M.F./N.C.L.C. scheme. Progress was, however, slow and gains were small. One key development occurred in 1932, when the anthracite district established a class scheme

[59] S.W.M.F. conference minutes, 27 June 1930; S.W.M.F., E.C. minutes, 28 Sept. 1930.

[60] *Plebs* (May 1930). Len Williams later succeeded Morgan Phillips as general secretary of the Labour Party. See Craik, op. cit., 184.

[61] N.C.L.C., Division 4, committee minutes, 28 Feb. 1931; N.L.S. Acc. 5120, Box 83, fo. 1.

[62] Neath I.L.P. minute books, 7 Mar., 12, 19 Apr., 5 July 1932. T. Nicholas papers, University College of Swansea Library; *Plebs* (September 1933).

[63] Edwards, C.L.C. S.W.M.F. scholar, 1919–21; later M.P. for Caerphilly.

with the N.C.L.C.[64] The anthracite district was somewhat less affected by the slump than the steam and coking coal areas in the eastern part of the region. Also, emigration had not depleted the pool of available lecturers in the way that it had in the Rhondda and Monmouthshire valleys. The services of the remarkable Nun Nicholas and other luminaries, such as D. R. Owen, James Griffiths and D. J. Williams, could still be called on.[65] Whilst the coalfield still tended to provide the bulk of class groups in south Wales (thirty-two out of forty-two in 1934), they were far more numerous (almost double in terms of students) in the western part of the coalfield by 1934–5.[66] There was not a single N.C.L.C. class in the Rhondda (though there was one at Pontypridd) during that autumn session, nor in the Aberdare and Rhymney Valleys, all former strongholds of I.W.C.E. It was possible in some areas to re-establish active class groups with a small number of class organizers and tutors, but relatively minor diversions of human or financial resources could trigger an organizational collapse. The precarious nature of such an organizational base is reflected in what happened in the Rhondda and in Merthyr in the mid-1930s. In 1933 the divisional committee of the N.C.L.C. encouraged local Labour Colleges and class groups to show a documentary film, *Russia Past and Present*, and whilst it seems to have proved an interesting departure for the N.C.L.C. in the region and was shown in eighteen different locations to over 2,000 people, it was a financial disaster. The local Labour College groups that decided to show it found that they could not recoup the outlay.[67] For some groups, including the Rhondda Labour College, it was the last straw, and they collapsed. In Merthyr, on the other hand, an enthusiastic group of tutors and students was able to mount five class groups in the autumn of 1934, with attendances of over a hundred students. By 1936 the local Labour College had collapsed, as those running it became involved in the hunger march and municipal elections.[68] It was obvious that if the I.W.C.E. movement was to survive in the eastern

[64] *Plebs* (November 1932).
[65] H. Francis and D. B. Smith, op. cit. 247–8.
[66] N.C.L.C., Division 4, committee minutes, 26 Jan. 1935, loc. cit.
[67] Ibid., 20 Jan. 1934.
[68] Ibid., 7 Nov. 1936.

part of the coalfield a Federation-wide scheme was essential.

This period saw the focus of activism in the coalfield move westward as the younger leaders of the Federation came to be drawn increasingly from the anthracite area. Many of these leaders, although trained by old-style, semi-syndicalist tutors such as Nun Nicholas, were members of the Communist Party and reflected the growing hold that active communists were having within the S.W.M.F. One of these younger leaders was Dai Dan Evans, from Abercrave, who had helped to build up a successful N.C.L.C. class group in his village from which was drawn the bulk of the leadership of the local Federation lodge. He was also one of the men responsible for the building up of a powerful rank and file grouping in the Amalgamated Anthracite Combine Committee.[69] Together with Ness Edwards, Dai Dan Evans began to agitate within the Federation for a coalfield-wide scheme in collaboration with the N.C.L.C.

The attitude of the Communist Party leadership towards the Labour College movement had always been critical, and it became even more so as Moscow sought to impose a Leninist orthodoxy on Marxist theory and teaching. The ideological gymnastics emanating from Moscow did much harm to the British party and made many of its members very vulnerable to isolation and victimization by the orthodox labour and trade union leadership. There was some resistance to the so-called 'new line', especially in south Wales, where many communists, such as Arthur Horner,[70] continued to work within existing working-class organizations and were reluctant to pursue to its fullest extent the party dogma of seeking to create completely separate communist-dominated organizations for working-class activity. Struggles by the S.W.M.F. against non-unionism and the rebuilding of its own strength, were deemed by the C.P.G.B. leadership in London to be 'reactionary' and mere 'reformism'. Horner counselled the party against the full implementation of this strategy, arguing that the communists could become 'a leadership without an army to

[69] Interview with D. D. Evans, S.W.M.L., Swansea; D. Francis, 'Dai Dan Evans, 1898–1974', *Llafur*, 1 (1974).
[70] H. Francis and D. B. Smith, op. cit., 153–4.

lead'.[71] In the field of workers' education the impact of the 'new line' was also felt; the C.P.G.B. tried to establish its own study circles. From the mid-1920s some of its most able young activists were sent to the Lenin school in Moscow for one- or two-year courses in Marxism–Leninism. Nevertheless, in south Wales many communists continued to work through the N.C.L.C. and saw this as the most practical way of providing long-term study in Marxist economics and history.

One area of tension which was to cause difficulties in the early 1930s was the growing centralization of control of the I.W.C.E. movement in the N.C.L.C. and, in particular, in the hands of its general secretary, J. P. M. Millar. Traditionally, the Labour College movement was closely associated with radical criticism of orthodox labour and trade union leadership; in south Wales it was inextricably bound up with the Unofficial Reform Committee and later with the Minority Movement. However, in his struggle to secure trade union affiliations, Millar steadily eroded the radical Marxian dimension of the N.C.L.C.'s work and gradually shifted the emphasis more and more towards training union activists rather than to challenging the capitalist system.[72] This was a trend which was designed to appear less threatening to union leaders whose support he needed to secure for the survival of the N.C.L.C. Millar also succeeded in eliminating all centres of opposition to his grip on the I.W.C.E. movement; by 1927 the Plebs League had been wound up, and the *Plebs* magazine became the house journal of the N.C.L.C., with Millar as its editor. The closure of the C.L.C. removed another focal point of opposition to his vision of a single I.W.C.E. agency providing courses for the labour movement. All that remained by the early 1930s was the semi-autonmous regional or divisional committees of the N.C.L.C. Millar was an enthusiastic supporter of postal courses, which were an important element of the work of the N.C.L.C. These courses, often giving tuition in useful subjects—such as written English and public speaking—which were undoubtedly beneficial to those active in the labour movement, were how-

---

[71] D. B. Smith, 'The re-building of the south Wales Miners' Federation, 1927–39: a trade union and its society' (University of Wales Ph.D. thesis, 1976), 302.

[72] M. Cohen, 'The Labour College movement between the wars', in B. Simon (ed.), op. cit., 118.

ever expensive to produce and administer, and many in the Labour College movement felt they diverted resources away from the local Labour Colleges and class groups. On the other hand, they were controlled centrally and (something which caused much adverse comment and bad feeling) were run by Millar's wife, Christine, a woman with a personality as formidable as that of her husband.[73]

Whilst one can admire Millar's determination and single-minded dedication to the cause of I.W.C.E., his skills of personnel management left much to be desired, and he acquired many enemies. Mark Starr described him as 'a mechanic—reliability in accounts came first, before everything'.[74] When Starr, a leading light of the Plebs League, resisted Millar's take-over of the publishing wing of the Plebs League, Millar took it as a threat to his position and he worked to isolate Starr within the Labour College movement—which contributed to Starr's decision to leave for the U.S.A. in 1928. In the process, I.W.C.E. lost one of the most effective popularizers of Labour College ideas and also the most seminal mind on pedagogical issues in the movement. In the early 1930s conflicts between Millar and some of his staff resulted in a whole series of administrative scandals, which seem to have been an abiding characteristic of the Labour College movement, and which did much to weaken rank and file activist support for the N.C.L.C.

In 1930 George Thomas, a communist and one of the south Wales C.L.C. students expelled from the college shortly before its closure, was appointed as a divisional organizer in Yorkshire. He soon fell foul of Millar and returned to south Wales, where he did much to keep the N.C.L.C. functioning in the Rhondda Valley through the terrible early 1930s. He became a severe critic of Millar and seems to have led an anti-Millar faction within the divisional committee. In 1931 an organizer with the Scottish Labour College called Younie was dismissed

[73] Figures for the take-up of postal courses in south Wales do not appear to exist. There are some figures for the take-up amongst S.W.M.F. students in the late 1930s, rising from 434 in 1936–7 to 609 in 1938–9. Sixty per cent of the courses taken by S.W.M.F. students were in 'practical' subjects such as written English, public speaking and chairmanship. N.C.L.C., E.C. minutes, Tables contained in Vols. 14 & 15, loc. cit.
[74] Interview with Starr, 5 Sept. 1983.

after making serious allegations about the way the Millars ran the N.C.L.C.[75] Thomas supported Younie's campaign for an inquiry and reinstatement. Eventually, the N.C.L.C. executive committee set up a committee of inquiry, including Ness Edwards, into the allegations. The committee found some questionable practices but came down on Millar's side. When Edwards reported the committee's finding back to the south Wales divisional executive committee in February 1932, it passed, against the vehement opposition of Ness Edwards, a motion highly critical of Millar and demanded that his wife be dismissed as head of the postal course department.[76] Thomas was subsequently elected as divisional delegate to the national executive committee of the N.C.L.C., and there followed a power struggle between Thomas and Ness Edwards, which eventually resulted in Thomas's removal from the national and divisional executive committees.[77] Frozen out of the N.C.L.C., in 1934 Thomas and Younie seem to have been involved in an attempt to establish branches of the Marx Memorial Library and Workers' School in south Wales. This scheme, based on a communist organization which ran classes in London and Manchester, does not seem to have come to fruition in south Wales, or, if it did, has left little evidence of its existence.[78] A few years later, the N.C.L.C. was convulsed by another scandal, involving allegations of dubious and inappropriate behaviour by the Millars by another dismissed regional organizer by the name of Ellis. By this time, however, Millar had secured further centralization of the N.C.L.C. with the last vestiges of regional autonomy eliminated; effective internal criticism of his autocratic style of administration became virtually impossible.[79]

[75] The details of this case can be studied in the N.C.L.C. collection at the National Library of Scotland, Acc. 5120 (second deposit), Box 2. See also M. Cohen, 'The Labour College movement between the wars' in B. Simon (ed.), op. cit., 111–12; Millar, op. cit., 109–10.

[76] N.C.L.C., Division 4, E.C. minutes, 25 Feb. 1932, loc. cit.

[77] Ibid., 14 Jan., 29 Apr., 18 Apr. 1933; Division 4, A.G.M. minutes, 18 Apr. 1933; E.C. minutes 13 Oct., 28 Nov. 1934.

[78] N.C.L.C., E.C. minutes, 13 Oct., 28 Nov. 1934; Division 4, E.C. minutes, 7 Sept. 1935, 19 Oct. 1935. On the Marx Memorial Library and Marx House Schools, see M. Cohen 'Revolutionary education revived: the communist challenge to the Labour Colleges, 1933–1945', in B. Simon (ed.), op. cit., 137–52.

[79] See A. Ellis, *A Secret History of the N.C.L.C.* (Birmingham, 1937); Millar, op. cit., 111–14.

From 1935 the Communist Party in south Wales seems to have abandoned any attempt to create a separate educational movement outside the N.C.L.C. Whilst there was little love lost between Millar and the communists, in the context of south Wales they came to a *modus vivendi* as the battle to secure a class scheme with the Federation transcended power struggles within the N.C.L.C. The early 1930s had seen the intellectual initiative within the working-class communities of south Wales pass away from the I.W.C.E. movement. Only in a few areas in the coalfield was the Communist Party able to give leadership to the resistance to the intellectual underpinnings of the social service response to unemployment. The N.C.L.C. proved remarkably unwilling, or unable, to adapt its organizational structures to cope with the jobless. The unemployed were a problem not an opportunity. In 1934 Len Williams, the regional organizer, stated that the unemployed were far less likely to maintain class attendance.[80] In so far as unemployment appears as an issue in class reports in *Plebs*, it is to explain some organizational failure or the collapse of a class because of the departure of a tutor to find work outside the region.[81] There is little evidence of attempts to link with rank and file unemployed groups such as the National Unemployed Workers' Movement or directly to challenge the social service agencies which were able to gain access to thousands of jobless south Wales workers. As much of the work of the settlements and unemployed clubs was practical and ameliorative, there was little point in courting the opprobrium that would follow any overt campaign, but none the less it exposed the weakness and limitations of the strategy of total independence which left the movement vulnerable to retrenchment by trade unions in times of recession.

In the early 1930s the N.C.L.C. bumped along in an organizational trough, managing to run about forty classes per session with average overall attendances of around 1,000.[82] Yet these figures hide enormous variations and some spectacular

---

[80] N.C.L.C. Division 4, A.G.M. minutes, 9 June 1934, loc. cit.

[81] Migration of tutors was a major source of difficulty. *Plebs* (Nov. 1930, Apr., Oct. 1932).

[82] Figures taken from quarterly returns for the winter sessions (Oct.–Dec., 1930–5). N.C.L.C., E.C. minutes, vols. 9–12, loc. cit.

areas of weakness. Mention has already been made of the fact that in the 1934–5 session there were no classes in the Rhondda, at a time when the Nobles, based at the Maes-yr-Haf settlement in Trealaw, were running no fewer than thirty unemployed clubs up and down the Rhondda Valleys, catering for over 6,000 men and 650 women. The W.E.A. in the Rhondda was running eighteen terminal courses and four one-year courses; Cardiff extra-mural department was running seven three-year tutorial classes and four preparatory classes.[83] Clearly, the Labour College movement could not rival this scale of activity, and although the I.W.C.E. made up in ideological commitment what it lacked in resources, the effect was the steady crumbling of the independent tradition.

The weakness of the Labour College movement might have continued, for in the later 1930s in most areas of the United Kingdom the N.C.L.C. saw stagnation and even a decline in activity, but not in south Wales.[84] The period after 1935 saw something of a revival in the fortunes of the I.W.C.E. movement in industrial south Wales which is closely associated with a rebirth of political activity and confidence in the ranks of the region's labour movement. In this new atmosphere, the older militant, anti-capitalist outlook generated by the Labour College movement took on a revived relevance as a new and defiant spirit gripped the communities, and not just the small groups of communist activists, that since 1926 had been shattered by the humiliation and trauma of defeat and impoverishment. The legacy of the years of revolutionary hope was still to be found in the coalfield, but it was now to undergo an up-turn in a very different context. There was no real economic revival in the later 1930s, and chronic unemployment still ravaged the Valleys: in 1936 nearly 45 per cent of the insured population in the Rhondda were jobless; of those nearly two-thirds were long-term unemployed.[85] Malnutrition and rickets stunted the young; emigration, sanctioned—indeed encour-

---

[83] J. Davies, 'Time to spare in Wales', in *Wales and the New Leisure* (Llandysul, 1935), 8; *W.E.A, South Wales, 29th Annual Report, 1935–36*.

[84] M. Cohen, 'The Labour College movement between the wars', op. cit., 132–3.

[85] The Pilgrim Trust, *Men Without Work* (Cambridge, 1938), 14–15.

aged—by the authorities, robbed the mining communities of their vitality and future.[86]

The Valleys had, however, learned to live with unemployment. They developed a culture of defiance against a means-testing government which was bent on asserting a greater degree of control over local Public Assistance Committees prone to liberality in the granting of uncovenanted benefits to the unemployed and their families. When, under the terms of the Unemployment Act of 1934, new scales of uniform relief were published, in the words of one writer, south Wales itself 'revolted against the statutory excesses of the means test'.[87] The new scales of benefit were seen as an attack on the living standards of whole communities. Thus, whole communities, not just the unemployed or organized labour, but shopkeepers, ministers of religion and medical practitioners, protested against the proposals of the government. The new scales were withdrawn, and a less abrupt system for the introduction of uniform scales of relief was put in their place. Some historians have queried whether the climb-down by the government was a direct consequence of the popular outcry,[88] but this is largely irrelevant because it was seen in south Wales as a victory for popular protest and gave heart to rank and file activists. When combined with other gains by the Federation, especially over the so-called non-political South Wales Miners' Industrial Union, the atmosphere by the end of 1935 was palpably different from that of only a couple of years earlier. Sustained campaigns against the phased introduction of new unemployment relief scales continued and, in the process, *de facto* popular fronts were established, whereby local communities united in opposition to all the detested paraphernalia of means testing and inadequate unemployment relief.[89]

This period was also significant because it allowed the Federation and the labour movement generally to reassert

[86] A. D. K. Owen, 'The social consequences of industrial transference', *Sociological Review*, XXIX, No. 4 (Oct. 1937).
[87] D. B. Smith, op. cit., 277–342.
[88] J. Stevenson, 'The making of unemployment policy, 1931–1935', in M. Bentley and J. Stevenson (eds.), *High and Low Politics in Modern Britain* (Oxford, 1983), 205–9.
[89] H. Francis and D. Smith, op. cit., 274.

leadership in the communities. Often led by communists, fellow travellers and left-wing Labour activists, the campaigns seemed to vindicate the claim that the organized working-class movement could embody the interests of the whole community, that its leadership was not, as Hilda Jennings and many of those active in the social service response claimed, sectional and divisive. By early 1936 the initiative in the stricken communities was passing away from the settlements and the unemployed clubs to local action committees of politically conscious but community-sensitive activists. Something which infuriated religious critics of the Communist Party, like the Methodist preachers Barker and Gwyther in the Rhondda, was that the Marxists were willing to steal the clothes of community action from the churches and chapels, and even, if necessary, infiltrate them.[90]

The new atmosphere was reflected in other developments, such as the community-wide response of south Wales to the civil war in Spain. This took its most tangible form with the large number of volunteers who went to fight for the International Brigade, south Wales miners forming the largest regional-occupational grouping among the British battalion; more vicariously, it was reflected in the Spanish Aid Committees which flourished throughout industrial south Wales.[91] The fight against fascism abroad and the means-testing government at home merged in a new spirit of aggressive hostility towards the existing economic and social order. While official Labour did all it could to dampen enthusiasm for popular and united front policies, and still discouraged links with communist organizations, the rank and file miners recognized ability, integrity and commitment, irrespective of party affiliation, and in 1936 elected Arthur Horner as president of the S.W.M.F. to replace Jim Griffiths, following his election to Parliament. The election did not herald the 'capture' of the S.W.M.F. by the Communist Party; the Federation's executive was still dominated by a respectable social democratic Labourism, embodied in men like Oliver Harris,

---

[90] Barker, op. cit., 43–6; C. Gwyther, *The Valley Shall be Exalted* (London, 1949), 315.
[91] H. Francis, *Miners against Fascism: Wales and the Spanish Civil War* (London, 1984),107–38.

Enoch Morrell and reconstructed militants like Will Main-waring. Furthermore Horner had resisted the excesses of the 'new line' and had, for a while, fallen out of favour with the C.P.G.B. leadership, but this was a new time, and the rise of Nazism meant that it was now valid in the eyes of King Street to court support from the former 'social fascists' of the Labour Party.[92]

It was in this context that the N.C.L.C. was, at long last, able to establish a coalfield-wide scheme with the S.W.M.F. In February 1936 a subcommittee of the S.W.M.F. executive committee was given the task of looking at the provision of education for S.W.M.F. members and of making recommendations. The subcommittee consisted of Ness Edwards, already a staunch advocate of an N.C.L.C. scheme, Gomer Evans, an executive committee member from the anthracite area and an N.C.L.C. tutor, and Dai Dan Evans, recently elected to the executive and an equally strong advocate of an N.C.L.C. scheme, together with Oliver Harris, general secretary of the Federation.[93] To nobody's surprise, the subcommittee supported an ambitious scheme of education with the N.C.L.C., involving the appointment of four full-time tutors and the creation of eighty-one new classes in the coalfield. This was to be paid for by a levy of threepence per annum per member. The key figure on this committee was undoubtedly Dai Dan Evans, the young communist member of the S.W.M.F. executive committee from the anthracite district. Exuding many of the best qualities of the old semi-syndicalist leaders from the Rhondda, he helped to build up a powerful rank and file movement in his district, based on the Amalgamated Anthracite Combine Committee. From this base, a new generation of militant union leaders mounted their challenge and reinvigorated the Federation, helping it to break out of the trough of defeat and despondency into which it had fallen after 1926. Possessed of what appeared to be inexhaustible energy, Dai Dan Evans helped to establish the anthracite district scheme with the N.C.L.C. in 1932. When the S.W.M.F. districts were abolished in 1933, he campaigned

---

[92] Francis and Smith, op. cit., 153–4, 311; L. J. Macfarlane, op. cit., 249–50.
[93] S.W.M.F., E.C. minutes, 25 Feb., 24 Mar. 1936.

to maintain the scheme by lodge affiliations to a West Wales
Labour College. He was a member of the N.C.L.C. divisional
executive committee for south Wales by August 1933. Whilst
still a working miner, by 1936 he was lodge secretary of his
pit in Abercrave, secretary of the local Labour college, *Plebs*
magazine agent for the area, and a class tutor, as well as being
elected to the Federation executive committee. Len Williams,
the regional organizer for the N.C.L.C., commenting on the
election of Dai Dan Evans to the Federation executive,
expressed the hope that there would now be rapid progress
towards the creation of a Federation scheme with the
N.C.L.C.[94] He was not to be disappointed, for within weeks
the Federation had affiliated, for the first time, to the
N.C.L.C.[95] After the S.W.M.F. established their scheme with
the N.C.L.C., Dai Dan Evans became the S.W.M.F. representative on the N.C.L.C. national executive committee and chairman of the south Wales division.

Evans was a key figure for another reason: he symbolized the
broad popular front strategy then being pursued by the
Communist Party in south Wales, and he ensured that the
N.C.L.C. was incorporated in it. This was a process greatly
assisted by the appointment, following the departure of
Len Williams to a full-time Labour party post in Leeds, of
Charlie Stead as south Wales organizer of the N.C.L.C.[96]
A former miner from the Rhondda who attended the Labour
College as an S.W.M.F. scholar from 1923 to 1925, he became
a member of the Communist Party and was one of the first
young British communists to be sent to the Lenin School in
Moscow, where he spent three years. Upon his return, he
became a full-time organizer with the party in south Wales,
in which capacity he was arrested and imprisoned for distri-
buting seditious literature outside a barracks. Thus, by the
summer of 1937 the divisional organizer and chairman were
active communists. This does raise the question of the extent
to which the Communist Party used its position of influence
in the division as a front for its activities and its objectives.

[94] *Plebs* (Feb. 1936).
[95] S.W.M.F., E.C. minutes, 24 Mar. 1936.
[96] N.C.L.C., E.C. minutes, 14 July 1936; *Plebs* (July 1936).

J. P. M. Millar, who was by this time very hostile to the C.P.G.B., claimed that he found evidence in south Wales divisional records that Stead was pressured by his party bosses to run the area in their interests, but that Stead resisted such pressure.[97] There is no such evidence available in the divisional N.C.L.C. records held in the National Library of Scotland. Nor is there any other indication of any inappropriate behaviour by Stead or Dai Dan Evans in their dealings with the N.C.L.C. in south Wales. It would, however, be ridiculous to suggest that their place of influence was other than very useful to the C.P.G.B. It brought them into frequent contact with mainstream members of the local labour movement at a time when the orthodox leadership of organized labour was anxious to isolate and marginalize the Communist Party. It must be remembered that even in the more militant atmosphere of the later 1930s the communists were a minority element, even within the N.C.L.C. in south Wales. In 1936 seventy-two students attending N.C.L.C. classes in south Wales were recorded as members of the C.P.G.B., whilst 586 were recorded as individual members of the Labour party; in 1937 the figures were sixty-six and 732 respectively.[98] There was, of course, a strong element among the Labour Party rank and file keen to develop a popular front policy with the communists, and they were probably well represented at the Marxist-orientated classes of the N.C.L.C. Thus, the Labour College movement probably contributed to the reinforcement of the new atmosphere and the revived anti-capitalist ethos of south Wales Labourism.

With the affiliation of the S.W.M.F., the N.C.L.C. in south Wales enjoyed a steady expansion of its activity in this new context.[99] In the autumn session of 1936, the south Wales division was able to put on sixty classes for nearly 1,500 students; by the autumn session of 1938 there were seventy-two classes for 1,620 students. The N.C.L.C. experience in south Wales was not shared nationally. The late 1930s were a time of actual decline in most parts of the U.K., and in June 1938 the N.C.L.C. held a

---

[97] Letter from J. P. M. Millar to the author, 2 Oct. 1972; Millar, op. cit., 82.

[98] N.C.L.C., Division 4, A.G.M. minutes, 11 June 1938.

[99] Millar ascribes the financial survival of the N.C.L.C. in the late 1930s in part to the affiliation of the S.W.M.F. in 1936. Millar, op. cit., 119.

meeting of regional organizers to address the issue. Many factors were cited, including counter-attractions such as the cinema and wireless broadcasting, but most agreed that the key problem was that many young activists were attracted by what appeared to be the more immediate thrill of campaigning on specific issues, 'a general atmosphere of wanting action'.[100] Many rival bodies on the left had grown up which were seen as diverting former and potential students away from Labour College classes: for example, the Hands off Spain and the Hands off China committees and, above all, the Left Book Club. Hunger Marches and anti-means test campaigns were also seen as a problem, but not in south Wales. The south Wales representatives at the meeting stated that there were no problems resulting from the remobilization of popular activism. Whilst the anti-Unemployment Act agitation of 1935 briefly affected class attendances, thereafter the N.C.L.C. seems to have revelled in its close involvement in agitations.[101] In 1936 Stead boasted of the presence of sixty N.C.L.C. students in the south Wales Hunger March of that year,[102] many acting as stewards or in the administration of support services. Nor did the growth of the Left Book Club create problems for the Labour College movement in south Wales. There appears to have been considerable overlapping of membership, and the occasional issues of duplication of effort and time and venue clashes seem to have been resolved quite amicably. Indeed, Dai Dan Evans said the Left Book Club was useful because it opened up contact with left-wing intellectuals, graduates and school teachers who could then be used as class tutors; it also was a valuable recruiting ground for N.C.L.C. students. By 1938 the south Wales N.C.L.C. was actually arranging classes for local branches of the Left Book Club.[103]

In seeking to explain this resurgence of rank and file activism and the recapture of the intellectual initiative by the organized working-class movements of south Wales, it is not possible to ascribe the cause to an overall economic revival, or to a

[100] N.C.L.C., E.C. minutes, organizers' meeting, 17 June 1938, loc. cit.
[101] *Plebs* (Feb. 1935).
[102] Ibid. (Dec. 1936).
[103] N.C.L.C., annual conference minutes, 18 June 1938, loc. cit.; Division 4, E.C. minutes, 11 Nov. 1939.

strengthening of the bargaining position of organized labour in the region. Instead, it is necessary to look once again at the 'socio-political filters' through which the activist element viewed the world. In the immediate post-war years, the Russian revolution and the imminent collapse of capitalism fostered a confident militancy which assumed that history was on the side of the workers and that victory was near at hand. In the 1930s the nature of the militancy was very different, for what they then faced was not a capitalism showing signs of collapse, but a new form of capitalist politics which was specifically geared to the destruction of organized labour and socialist politics. In addition, what now faced them was not a world revolution but a world war.

3. 'FASCISM AND THE WAR DANGER'

The rise of fascism abroad and the imminent danger of war fostered a new atmosphere in the 'loose democracy' of south Wales working-class activism. There arose a demand for more knowledge of the international situation, a desire to hear experts, to listen to first-hand accounts from exiles and refugees, to debate the issues and campaign against both an inexorable drift to war and the expansion of fascism in Europe—something which appears, with the benefit of hindsight, more contradictory today than it did in the late 1930s. This trend is discernible in both traditions of workers' education in south Wales, and to a significant extent it shaped and changed the nature of the education supplied by both the N.C.L.C. and the W.E.A.

Economics, the basic subject taught in Labour College classes since the inception of the movement, at long last lost its dominance in south Wales to 'modern problems', economic geography and imperialism, as class subjects.[104] However, the new atmosphere was most clearly revealed in the escalating demand for day and weekend schools. Always a feature of N.C.L.C. work, they blossomed in the late 1930s. In 1936–7 there were twenty N.C.L.C. day schools in south Wales, with

---

[104] In 1936–7 there were 61 classes on economics and 24 on 'modern problems', in 1937–8 18 on economics and 34 on 'modern problems'. N.C.L.C., E.C. minutes, quarterly tables, vols. 13, 14, loc. cit.

total attendances of 2,243; the following year there were thirty-one day schools, with total attendances of 5,716.[105] The bulk of these were on some aspect of the international crisis, often with noted left-wing experts, such as Maria Saran and Lester Hutchison, speaking on the rise of Hitler or the Popular Front government in France. It was Spain, however, which excited the deepest interest and concern. On his return from Spain, Will Paynter was much in demand by N.C.L.C. classes for his direct experience of the conflict.[106]

Spain did much to revive popular enthusiasm for the Labour College movement in south Wales because of the movement's full integration within the campaign in support of the Republican government, and also because it afforded opportunities for young activists to place the conflict in a wider perspective. Forty-one of the Welsh recruits to the International Brigade had attended N.C.L.C. classes, but the movement offered other forms of practical support.[107] Dai Dan Evans took evident pride in reporting, in the April 1937 edition of *Plebs*, that the Swansea Valley Labour College had raised £90 for the Spanish Aid Committee. Resolutions attacking the British government's non-intervention policy and in support of the International Brigade were passed at the N.C.L.C. south Wales divisional conference of 1938.[108] From the autumn of 1937, the *Plebs* magazine started carrying grim items recording the deaths of former Labour College movement students, many from south Wales, in the ranks of the International Brigade.[109] The close links between the I.W.C.E. movement and the Spanish Republican cause are illustrated by a dinner arranged by the Amalgamated Anthracite Combine committee, in the spring of 1939, to honour those of its members who had just returned from fighting with the International Brigade. Charlie Stead reported that it was in many ways also an N.C.L.C./

[105] Division 4, E.C. minutes, 18 Sept. 1937.
[106] *Plebs* (Sept. 1937, Feb., Apr. 1938).
[107] H. Francis, op. cit., 196.
[108] N.C.L.C., Division 4, A.G.M. minutes, 11 June 1938. The first recorded collection of money for the Spanish Republic by a Labour College group was by the Upper Swansea Valley Labour College in Sept. 1936, *Plebs* (Oct. 1936).
[109] The first former N.C.L.C. student from south Wales killed in Spain was Sam Morris from Ammanford, *Plebs* (Sept. 1937). The N.C.L.C., divisional E.C. noted the deaths of five others by 24 Sept. 1938.

C.L.C. reunion dinner.[110]

Whilst the revival of the I.W.C.E. movement was closely linked with the development of a genuine enthusiasm amongst rank and file labour activists for anti-fascist/popular front policies and campaigns, the nature of this revival was very different from the atmosphere obtaining in the later war and early post-war years. The I.W.C.E. movement never managed to gain the ascendancy amongst activists that it had achieved twenty years earlier. The W.E.A. now had strength in depth in industrial south Wales, an organizational base, and a fund of enthusiasm and good will amongst hundreds of students and dozens of tutors, which the N.C.L.C. was incapable of matching in any effective way. Additionally, the new atmosphere was, unlike that of the era of revolutionary posturing, one to which the W.E.A. found it very easy to adapt. The W.E.A. in south Wales was in many ways better placed to deal with the upsurge in interest in foreign and defence policy issues than the Labour College movement. It was closely linked with the League of Nations Union and with the radical establishment which still carried forward the older pre-Lloyd George, anti-war sentiment which had always been such an important, if not universal, characteristic of late nineteenth-century Welsh Noncon-formity and popular liberalism.[111] In the so-called Peace Ballot of 1935, the Welsh returns recorded the highest votes in favour of various forms of arms limitation measures.[112] As early as the 1928–9 session, Illtyd David, who developed an early enthusiasm for international relations, was arranging day schools for the W.E.T.U.C. on 'International labour legislation', European tariffs and 'Safeguarding' and 'Anglo-American relations'; he also arranged joint W.E.T.U.C./ League of Nations Union classes on international relations in Port Talbot and Ogmore Vale. A lecturer from the University of Geneva gave talks to W.E.A. class groups in the west of the coalfield on the topic 'Present-day Germany', with particular reference to the political consequences of economic distress.[113]

---

[110] *Plebs* (Apr. 1939).
[111] G. J. Jones, *Wales and the Quest for Peace* (Cardiff, 1969), 97–158.
[112] Francis, op. cit., 31–2.

It is, however, for the session 1936–7 that widespread change in the subject interest of students is detectable. Of the 189 W.E.A. classes held in south Wales that year, eighty-seven were in economics and related disciplines, and thirty-four were in international relations. By 1938 the figures were twenty-eight and sixty respectively. The parallels with the N.C.L.C. experience are apparent in other respects, because it was in the day schools and weekend schools that the dramatic upsurge in interest was most striking. Here, the change is detectable fairly early. In 1936, of the twenty-one public lectures arranged by the district, sixteen were on topics falling broadly under the heading of international relations.[114] Many of those who were prominent in the debates on foreign and defence issues had no interest in the conflict between the two traditions of workers' education, and spoke at day schools and public lectures arranged by both organizations. Thus, when a long-standing 'trouble-maker' in the field of foreign policy, H. N. Brailsford, came to south Wales in 1936, he delivered four lectures for the W.E.A. and addressed two day schools for the N.C.L.C. in Swansea and Cardiff.[115] By the late 1930s there were those on the left of south Wales politics who seemed to have few qualms about associating with the W.E.A. Aneurin Bevan, whose election agent, Archie Lush, was very active with the south Wales association, used it on several occasions in this period to voice criticisms of the government's foreign policy, especially with regard to the expansionary fascist powers. In June 1936 he addressed a day school organized by the Barry W.E.A. under the title 'Fascism and the war danger' in which he advocated an alliance between Britain, the Soviet Union and 'Popular Front' France to check the ambitions of Nazi Germany, which he portrayed as the real enemy of peace.[116] It was an analysis which seems to have found favour. The W.E.A. in south Wales was still leftward-leaning, even though the association continued to emphasize its non-partisan stance. Over the issue of the Spanish civil war, the bulk of opinion in the

[113] *W.E.A., South Wales, 22nd Annual Report, 1928–29.*
[114] These figures are taken from the south Wales W.E.A. annual reports from 1935 to 1939.
[115] *W.E.A., South Wales, 29th Annual Report, 1935–36*; *Plebs* (Mar. 1936).
[116] *Chwarae Teg* (Aug. 1936). Archie Lush chaired the district's organization subcommittee established in 1936.

W.E.A. in the region was strongly pro-Republican. D. R. Grenfell, M.P. for Gower and brother of Swansea W.E.A. organizer, Mansell Grenfell, addressing the Swansea W.E.A. in late 1936, spoke warmly in support of the Republicans and condemned Franco.[117] Eight of the Welshmen who fought with the International Brigade definitely attended W.E.A. classes, but mostly in addition to N.C.L.C. classes.[118] Only one very active W.E.A. student, Jim Brewer, went to Spain. A member of Nye Bevan's constituency Labour Party, he was also active with the N.U.W.M. and took part in the 1936 Hunger March. He was also, before leaving for Spain, a part-time area organizer for the W.E.A.[119] This was an unusual combination, but it reflected the fluidity of activity in the coalfield and the breakdown of the rigid distinctions in workers' education which had obtained in previous decades. The openness of the W.E.A. is also reflected in the fact that it was possible for a supporter of the Nationalist cause in Spain to gain a hearing. The Pontypool branch of the W.E.A. had a strong Roman Catholic element in its membership, and a leading local Catholic layman was invited to give a talk on the Spanish civil war. It consisted of a fierce tirade against the Republican cause.[120] This was an unusual event; the south Wales W.E.A. reflected the broad consensus on the left about the fascist threat and therefore could not easily be bracketed by its I.W.C.E. critics as reactionary or hostile to the interests of organized labour.

The ability of the W.E.A. to adapt to the new atmosphere in south Wales was a major difficulty as far as the N.C.L.C. in south Wales was concerned. In 1937 Charlie Stead produced a report which contrasted the relative strengths of the two traditions and showed that it would be an uphill task for the N.C.L.C. to match, let alone surpass, the W.E.A. in the coalfield and the rest of the region. Stead calculated that the association was responsible for some 265 classes in south Wales, with total attendances of over 5,000; the divisional N.C.L.C. was responsible for 142 classes, with gross attendances of over

[117] South Wales Post, 22 Dec. 1936.
[118] Francis, op. cit., 196.
[119] Interview with H. Francis, 29 Nov. 1969 (S.W.M.L., Swansea); W.E.A., South Wales, 30th Annual Report, 1936–37.
[120] Pontypool Free Press, 17 Sept. 1937.

3,000.[121] These figures, which put a very generous gloss on the N.C.L.C. class numbers and attendances, were still a salutary jolt to those who may have been taken in by the scale of the N.C.L.C. revival after 1936. Stead stated that his plan was for the N.C.L.C. in south Wales to increase class group numbers to 250, with gross attendances of over 5,000, that is, nearly matching the W.E.A. Stead also planned some fifty day schools for the 1938–9 session. These figures were never reached, though the day-school attendances soared as the international situation deteriorated.[122]

Stead's comments are interesting because they reflected a growing concern about the strength of the south Wales W.E.A. amongst N.C.L.C. activists. It was a justified anxiety; the association, in conjunction with the extra-mural departments, was now the dominant tradition in south Wales. Even in the coalfield the W.E.A./extra-mural classes numbered approximately 200 by 1937.[123] Nor could the N.C.L.C. comfort itself with the belief that these courses were mainly attended by middle-class, white-collar workers and teachers; the W.E.A. students were overwhelmingly working-class, approximately 80 per cent in the case of the shorter W.E.A. courses and 60 per cent in the case of the university tutorial classes.[124] However, even in the more select tutorial classes coalminers constituted the largest single occupational group. In the session 1936–7, five hundred members of the S.W.M.F. were attending W.E.A. classes in south Wales. If to this total are added the 359 south Wales miners attending university tutorial classes, it clearly already came close to challenging the 973 Federation members attending N.C.L.C. classes at that time.[125] The situation from the N.C.L.C. perspective actually worsened in subsequent years; in the autumn session

[121] N.C.L.C., Division 4, E.C. minutes, 18 Sept. 1937. Stead did point out that 40 per cent of W.E.A. work in south Wales was in non-political areas such as Bible study, music and drama, though this would have been of limited comfort to Labour College activists.

[122] *Plebs* (May 1938).

[123] B. B. Thomas, op. cit., table IV.

[124] Ibid., table XV; W.E.A. District annual reports, 1935–6, 1936–7, 1938–9.

[125] In the year that the S.W.M.F./N.C.L.C. scheme came into existence, the south Wales W.E.A. sought to publicize the fact that the association's services were used by a very large number of Federation members, *W.E.A., South Wales, 30th Annual Report, 1936–37*; see also *Daily Express*, 24 July 1937. The next largest grouping in W.E.A. classes was the N.U.T. (163), followed by the I.S.T.C. (148).

of 1938–9 it appears likely that more south Wales miners were attending W.E.A./extra-mural-type classes than were attending N.C.L.C. classes.[126]

Whilst the late 1930s were characterized by a desire on the left to secure at least a semblance of unity against the fascist threat, the strength of the W.E.A. tradition of education in south Wales did lead to a revival of overt hostility to the association by supporters of I.W.C.E. Sydney Jones, the ex-C.L.C. student and veteran N.C.L.C. lecturer, led a campaign to stop Labour local authorities giving financial support to W.E.A. classes. 'It is an impossible situation to see S.W.M.F. men sitting as councillors on bodies supporting the capitalistically subsidised W.E.A.,' said Jones in January 1937. 'It is as much our duty to prevent money being given to Coleg Harlech as to teach I.W.C.E. ... The so called impartial education is now more dangerous than ever when the working class is fighting for its very existence.'[127] At the national N.C.L.C. conference in June 1937, south Wales representatives took a particularly aggressive anti-W.E.A. stance. Dick Beamish, a Labour College lecturer from the western part of the coalfield, moved a resolution from the south Wales division demanding a campaign amongst socialist councillors to stop rate support to 'capitalist subsidised educational bodies'. Beamish complained bitterly about the financial aid being given by Labour councils in south Wales to the W.E.A.[128] The resolution was passed but there was little in the way of an effective campaign against the W.E.A., and the N.C.L.C. in south Wales was forced to reconsider its general teaching strategy in the face of the organizational strength of the association and the extra-mural departments. One issue which resurfaced at this time was the hardy perennial of whether the Labour College movement in

---

[126] In the autumn quarter of 1938–9, 889 members of the S.W.M.F. were attending N.C.L.C. classes. In that session 1,178 south Wales miners attended W.E.A. classes and 309 attended extra-mural classes. N.C.L.C., E.C. minutes, quarterly returns vol. 15, loc. cit; B. B. Thomas, op. cit., table XV; *W.E.A., South Wales, 32nd Annual Report, 1938–39*. Even allowing for some double counting on the shorter W.E.A. courses, it looks as if more S.W.M.F. members were attending W.E.A./extra-mural courses in this session.

[127] N.C.L.C., Division 4, E.C. minutes, 9 Jan. 1937; see also his speech to the Division 4, A.G.M., 11 June 1938.

[128] N.C.L.C., annual conference minutes, 20 June 1937. The resolution was passed by twenty-one votes to ten.

south Wales should break with national practice and pay tutors. Vehement resistance from Millar and the executive committee of the N.C.L.C. was eventually overcome when the S.W.M.F. executive committee itself insisted that, if their scheme was to be effective, tutors would have to be paid fees for their work, as had been the case with the old district schemes.[129] Thus, whilst the Labour College movement had seen a revival in its fortunes, compared with the grim days at the beginning of the decade, enthusiasm was tempered by the knowledge that the rival tradition was now well entrenched in the coalfield and throughout industrial south Wales. It was also true that many active on the left in the region, and many trade unionists including large numbers of S.W.M.F. members, cared little for the rivalry between the two workers' education movements, and used facilities when they were available and met their needs.

This was a south Wales very different from the late Edwardian and immediate post-war years. The Federation was no longer quite the all-powerful agency it had been, it no longer exerted the influence over working-class activists that it had in previous decades. South Wales generally was now open to far more influences: the rise of the new mass communications, the wireless, the cinema and the cheap, mass-circulation national daily press were changing the region's cultural fabric, as they were in other areas of the United Kingdom. The distinctly Welsh nature of the region was being eroded far too quickly for the Cardiff–Barry coterie's ideal of popular culture to be created as a viable alternative to the appeal of working-class internationalism. Yet emigration, contact with the cultural values of Hollywood and Fleet Street, and the long-term effects of state education were just as damaging to the attempts to create an alternative independent proletarian culture. That is why the study of 'Little Moscows' has proved so interesting, because they were brave, Canute-like attempts by isolated communities to resist the on-rushing waves of capitalist cultural uniformity. Yet even in Mardy, the archetypal

---

[129] N.C.L.C., Division 4, E.C. minutes, 30 October 1937; S.W.M.F. E.C. minutes, 24 Jan. 1938; N.C.L.C., E.C. minutes, 8 Mar. 1938.

'Little Moscow', there existed viable branches of the League of Young Britons and the Women's Unionist Association.[130] The intellectual horizons of the left also expanded and encompassed not just the economic and historical determinism of Nun Nicholas but also the literary skills of Lewis Jones and even public lectures arranged by a local Labour College on 'Welsh revolutionary poets'.[131]

The effects of several decades of workers' education, of all types, on the several thousand labour activists in the region also need to be taken into account in understanding the changed atmosphere. In south Wales the workers' education movement reflected and reinforced trends; it did not initiate them. It responded, with varying degrees of effectiveness and alacrity, to the changing circumstances of the working class in general and the organized labour movement in particular. By the end of the 1930s the two traditions of workers' education had helped to create a loose, rather disparate, alliance of trade union activists, local politicians, academics, ministers of religion and school teachers who shared a rather nebulous consensus about the political direction in which they wished to see society move. This consensus had been achieved by individuals, not imposed by any single agency of workers' education, and the impact on individuals varied; but by the aggregation of their experience a new world view had been created which was to form the outlook, tempered by the experience of another world war, of the labour movement in south Wales for the next three decades.

There are no 'typical' examples of the way in which contact with workers' education shaped the development of individuals in the context of the 1930s, but two examples drawn from the Maesteg area may illustrate how workers' education could determine the direction of personal development, sometimes away from the perceptions of society suggested by their original milieu. Rosser Thomas came from a well-respected, lower middle-class family in Maesteg with close connections with

---

[130] D. B. Smith, op. cit., 167. See also S. Macintyre, *Little Moscows* (London, 1980), 23–45.

[131] See D. B. Smith's introduction to Jones's two novels, *Cwmardy* and *We Live* (reprinted London, 1978). The lecture on Welsh revolutionary poets was delivered at Gwaun-Cae-Gurwen in spring 1936, *Plebs* (Mar. 1936).

colliery management.[132] Thomas attended Maesteg secondary
and Cowbridge grammar schools, before going to University
College, Aberystwyth, to read French. Conscious of the poverty
and deprivation of the valley towns, he was also concerned about
the rise of fascism, a concern which was deepened by his experiences of Popular Front France in 1936–7. He became active with
the left-wing Labour Club in Aberystwyth, most of whose members were also members of, or closely allied to, the Communist
Party. On his return to Maesteg as a trained but unemployed
school teacher, he became active with the C.P.G.B. in the
Ogmore and Llynfi Valleys. 'Discovered' by Charlie Stead, he
was seen as the ideal person to take N.C.L.C. classes, which he
did well into the war period.[133] Thomas felt that his inability
to buy source books and his lack of experience about the realities
of life caused him to have doubts about the quality of his teaching
for the Labour College movement. Yet in many ways Thomas
represented a significant new element on the left: academics
and intellectuals won over by the fascist threat and by a revul-
sion against the economic disorder and deprivation caused by
unplanned and undirected capitalism. Later, however,
Thomas ceased to be politically active and his teaching career
abosorbed his interest and enthusiasm.

Gwyn Phillips was rather older than Rosser Thomas. Born
into a Maesteg mining family, school gave him only the elementary skills of literacy and numeracy; it was the Welsh-speaking
Presbyterian chapel which shaped his earliest views of the
world.[134] He remembers Bible study classes spilling over into
debates about politics and social conditions. He soon developed a passion for evening classes and public lectures put on
by organizations such as the Y.M.C.A. and the League of
Nations Union. He clearly recalled a public lecture by one of
the first communist M.P.s, S. Saklatvala. From the mid-
1920s, along with his two elder brothers, he started to attend
W.E.A. classes taken by the Revd William Edwards, a well-
known local Nonconfomist preacher and very effective adult

[132] This account of Rosser Thomas's early career is based on an interview, 15 Dec.
1977.
[133] *Plebs* (Feb. 1940).
[134] This account of Gwyn Phillips's early career is based on an interview, 17 July
1978.

class teacher. William Edwards started life as a builder's labourer, but took the chapel route to self-improvement and through his own reading was able, like many other preachers in inter-war south Wales, to impart knowledge to other working people beyond the purely religious and spiritual fields through the agency of the W.E.A.[135] The message of public service was always paramount and it left its mark on Gwyn Phillips. Under Edwards, Phillips remembered studying elementary psychology, philosophy, astronomy, economics and English literature. Although a staunch trade unionist and active member of the Federation, Phillips had no contact with the local N.C.L.C. which, by the late 1920s in Maesteg, was strongly pro-communist in outlook. He was a great admirer of Vernon Hartshorn, miners' agent and local M.P., whose belief that trade unionism should extend beyond the workplace and into wider community service was something which guided Phillips's subsequent political ideas. Active in the St John's lodge of the S.W.M.F., he held a number of posts including that of miners' examiner, he later became full-time secretary of Penallta lodge, a post previously held by Ness Edwards. Although Gwyn Phillips had strong Welsh nationalist leanings, he supported the nationalization programme of the 1945 Labour government and subsequently became an industrial relations officer with the National Coal Board in Monmouthshire.

Whilst these two men came from different backgrounds and, through contact with different traditions of workers' education, tended to adopt somewhat different perceptions of the world, they shared a good deal. They were both distressed by the drift to war, but they were equally hostile to fascism and the Nazi menace. They both felt that private ownership of the mines was a cause of much of the deprivation and unemployment in the south Wales Valleys; therefore they favoured state ownership of the coal industry. They also favoured extended welfare provision and a state health service. In seeking to understand the major political changes of the 1940s, a good deal of attention has been focused on the radicalizing experience of total war. Yet long before the war began to change popular atti-

---

[135] See south Wales, W.E.A. district annual reports, 1927–8, 1928–9.

tudes, in the ranks of Labour activists in south Wales there already existed a well-informed hostility to the existing social and economic order, and one that had converted a generalized anti-capitalist ethos into a sustained demand for political change and social and economic reform. The late 1930s saw a successful reconciliation of those who defined their class-consciousness in community terms and those who defined their community sense in class terms. This was ameliorative and not revolutionary: the communists who advocated 'popular front' policies had to be reformist, while the voluntaryists of the W.E.A. could not seriously maintain that the social service response was adequate to the challenges of chronic unemployment and large-scale deprivation. Thus, within the working-class communities of south Wales there were, through the agencies of the two traditions of workers' education, several thousand men and women, local opinion-formers, who could shape the ideas and attitudes of those around them when the experience of total war moved popular sentiment in a radically collectivist direction.

EPILOGUE

1. WORKERS' EDUCATION IN THE POST-WAR WORLD

The Second World War created new opportunities for adult education and, in a sense, the W.E.A. saw many of its aims and methods justified. The Army Bureau of Current Affairs (A.B.C.A.), established to develop a sense of mission and purpose among the armed forces, drew on W.E.A. tutors and techniques, and even used Coleg Harlech as its base for training army education officers. Thomas Jones's influence was felt in yet another major area of adult educational development.[1] However, as in the First World War, the short-term impact on the W.E.A. was not beneficial. The last years of peace, from 1936 to 1939, had seen the south Wales W.E.A. still thriving under the patronage of the social service agencies, with grants of money sufficient to sustain eight full-time organizing staff in addition to the district secretary. This 'halcyon period', as it was described in an H.M.I. report in 1954, came to an abrupt end in the session 1940–1.[2] The termination of temporary grants and the enlistment of members of the organizing staff saw the district reduced to only two full-time officials. The association was to bump along with this limited administrative support until the mid-1950s. Whilst the need for more state-supplied adult education was widely accepted in the radicalized atmosphere of wartime Britain, the precise place and role of the W.E.A. and workers' education in general in such provision was never fully resolved. The W.E.A. participated in the 'White Paper chase' of 1942, making proposals for a new post-war adult education service, but one which still preserved the association's special role and function. It still maintained that the W.E.A. should retain its voluntary nature, free

[1] Stead, op. cit. (1977), 85–8.
[2] *Report by H.M. Inspectors: A Survey of the Work of the South Wales District of the Workers' Educational Association* (London, 1954), 2.

of state control, so that its essentially democratic objectives could be maintained, the wishes of students expressed and its provision adapted to their needs.[3]

Fears that state provision for adult education might eclipse the association proved groundless. The 1944 Education Act did place a new statutory responsibilty on education authorities to provide an adult education service, but the value of the W.E.A. as an administratively economical provider of classes was too good in the austerity years to allow it to lose its niche.[4] On the other hand, the association drifted along as a supplier of liberal, non-vocational classes, and what was known as its 'social emancipation' role continued to atrophy in south Wales as elsewhere.

It was in the early 1950s, rather than in the war and immediate post-war years, that the W.E.A. experienced a period of reassessment and heart-searching about its role and relevance. This was partly in response to financial difficulties but also because society was changing rapidly, with greater affluence, social mobility, and distractions such as television. The continued expansion of university extra-mural provision deepened further the crisis of confidence and identity. There were those who, by the mid-1950s, felt that in some ways the W.E.A. had discharged its responsibilities to the working class. Eric Ashby stated in 1955 that 'the social emancipation of what used to be called the working classes and the rise to political power of the Labour party were guided and stabilized by men who had acquired from the W.E.A. tutorial classes the undogmatic mind', and who sought solutions to social problems with the 'critical objectivity of the student rather than the impassioned prejudice of the agitator'.[5] There were moves to drop the word 'workers' from the name of the association and to refocus attention on an élite of true scholars, whose numbers might be small but whose social and political influence would be great.[6] There was also, as one recent study has shown, an intrusion of Cold War values into some sectors of

[3] *Educational Reconstruction: A W.E.A. Programme* (London, 1942), 31. See also *Adult Education after the War* (London, 1942).
[4] Kelly, op. cit., 337–43.
[5] E. Ashby, *The Pathology of Adult Education* (Belfast, 1955), 9.
[6] Kelly, op. cit., 378; Ashby, op. cit., 21.

adult education, with strong whiffs of McCarthyism even drifting into the W.E.A.[7] These pressures were resisted, and there
was instead an attempt to re-establish at least some sense of
social mission, which centred on efforts to revitalize the
alliance with the trade unions, which had become routine
and unchallenging. The result was not a dramatic new call to
establish the educational foundations of a participatory democracy, but far more classes in practical trade union studies and
the new discipline of industrial relations. It was a time when it
was widely believed, even by the Conservative governments of
the period, that 'good' industrial relations, necessary for a successful modern economy, would result from a better-*trained* and
active union membership. The training tended to stress non-
conflictual approaches to employer–employee relations and it
encouraged resort to structured negotiations and mutually
beneficial agreements. There was a reinstatement of the principles of mutuality, which had been under attack from anti-
capitalist forces within the labour movement since the days of
the Lib-Labs.[8] There was an explicit downgrading of the
'social emancipation' aspect of W.E.A. work.[9] The new 'training' approach was also something of a departure from the essentially non-vocational principles of Mansbridge and the early
W.E.A. It was a trend which some found unpalatable. Nevertheless, it was decided by the W.E.A. nationally that some
initiative in the field of trade union education was vital for
the long-term survival of the association.

In south Wales this new initiative took practical form in the
W.E.A./W.E.T.U.C pilot scheme for trade union studies, one of
which was based in Port Talbot. There were two other schemes,
on Tyneside and Teesside.[10] Port Talbot, a steel town, was
within the area in which the W.E.T.U.C. had managed to
build up a body of support amongst members of the I.S.T.C.,
T.G.W.U., and the General and Municipal workers. By the
mid-1950s the direct involvement of the unions in the work of

[7] R. Fieldhouse, *Adult Education and the Cold War: Liberal Values under Siege* (Leeds, 1985).
[8] J. McIlroy, 'The triumph of technical training?' in B. Simon (ed.), op. cit., 208–18.
[9] *Trade Union Education. A Report From a Working Party set up by the Workers' Educational Association* (London, 1953), 28.
[10] Corfield., op. cit., 123–32.

the local W.E.A. was negligible. There were no classes directly aimed at trade unionists or even organized jointly with them. The men selected to run the scheme in Port Talbot had impeccable trade union backgrounds: both the organizer, R. C.(Dick) Lewis, and the tutor/organizer, W. E.(Eddie) Jenkins, were ex-miners who had attended Coleg Harlech on scholarships from the south Wales area of the National Union of Mineworkers, a shortlived scheme of the late 1940s and early 1950s.[11] Echoes of the broader 'social emancipation' factor could be detected in the work of the scheme, which operated under the motto, 'Knowledge is power', and Dick Lewis certainly saw the pilot scheme as an integral part of his work for the labour movement.[12]

With the establishment of the Abbey steelworks in the late 1940s and early 1950s, the Port Talbot/Neath area enjoyed something of an economic boom. Associated industries, such as the Metal Box Company, provided new opportunities for the W.E.A. in industries in which their old trade union allies were well established. The old problems which afflicted workers' education in the inter-war years, such as structural unemployment, emigration and poverty, were replaced by others related to the new prosperity, such as the distractions of television and consumer materialism. The curriculum was, therefore, heavily weighted towards courses of direct relevance to trade unionists in their day-to-day activities, with much of the work conducted by means of single and linked weekend schools. In the 1955–6 session, all but three of sixteen such schools were on industrial relations topics. The day schools and short courses were slightly more varied in character, but it was the linked weekend schools which proved to be the most successful innovation in terms of recruitment and impact. The pilot schemes can in retrospect be seen to have been part of the 'technicization' of workers' education, with the displacement to some extent of educational values by those of training. In

[11] Stead, op. cit. (1977), 93; interview with R. C. Lewis, 9 July 1979. See also the two annual reports of the Port Talbot and District Pilot Scheme for Trade Union Education, 1955–6 and 1956–7, W.E.A. records, Cardiff.

[12] Interview with R. C. Lewis. At the time of his appointment as pilot scheme organizer, Dick Lewis was secretary of the Maesteg District Labour Party and chairman of the Ogmore Constituency Labour Party.

this process, the 'social emancipation' factor seems to have become more and more attenuated.[13]

The W.E.A. in south Wales, with its extensive links with the trade union, local authority and academic worlds, has proved to be a very fertile spawning ground for local, national and even international politicians, not so much amongst its students as amongst its full-time staff. At various times officials of the south Wales district have held important offices in local government. Five south Wales Labour M.P.s, including the former leader of the Labour Party, and two members of the European Parliament are former employees of the south Wales district of the association.[14] It is not surprising that those with a commitment to Labour politics have found the association a valuable base on which to build their ambitions, but it is perhaps ironic that this process was taking place as the W.E.A. was diluting its broader political perspective.

The loss of 'vision' and the drift towards a training mentality in the field of workers' education was also apparent in the work of the W.E.A.'s great rival, the N.C.L.C. Under Millar the Labour College movement became more and more locked into the needs of the trade union movement for 'training' courses, and its political perspectives, still nominally Marxian, were anti-left in general and anti-communist in particular.[15] By the mid-1950s the drift from the revolutionary principles of the early I.W.C.E. movement was so pronounced that there was a strong lobby within the leadership of the south Wales area of the N.U.M. for a break with the N.C.L.C. and the establishment of an independent education service directly under the control of the area. The leading advocate of this policy was none other than Dai Dan Evans, who had done so much to create the S.W.M.F./N.C.L.C. scheme in the 1930s. Evans criticized the failure of the N.C.L.C. to provide fundamental training in the social sciences, for in effect failing to educate workers in the Marxian critique of capitalism. His

[13] For an evaluation of the pilot schemes, see Corfield, op. cit., 123–8. See also H. A. Clegg and R. Adams, *Trade Union Education* (London, 1959).

[14] Neil Kinnock, Allan Rogers, Ron Davies, Rhodri Morgan, Llewellyn Smith (M.E.P. and M.P.), and Wayne David.

[15] J. McIlroy, 'The demise of the National Council of Labour Colleges', in B. Simon (ed.), op. cit., 186–99; see also Lowe, op. cit., 159.

supporters also criticized the way in which the scholarship
scheme with Coleg Harlech was resulting in the departure of
recipients from the ranks of the industry and the union, a trend
well illustrated by the two men appointed to run the Port
Talbot pilot scheme.[16]

The Coleg Harlech scholarships were dropped, and the
scheme with the N.C.L.C. was terminated in favour of the
south Wales area's own scheme. It involved the appointment
of a full-time education officer, who would take ninety-nine
students, selected on a competitive basis, for an intensive
fifteen-week course based on day-release classes, the union making up the lost wages. The subject orientation was unambiguously geared towards the 'institution of a socialist society'.[17]
One-third of the classes were on political economy, one-third
on social history; the remainder were concerned with the
history of the miners' union, and only five out of forty-five
were concerned with practical union matters, such as branch
administration. The south Wales N.U.M. was thus cutting
directly across the grain of the developments of the 1950s in
workers' education, and it was clearly an attempt to restore
the original values of I.W.C.E. at a time when all the other
agencies of workers' education, not least the N.C.L.C., seemed
intent on abandoning them. The appointment in 1957 of the
communist sociologist, Ronald Frankenburg, as the full-time
education officer guaranteed both the quality of the education
supplied and its strong political content.[18] Ironically, this was
perhaps as close as any south Wales miners' coalfield-wide educational scheme came to meeting the ideals of Ablett and his
early supporters.

The loss of the south Wales N.U.M. scheme was a part of the
steady decline of the N.C.L.C. caused by the changing
demands of the unions and the interests of their members in a
time of prosperity and apparent economic stability. The nominal commitment to Marxism alienated the pragmatists of the

---

[16] National Union of Mineworkers (N.U.M.), South Wales Area, minutes of
area delegate conference, 9 Nov. 1954; South Wales Area, E.C. minutes, 11 January
1955.
[17] 'Education department' report, *N.U.M. South Wales Area, Annual Conference Report,
1957–58*, 124–30.
[18] Frankenburg was not the first full-time education officer appointed by the south
Wales N.U.M.; D. J. Phillips (the brother of Gwyn Phillips) was initially appointed
to the post, but he died suddenly just before taking up the job.

Labour right, and the anti-left stance and authoritarianism of
Millar and the N.C.L.C. leadership alienated the activists of
the Labour, communist and Trotskyist left. In 1964 the
N.C.L.C. was absorbed into the T.U.C. education service,
where all the last vestiges of its Labour College origins rapidly
withered.[19] Only the south Wales N.U.M. scheme retained any
commitment to I.W.C.E. ideals. With the ending of the area
educational scheme in the early 1970s, the I.W.C.E. movement became organizationally defunct.

2. Conclusion

In seeking to assess the impact of workers' education on the
development of the organized working-class movement in
south Wales it would be useful to have a set of criteria against
which to measure success and failure. If such criteria were to be
based on the number of senior union leaders and national
politicians whose careers were touched by involvement with
one or other of the agencies of workers' education, there can
be little doubt that the Central Labour College was the most
spectacularly successful. It had an enormous impact on the
south Wales miners' union. By the 1930s, the executive committee and its senior offices were already well staffed by ex-students
and tutors of the Labour College. Similarly in the political field,
by the time of the 1945 election the coalfield was represented by
thirteen M.P.s sponsored by the miners' union, eight of whom
were former students of the Central Labour College. Three
became cabinet ministers, two of whom, Aneurin Bevan and
James Griffiths, presided over the creation of the post-war
welfare state. Two general secretaries of the M.F.G.B. were
ex-C.L.C. scholars, Frank Hodges and Arthur Cook. The
growth of the Communist Party was shaped by men like Idris
Cox, who became editor of the *Daily Worker* and later secretary
of the party's international department. There were, too, ex-
Labour College men like Lewis Jones, the first communist to
be elected to Glamorgan County Council, who also provides
an insight into the world view of coalfield activists in the
1930s through his novels, *Cwmardy* and *We Live*. There were

[19] Millar, op. cit., 157–69.

those whose careers within the labour movement took them out of south Wales: Will Coldrick and Will Owen became Labour M.P.s in England; Bryn Roberts built up the National Union of Public Employees; the list could go on and on.

Yet if another criterion is taken, that is, of the movement with a distinct political ideology underpinning its teaching which reached the greatest number of workers, then clearly the non-residential Labour College movement, and especially the N.C.L.C., must be regarded as the most influential and effective of the traditions. It was through the N.C.L.C. that thousands of young trade unionists were imbued with a strong anti-capitalist ethos, based on Marxian economics and the materialist conception of history. The Labour College movement, far more than any political party, reinforced a socialist rhetoric and the language of class conflict. In south Wales the outlook of the miners' union was to a large extent forged in the Labour College classes, where hundreds of lodge secretaries and chairmen were taught their craft in the context of an unambiguously class-conscious world view. It was at this level of activism that the Labour College movement probably made its really significant mark. The élite who attended the Central Labour College were already marked for leadership, men whose intellect and abilities had been recognized by their fellow workers. Nor did this section belong to the even more rarefied group of working-class autodidacts whose role in the development of the I.W.C.E. movement has been well analysed in the works of Jonathan Ree and Stuart Macintyre. Whilst these studies have brought a welcome analytical light to bear on figures such as Tommy Jackson and Fred Casey and, in the case of south Wales, Nun Nicholas, there is a danger that their significance can be overstated. Such figures were rare, perhaps mercifully rare. Also, by the 1920s the extent to which they could be described as truly self-taught may be questioned. In the Valleys and towns of industrial south Wales there was a whole range of agencies providing learning for adults, from the adult classes of chapel Sunday schools, the Co-operative Societies, the Y.M.C.A. and the League of Nations Union to the I.L.P. and the Communist Party. Above all, there were public and institute libraries, which sprang up in the Edwardian era, and also the informal

sources of learning in the pit, workshop, public house and
barber shop. All this in addition to the expanding provision
made by the extra-mural departments of the university and
the workers' education movement. It was possible, in the first
half of this century, to be very well read and very well
informed, and indeed there were many such men and women
in the industrial towns and villages of inter-war south Wales.
They were not part of that rare collection of disparate intellects
who could truly be called autodidacts, but intelligent working-
class people interested in the world and seeking to understand
their place in it. They were the kind of people whom the oral
historian George Ewart Evans recalled from his early life in
depression-hit south Wales. 'Most of the miners were unemployed, just as I was, and I used to meet them on the lee-side
of a stone wall. They used to talk about everything under the
sun from Marx, to Feuerbach, Engels and Plekhanov—and
some of them had actually read them.'[20] This was the real
market for workers' education, this large group who became
the activists, union officers and local councillors. They were
local opinion-formers who helped to shape the political attitudinal base of industrial south Wales, especially the coalfield.
It was the world view of this group that the Labour College
movement did most to mould.

Yet if sheer numbers are to be the criterion by which the
influence of a tradition of workers' education is to be assessed,
then the orthodox, collaborationist W.E.A. tradition has to
be seen as the most successful. Working in alliance with the university's extra-mural departments and, to a lesser extent, the
local authority evening classes, the W.E.A. touched the lives
of far more people than did any other tradition. The criticism
that the W.E.A. was really aimed at the adult educational
needs of the middle and professional classes may or may not
be valid in other areas of the U.K.; in inter-war south Wales,
particularly in the 1930s, the W.E.A. catered to an overwhelmingly working-class clientele. Nor can the W.E.A. simply
be seen as just another agency of social control. Its role was far
more ambivalent; it could disseminate a non-conflictual perspective on the social and economic order, but it could also—

[20] G. E. Evans, 'Approaches to interviewing', *Oral History*, 1, No. 4 (1973), 57.

sometimes clandestinely, sometimes overtly—be a vehicle for anti-capitalist and anti-conservative sentiment. It did, however, play an important part in maintaining contact between leaders of working-class opinion and those who belonged to the lower professional classes in south Wales, the teaching profession and ministers of religion, whose influence could have been marginalized during the days when the powers of the institutions of working-class independence, especially the Miners' Federation, were at their height. It also carried the mentality of its founders: it was imbued with Idealist values, with their stress on social and public service, and their innate belief in community and mutuality. This came to the fore in the era of structural unemployment, and consolidated the association in south Wales. The links with the irremediably reformist leaders of unions, like the steelworkers and the transport workers, also perhaps helped to curb the influence of the more advanced anti-capitalist ideologues who held sway in parts of the coalfield.

The W.E.A. was ultimately the more successful tradition because of its adaptability. It was always willing to seek out opportunities in the rapidly changing society that was twentieth-century south Wales. Only in the era of revolutionary posturing, from 1916 to 1921, did it seem that the Labour College movement might overwhelm the W.E.A. It was not so much the ideological commitment of the I.W.C.E. movement which was to prove its ultimate source of failure, but rather its obsession with independence. Success depended on the willingness and the ability of organized labour to fund the movement. The terrible defeats of 1921 and 1926 showed the strategic limitations of independence. Mark Starr saw and predicted these limitations; he advocated a strategy of principled opportunism, but his views were rejected, ignored, or implemented in a half-hearted and a far too cynical fashion. In these circumstances, what for the W.E.A. was to prove its great opportunity, heavy structural unemployment, became for the N.C.L.C. a source of weakness, decay and, on occasion, collapse.

The close links between the Labour College movement and the semi-revolutionary working-class movements of the 1910–26 period, combined with the subsequent prominence of many of the products of the Central Labour College, have fascinated some Labour historians. That the I.W.C.E. movement derived much of its impetus and support from the south Wales coalfield has also resulted in a tendency for it to be credited with a significance in the history of the region beyond what it deserves. The influence of Ablett and the Plebs League on the militancy of the coalfield in 1910–14 was much overstated at the time—by friends and enemies of the movement—and too many historians have accepted these inflated accounts in an uncritical fashion. The I.W.C.E. movement was actually a symptom and not a cause of the turmoil in the coalfield. In truth, prior to the First World War, both traditions of workers' education in south Wales clung to existence by their finger nails as each sought a formula that would appeal to the activist element in the labour movement. This is not to deny that the Labour College movement was a formative influence on the south Wales labour movement, but rather to argue that more should be made of the W.E.A., whose ultimate legacy was just as powerful and, perhaps, more profound.

Both traditions, against the wishes of their founders and early supporters, became agencies of social mobility. As the expanding labour movement evolved an informal career structure, they both provided routes of escape from the harsher realities of working-class life in industrial south Wales. At a time when organized labour has never been weaker, and more marginalized politically, the old imperatives which created the workers' education movement seem to have disappeared. This may be a temporary phenomenon, but it is a trend reinforced by other social changes. The post-war expansion of secondary education, the growth in further and part-time education, and the opening out of new avenues of access to higher education may mean that the demand for workers' education, especially as an agency of social mobility, has all but dried up. The trend towards 'technicization' of trade union education has continued, but the service is in crisis with even state-supported provision of trade union education suffering from a loss of membership and unemployment. It may be that the refocusing of attention away from 'raising the whole class', which governed both traditions but which may now be outdated, and towards specific social groups, especially women and the ethnic minorities, will revitalize the movement.

Certainly the shift will result in the effective abandonment of any attempt to define the role of workers' education in collective terms. The laudable desire to break down factitious barriers to personal development is seen as a valid objective in itself. Individual mobility is seen as proof of success; equal opportunities are an adequate substitute for cultural and intellectual equality. This is progress of a sort, but not quite what the founders of either tradition of workers' education had in mind.

BIBLIOGRAPHY

1. MANUSCRIPT COLLECTIONS

2. REPORTS

3. NEWSPAPERS AND PERIODICALS

4. ORAL TESTIMONY

5. UNPUBLISHED THESES

6. BIOGRAPHIES AND MEMOIRS

7. OTHER BOOKS AND PAMPHLETS

8. ARTICLES IN BOOKS AND JOURNALS

1. MANUSCRIPT COLLECTIONS:

Gwent Record Office
Minute book, S.W.M.F., Abercarn lodge

National Library of Wales
Edgar L. Chappell, personal collection
W. H. Mainwaring, personal collection
D. Lleufer Thomas, personal collection

N.C.L.C. Collection, National Library of Scotland, Edinburgh
Acc. 5120 (first deposit)
Labour College, correspondence and related papers, 1909–29
Minute books, Labour College, Board of Governors, 1919–29
N.C.L.C., Division IV, A.G.M. and council minute book, 1930–40
Acc. 5120 (second deposit)
N.C.L.C., national executive committee minutes, 1921–40
Acc. 6889
Minute books and related papers, Labour College, Board of
    Governors, 1910–29

Private Collections
W. Gregory (Croydon)
J. P. M. Millar (Dartmouth)
J. Thomas (Manchester)

Public Record Office. London
Board of Education papers, ED/24

Ruskin College Library, Oxford
Correspondence between T. I. Mardy Jones and Bertram Wilson, 1909

South Wales Miners' Library, Swansea
John Thomas, 'The economic doctrines of Karl Marx and their influence on the industrial areas of South Wales, particularly among the miners', MS essay submitted to the National Eisteddfod, Ammanford, 1922
J. S. Williams (Dowlais), miscellaneous personal papers

University College of Swansea, Department of Adult Education Library
Minute books, W.E.A., Swansea branch, 1927–40

University College of Swansea Library
Minute books, S.W.M.F, executive committee and conferences, 1908–40. South Wales area, N.U.M., 1947 onwards
Minute books, S.W.M.F., Rhondda No. 1. District, 1900–31
Minute books, S.W.M.F. Blaenavon lodge, 1904–37
Minute books, Cardiff, Penarth and Barry Coaltrimmers' Union, 1881–1941
Minute books, Neath branch, Independent Labour Party, 1923–32
Edmund Stonelake (Aberdare), MS of unpublished autobiography
George Thomas (Porthcawl), miscellaneous papers
D. J. Williams (Neath), miscellaneous papers

W.E.A. Head Office, Library, Temple House, London
Minute books, W.E.A. executive committee, 1903–40
Minute books, Central Labour College, provisional committee and Board of Governors, 1909–16

W.E.A. South Wales District, Records, Cardiff
Minute books, South Wales district committee, 1907–10. Wales district committee, 1911, 1914–25. South Wales district council, 1925–29
Minute books, Wales district executive committee, 1918–25. South Wales district executive committee, 1925–9, 1930–8
Minute books, W.E.T.U.C. Divisions I and II, 1920–38

Minute book, joint committee, Carnegie Coalfield Distress Fund, 1929–30

Minute book and reports, Joint Committee for the Promotion of Educational Facilities in the South Wales and Monmouthshire Coafield, 1930–3

Minute book, South Wales Council of Social Service, Education Committee, 1934–5

Miscellaneous papers and correspondence, Wales and South Wales district of the W.E.A., 1914–40

Miscellaneous memoranda of the national W.E.A.

'Proposed statement on the Education Bill to be submitted to the President of the Board of Education by the W.E.A.(Welsh District)', *c.* 1917

Correspondence with the Llantwit Branch, W.E.A., 1917–18

2. REPORTS

Annual Reports
Workers' Educational Association, 1905–40
The Wales and South Wales Districts of the W.E.A. 1912–40
University of Wales Extension Board, 1920–40
Central Joint Advisory Committee on Tutorial Classes, 1908–29

Government Publications
Board of Education, Report of the Consultative Committee on Attendance, Compulsory or Otherwise, at Continuation Schools vol.1, Report and appendices (Cmnd. 4757), 1909; vol.2, Summaries of evidence (Cmnd. 4758), 1909

Commission of Enquiry into Industrial Unrest: Division No. 7. (Wales and Monmouthshire) (Cmnd. 8668), 1917

Royal Commission on University Education in Wales, Final Report (Cmnd. 8993), 1918; vol. III, Minutes of evidence, (Cmnd. 8993), 1918

Ministry of Reconstruction, Final Report of the Adult Education Committee (Cmnd. 321), 1919

Welsh Department, Board of Education, Report of the Board's Inspector of Tutorial Classes, conducted in the Session 1922–23 (London, 1923)

Welsh Department, Board of Education, Report on Adult Education in Wales, Memorandum No. 5 (London, 1936)

Ministry of Education, Report by H.M. Inspectors on a Survey of the Work of the South Wales District of the Workers' Educational Association (London, 1954)

Other Printed Reports
Statement of the Views of the Council, Workers' Educational Association, Welsh District, to the Royal Commission on University Education in Wales (Cardiff, 1917)
University of Wales Extension Board, Survey of Adult Education in Wales (Cardiff, 1940)

3. NEWSPAPERS AND PERIODICALS

(a) Newspapers:

Barry Dock News
Barry Herald
Daily Herald
Free Press of Monmouthshire
Glamorgan Free Press
Glamorgan Gazette
Herald of Wales
Llais Llafur
The Pioneer (Merthyr)
Merthyr Express
Rhondda Leader

Rhondda Socialist
South Wales Argus
South Wales Weekly Argus
South Wales Daily News
South Wales Echo
South Wales Gazette
South Wales Post
South Wales Worker
Sunday Worker
The Times
Western Mail

(b) Periodicals:

Anvil
Cambria
Communist Review
Highway
Journal of the Iron and Steel Confederation

Labour Monthly
Plebs
Railway Review
Welsh Outlook
Workers' Life

4. ORAL TESTIMONY

(a) Interviews Conducted solely by the Author
Dr Illtyd David (Swansea)
Mr D. T. Guy (Cardiff)
Mr R. C. Lewis (Bridgend)

Mr J. P. M. Millar (Dartmouth)
Mr Amos Moules (Swansea)
Mr Gwyn Phillips (Hengoed)
Mr Mark Starr (New York)
Dr John Thomas (Manchester)
Mr Rosser Thomas (Maesteg)

(b) Interviews Conducted jointly with Members of the S.S.R.C. Coal-field History Project, 1972–4. Transcripts held at the South Wales Miners' Library, Swansea
Mr W. Coldrick (Bristol) with D. Egan
Mr Glyn Evans (London) with H. Francis
Mr W. Gregory (Croydon) with H. Francis
Mr James Griffiths (Putney) with H. Francis
Mr Len Williams (Neath) with D. Egan
Mr W.H. Williams (London) with H. Francis

(c) S.S.R.C. Coalfield History Project Interview Transcripts consulted at the South Wales Miners' Library, Swansea
J. Brewer
I. Cox
D. J. Davies
D. D. Evans
N. Gittins
M. Goldberg
E. Greening
L. Jeffreys
A. Lush
H. Morgans
T. Nicholas
W. Paynter
W. Picton
O. Powell
W. Rees
E. Thomas
G. Thomas
M. Thomas (two interviews)
W. C. Thomas
J. L. Williams

5. UNPUBLISHED THESES

J. A. Cartwright, 'A study in British syndicalism: the miners of south Wales, 1906–14' (University of Wales M.Sc. thesis, 1969)

D. A. Eastwood, 'The full man: adult education in Cardiff, 1860–1960' (University of Wales M.Ed. thesis, 1970)

K. O. Fox, 'The emergence of the political labour movement in the eastern sector of the south Wales coalfield' (University of Wales M.A. thesis, 1965)

H. Francis, 'The south Wales miners and the Spanish civil war: a study in internationalism' (University of Wales Ph.D. thesis, 1977)

R. Frow, 'Independent working class education, with special reference to south Lancashire' (University of Manchester M.Ed. thesis, 1968)

C. E. Gwyther, 'Methodism and syndicalism in the Rhondda Valley, 1906–26' (University of Sheffield Ph.D. thesis 1967)

I. W. Hamilton, 'Education for revolution: the Plebs League and the Labour College movement' (University of Warwick M.A. thesis, 1972)

L. S. Jones, 'Church and Chapel in Wales as sources and centres of education' (University of Liverpool M.A. thesis, 1940)

R. Lewis, 'Leaders and teachers: the origins and development of the workers' education movement in south Wales, 1906—40' (University of Wales Ph.D. thesis, 1980)

J. H. Roberts, 'The N.C.L.C.: an experiment in workers' education' (University of Edinburgh M.Sc. thesis, 1970)

D. B. Smith, 'The rebuilding of the South Wales Miners' Federation, 1927–39: a trade union and its society' (University of Wales Ph.D thesis, 1976)

J. Thomas, 'The south Wales coalfield during government control, 1914–21'(University of Wales M.A. thesis, 1925)

M. Turner, 'The miners' search for self-improvement: the history of the evening classes in the Rhondda Valley from 1862–1914' (University of Wales M.A. thesis, 1967)

M. G. Woodhouse, 'Rank and file movements among the miners of south Wales, 1910–26' (University of Oxford D.Phil. thesis, 1970)

6. Biographies and memoirs

Barker, R. J., *Christ in the Valley of Unemployment* (London, 1936)
Butterworth, K., *William Noble and his Wife Emma* (London, 1962)
Davies, P., *A. J. Cook,* (Manchester, 1987)
Edwards, W. J., *From the Valley I Came* (London, 1956)
Evans, E. W., *Mabon* (Cardiff, 1959)
Finch, H., *Memoirs of a Bedwellty M.P.* (Newport, 1972)
Foot, M., *Aneurin Bevan, 1897–1945* (London, 1975)
Furniss, H. S., *Memories of Sixty Years* (London, 1931)
Glasgow, G., *Ronald Burrows: A Memoir* (London, 1924)
Griffiths, J., *Pages From Memory* (London, 1969)
Hodges, F., *My Adventures as a Labour Leader* (London, 1925)
Horner, A., *Incorrigible Rebel* (London, 1960)
Jones, T., *Welsh Broth* (Aberystwyth, 1950)
Idem, A Diary with Letters, 1931–51 (London, 1954)
Middlemass, K., (ed.), *Whitehall Diaries*: vol. 1, *1916–25* (London, 1969)
Lawson, J., *A Man's Life* (London, 1932)
Mackenzie, M., (ed.), *J. S. Mackenzie* (London, 1936)
Paynter, W., *My Generation* (London, 1972)
Watkins, H., *Unusual Students* (Liverpool, 1947)
Watkins, P. E., *A Welshman Remembers* (Cardiff, 1944)
White, E., *Thomas Jones, Founder of Coleg Harlech* (Aberystwyth, 1977)
Zimmern, A., *My Impressions of Wales* (London, 1921).

7. Other books and pamphlets

Ablett, N., *Easy Outline of Economics* (Sheffield, 1919)
Addison, P., *The Road to 1945* (London, 1975)
Arnot, R. P., *A History of the South Wales Miners, 1898–1914* (London, 1967)
Idem, A History of the South Wales Miners, 1914–1926 (Cardiff, 1975)
Ashby, E., *The Pathology of Adult Education* (Belfast, 1955)
Atkins, J. A., *Neither Crumbs nor Condescension: The Central Labour College, 1909–1915* (Aberdeen, 1981)
Barker, R., *Education and Politics* (Oxford, 1972)
Beveridge, W., *Full Employment in a Free Society* (London, 1944)

Bracher, S. V., *Herald Book of Labour Members* (London, 1922)

Brown, G., (ed.), *Industrial Syndicalist* (Nottingham, 1974)

Bull, B. M., *The University Settlement in Cardiff*, (Cardiff, 1965)

Calder , A. *The People's War* (London, 1969)

Challinor , R. *The Origins of British Bolshevism* (London, 1977)

Clarke, P. F., *Lancashire and the New Liberalism* (Cambridge, 1971)

Clegg, H. A., and R. Adams, *Trade Union Education* (London, 1959)

Cole, G. D. H., *The British Working Class Movement* (London 1944)

Idem, A Short History of the British Working Class Movement, 1789– 1946 (London, 1948)

Idem and R. Postgate, *The Common People* (London, 1975)

Cook, C., *The Age of Alignment* (London, 1975)

Corfield, A. J., *Epoch in Workers' Education* (London, 1969)

Craik, W. W., *Students' Outlines* (Halifax, 1919)

Idem, Central Labour College (London, 1964)

Dangerfield, G., *The Strange Death of Liberal England*, (London, 1966)

Daunton, M. J., *Coal Metropolis: Cardiff 1870–1914* (Leicester, 1977)

Davies, G., *Welsh School of Social Service, 1911–1925* (Cardiff, 1926)

Edwards, N., *History of the South Wales Miners' Federation* (London, 1938)

Idem, The Industrial Revolution in South Wales (London, 1938)

Ellis, A., *A Secret History of the N.C.L.C.* (Birmingham, 1937)

Ellis, E. L., *T.J.: A life of Dr Thomas Jones, C.H.* (Cardiff, 1992).

Emy, H. V., *Liberals, Radicals and Social Politics* (Cambridge, 1973)

Evans, D., *Labour Strife in the South Wales Coalfield 1910–1911* (Cardiff, 1963)

Evans, E. W., *The Miners of South Wales* (Cardiff, 1961)

Evans, W. G., *Education and Female Emancipation: the Welsh Experience, 1847–1914* (Cardiff, 1990)

Fieldhouse, R., *Adult Education and the Cold War: Liberal Values under Siege* (Leeds, 1985)

Fisher, H. A. L., *History of Europe;* vol. I. (London, 1937)

Francis, H., *Miners against Fascism: Wales and the Spanish Civil War* (London, 1984)

Idem and D. B. Smith *The Fed* (London, 1980)

Glynn, S. and G. Oxborrow, *Interwar Britain: A Social and Economic History* (London, 1976)

Gordon, P. and J. White, *Philosophers as Educational Reformers: The Influence of Idealism on British Educational Thought and Practice* (London, 1979)

Gregory, R., *The Miners and British Politics, 1906–14* (Oxford, 1968)

Griffin, A. R., *The Miners of Nottingham* (London, 1962)

Haldane, R. B., *The University and the Welsh Democracy* (London, 1922)

Harrison, J. F. C., *Learning and Living, 1790–1960* (London, 1961)

Harrop, S. (ed.), *Oxford and Working Class Education* (Nottingham, 1987)

Hay, W. F., *Education and the Working Class* (Liverpool, 1920)

Hinton, A., *The First Shop Stewards Movement* (London, 1972)

Hodgen, M. T., *Workers' Education in England and the United States* (London, 1925)

Holton, R., *British Syndicalism* (London, 1976)

Hopkins, P. G. H., *Workers' Education: An International Perspective* (Milton Keynes, 1985)

Jenkins, D. W. T., *Adult Education in Wales* (Cardiff, 1966).

Jennings, H., *Brynmawr* (London, 1934)

Jones, A. J., *The Adolescent and the Continuation School* (Cardiff, 1919)

Jones, G. J., *Wales and the Quest for Peace* (Cardiff, 1969)

Jones, L., *Cwmardy* (London, 1978)

Idem, We Live (London, 1978)

Jones, R. M. (ed.), *The Miners' Next Step: Being a Suggested Reorganisation of the Federation* (London, 1972)

Idem, The North Wales Quarrymen, 1874–1922 (Cardiff, 1982)

Jones, S. G., *Workers at Play: A Social History of Leisure, 1918–1939* (London, 1986)

Kendall, W., *The Revolutionary Movement in Britain, 1900–21* (London, 1969)

Kelly, T., *A History of Adult Education in Great Britain* (Liverpool, 1970)

Kirby, M. W., *The British Coalmining Industry, 1870–1946* (London, 1970)

Klugman, J., *History of the Communist Party of Great Britain*, vol. I (London, 1968)

Lawson, J., *A Man's Life* (London, 1932)

Lewis, E. D., *The Rhondda Valleys* (London, 1959)

Lowe, J., *Adult Education in England and Wales: A Critical Survey* (London, 1970)

Lush, A. J., *The Young Adult* (Cardiff, 1941)

Macfarlane L. J., *The British Communist Party: Its Origins and Development until 1929* (London, 1966)

Mackenzie, J. S., *Introduction to Social Reform* (London 1890)

Mansbridge, A., *University Tutorial Classes* (London, 1913)

Marwick, A., *The Deluge* (London, 1965)

McKibbin, R. I., *The Evolution of the Labour Party, 1910–24* (Oxford, 1974)

Molyneux, F., G. Low, and G. Fowler, (eds), *Learning for Life: Politics and Progress in Recurrent Education* (London, 1988)

Morgan, H., *The Social Task in Wales* (London, 1919)

Morgan, J., *Conflict and Order: The Police and Labour Disputes in England and Wales, 1900–1939* (Oxford, 1987)

Morgan, K. O., *Wales in British Politics, 1868–1922* (Cardiff, 1963)

Idem, Consensus and Disunity: The Lloyd George Coalition Government, 1918–1922 (Oxford, 1979)

Idem, Rebirth of a Nation: Wales 1880–1980 (Oxford and Cardiff, 1981)

N.C.L.C., *Education for Emancipation* (London, 1933)

Owen, C., *Address to the Second Annual General Meeting of the Cardiff University College Past Students' Association* (Cardiff, 1900)

Passmore, J., *A Hundred Years of Philosophy* (London, 1970)

Paul, E. and C. Paul, *Proletcult* (London, 1921)

Pelling, H., *Social Geography of British Elections, 1885–1910* (London, 1967)

Idem, Popular Politics and Society in Late Victorian England (London, 1968)

Pilgrim Trust, *Men Without Work* (Cambridge, 1938)

Pribicevic, B., *The Shop Stewards' Movement and Workers' Control, 1910–22* (Oxford, 1959)

Price, T. W., *The Story of the Workers' Educational Association* (London, 1923)

Ree, J., *Proletarian Philosophers: Problems in Socialist Culture* (Oxford, 1984)

Renshaw, P., *The General Strike* (London, 1976)

Robbins, K., *The Abolition of War* (Cardiff, 1976)

Saddler, M. E., *The Development of University Extension*, (Philadelphia, 1892)

Seed, W. H., *The Burning Question of Education* (Oxford, 1909)

Simon, B., *Education and the Labour Movement, 1870–1920* (London, 1965)

Idem, B. Simon (ed.), *The Search for Enlightenment: The Working Class and Adult Education in the Twentieth Century* (London, 1990)

Smith, D. B. (ed.), *A People and a Proletariat: Essays in the History of Wales, 1780–1980* (London, 1980)

Smith, H. P., *Labour and Learning* (Oxford, 1956)

Starr, M., *A Worker Looks at History* (Oxford, 1917)

Idem, A Worker Looks at History (London, 1925)

Idem, A Worker Looks at Economics (London, 1925)

Idem, Lies and Hate in Education (London, 1929)

Stead, P., *Coleg Harlech: The First Fifty Years* (Cardiff, 1977)

Stocks, M., *The W.E.A.: The First Fifty Years* (London, 1953)

Skelley, J. (ed.), *The General Strike, 1926* (London, 1976)

Tanner, D., *Political Change and the Labour Party* (Cambridge, 1990)

Thomas, B. B. (ed.), *Harlech Studies* (Cardiff, 1938)

Thomas, D. L., *Labour Unions in Wales: Their Early Struggles for Existence* (Swansea, 1901)

Thomas, J., *The Economics of Coal* (London, 1919)

Idem, The Miners' Conflict with the Mineowners (London, 1921)

Waites, B., *A Class Society at War: England 1914–1918* (Leamington Spa, 1987)

Watkins, P. E., *Adult Education amongst the Unemployed of South Wales* (London, 1935)

Idem, Educational Settlements in South Wales and Monmouthshire (Cardiff, 1940)

Williams, C. R., *Jubilee Year, The South Wales District of the Workers' Educational Association* (Cardiff, 1957)

Williams, D. J., *Capitalist Combination in the Coal Industry* (London, 1924)

Williams, W. H., *The Miners' Two Bob* (London, n.d.)

Winter, J. M., *Socialism and the Challenge of War* (London, 1974)

Wrigley, C. J., *David Lloyd George and the British Labour Movement* (London, 1976)

W.E.A., *Aims and Standards in W.E.A. Classes* (London, 1938)

Idem, Adult Education after the War (London, 1942)
Idem, Educational Reconstruction: A W.E.A. Programme (London, 1942)
Idem, Trade Union Education (London, 1953)
Idem, Summary and Short Statement of Evidence to the Russell Committee on Adult Education (London, 1970)
Yorke, P., *Ruskin College, 1899–1909* (Oxford, 1977)

8. ARTICLES IN BOOKS AND JOURNALS

Bowie, J. A., 'The miners' mind', *English Review*, 40 (February 1925)
Brennan, T., 'The White House', *Cambridge Journal*, VII, No. 4 (1954)
Brown, G., 'Educational values and working class residential adult education', in *Residential Adult Education: Values, Policies and Problems* (Society of Industrial Tutors, 1978)
Bulmer, M. I. A., 'Sociological models of the mining community', *Sociological Review*, No. 23 (1975)
Burrows, R., 'Evolution or revolution', *Welsh Outlook* (January 1914)
Carter, G. R., 'The coal strike in south Wales', *Economic Journal*, XXV, No. 99 (1915)
Idem, 'The sequel of the coal strike and its significance', *Economic Journal*, XXV, No. 100 (1915)
Church, R., 'Edwardian labour unrest and coalfield militancy, 1890–1914', *Historical Journal*, 30, No. 4 (1987)
Clarke, P. F., 'Electrical sociology of modern Britain', *History*, No. 57 (1972)
Cohen, M., 'The Labour College movement between the wars', in B. Simon (ed.), *The Search for Enlightenment: The Working Class and Adult Education in the Twentieth Century* (London, 1990)
Idem, 'Revolutionary education revived: the communist challenge to the Labour Colleges, 1933–45; in B. Simon (ed.), *The Search for Englightenment: The Working Class and Adult Education in the Twentieth Century* (London, 1990)
Cox, K. R., 'Geography, social contexts and voting behaviour in Wales, 1861–1951' in S. Allardt and E. Rokkan (eds.), *Mass Politics* (New York, 1973)

Davies, J., 'Time to spare in Wales', in *Wales and the New Leisure* (Llandysul, 1935)

Davies, J. E., 'Educational settlements in south Wales with special reference to the Merthyr Tydfil Settlement', *Transactions of the Honourable Society of Cymmrodorion*, pt. 2 (1970)

Davies, P., 'The making of A. J. Cook: his development within the south Wales labour movement', *Llafur*, 2, No. 3 (1978)

Davies, W. H., 'The south Wales miner', *Welsh Outlook* (February 1929)

Egan, D., 'The Swansea conference of the British Council of Soldiers' and Workers' Delegates, July 1917: reactions to the Russian revolution of February 1917 and the anti-war movement in south Wales', *Llafur*, 1, No. 4 (1975)

Evans, D. E., 'Adult education in Wales', *Transactions of the Honourable Society of Cymmrodorion* (1926–7)

Evans, G. E., 'Approaches to interviewing', *Oral History*, 1, No. 4 (1973)

Fieldhouse, R., 'Voluntaryism and the state in adult education: the W.E.A. and the 1925 T.U.C. education scheme', *History of Education*, 10, No. 1 (1981)

Fryer, R., 'The challenge to working-class education', in B. Simon (ed.), *The Search for Englightenment* (London, 1990)

Francis, D., 'Dai Dan Evans (1898–1974)', *Llafur*, 1, No. 3 (1974)

Francis, H., 'Survey of Miners' Institute and Welfare Libraries', *Llafur*, 1, No. 2 (1973)

Idem, 'The origins of the South Wales Miners' Library', *History Workshop*, No. 2 (1976)

Idem, 'South Wales', in J. Skelley (ed.), *The General Strike, 1926* (London, 1976)

Harrison, B., 'Oxford and the labour movement', *Twentieth Century British History*, 2, No. 3 (1991)

Hopkin, D. R., 'Patriots and pacifists in Wales, 1914–1918', *Llafur*, 1, No. 3 (1974)

Idem, 'A. J. Cook in 1916–18', *Llafur*, 2, No. 3 (1978)

Idem, 'The great unrest in Wales, 1910–1913: questions of evidence', in D. R. Hopkin and G. S. Kealey (eds.), *Class, Community and the Labour Movement: Wales and Canada, 1850–1930* (Cardiff, 1989)

Jenkins, G., 'The *Welsh Outlook*, 1914–33', *National Library of Wales Journal*, xxxiv (Winter, 1986)

Jenkins, R. T., 'Syndicalist education', *Welsh Outlook* (April 1918)

Jenkinson, A. J., 'Reflections on a pamphlet entitled "The miners' next step"', *Economic Review*, 22 (July 1912)

Jennings, B., 'Revolting students: the Ruskin College dispute, 1908–9', *Studies in Adult Education* (April 1977)

Idem, 'The making of the Oxford report', in S. Harrop (ed.), *Oxford and Working Class Education* (Nottingham, 1987)

Jennings, H., 'A social survey of Brynmawr', *Cambria* (Summer 1930)

James, G., 'The chief task of adult education in Wales', *Welsh Outlook* (February 1933)

Jones, S., 'Fellowship in the coalfield', *Welsh Outlook* (March 1929)

Kenney, R., 'The brains behind the labour revolt', *English Review* (March 1912)

Lambert, W. R., 'Some working class attitudes towards organised religion in nineteenth century Wales', *Llafur*, 2, No. 1 (1976)

Lewis, J. P., 'The Anglicization of Glamorgan', *Transactions of the Glamorgan Local Historical Society*, 4 (1960)

Lewis, R., 'South Wales miners and the Ruskin College strike of 1909', *Llafur*, 2, No. 1 (1976)

Idem, 'The Central Labour College: its decline and fall, 1919–1929', *Welsh History Review*, 12, No. 2 (1984)

Idem, 'Protagonist of labour: Mark Starr, 1894–1985', *Llafur*, 4, No. 3 (1986)

Idem, 'The inheritance: adult education in the Valleys between the wars', in H. Francis (ed.), *Adult Education in the Valleys: The Last Fifty Years* (Cardiff, 1987)

Macintyre, S., 'Joseph Dietzgen and British working class education', *Bulletin of the Society for the Study of Labour History*, No. 29 (1974)

Mansbridge, A., 'Trade unionism, cooperatives and university extension', *University Extension Journal* (1903)

Marwick, W. H., 'Workers' education in early twentieth century Scotland', *Journal of the Scottish Labour History Society* (1974)

Miall, J. H., 'Talks with miners in the Rhondda Valley', *Fortnightly Review*, 120 (1926)

Millar, J. P. M., 'Forty years of independent working class education', *Adult Education*, XXI (1948)

Morgan, K. O., 'The New Liberalism and the challenge of Labour: the Welsh experience, 1885–1929', *Welsh History Review*, 6, no. 3 (1973)

Idem, 'Socialism versus syndicalism: the Welsh miners' debate', Society for the Study of Labour History, *Bulletin*, No. 30 (Spring 1975)

Idem, 'Post-war reconstruction in Wales, 1918–45', in J. Winter (ed.), *The Working Class in Modern British History* (Cambridge, 1983)

Môr-O'Brien, A., 'Patriotism on trial: the strike of the south Wales miners, July 1915', *Welsh History Review*, 12, No. 1 (1984)

Idem, 'Keir Hardie, C. B. Stanton and the First World War', *Llafur*, 4, No. 3 (1986)

Neville, R. G., 'The Yorkshire miners and education', *Journal of Educational Administration and History*, VIII, No. 2 (July 1976)

Owen, A. D. K., 'The social consequences of industrial transference', *Sociological Review*, XXIX, part 4 (1937)

Parry, C., 'Gwynedd politics, 1900–20', *Welsh History Review*, 6, No. 3 (1973)

Ritchie, A. E., 'Reply to J. A. Bowie', *English Review*, 40 (April 1925)

Simon, B., 'The search for hegemony, 1910–26', in B. Simon (ed.), *The Search for Englightenment* (London, 1990)

Smith, D. B., 'The struggle against company unionism in the south Wales coalfield, 1926–39', *Welsh History Review*, 6, No. 3 (1973)

Idem, 'Tonypandy 1910: definitions of community', *Past and Present*, No. 87 (May 1980)

Idem, 'Wales through the looking glass', in D. B. Smith (ed.), *A People and a Proletariat* (London, 1980)

Stead, P., 'Vernon Hartshorn: miners' agent and cabinet minister', *Glamorgan Historian*, 6 (1969)

Idem, 'The Welsh working class', *Llafur*, 1, No. 2 (1973)

Idem, 'Miners and education', *New Edinburgh Review*, No. 32 (1976)

Idem, 'The language of Edwardian politics', in D. Smith (ed.), *A People and a Proletariat* (London, 1980)

Stevenson, J., 'The making of unemployment policy, 1931–35', in M. Bentley and J. Stevenson (eds.), *High and Low Politics in Modern Britain* (Oxford, 1983)

Thomas, B., 'Migration of labour into the Glamorganshire coalfield, 1861–1911', *Economica*, X (1930)

Thomas, B. B., 'Adult education and the industrial worker', *Welsh Outlook* (October 1929)

Thomas, D. H., 'Coleg Harlech and the worker', *Cambria* (1931)

Thomas, D. L., 'University tutorial classes for working people', *Transactions of the Honourable Society of Cymmrodorion* (1916)

Thomas, J., 'The present and future prospects of the south Wales miners', *Communist Review* (January 1922)

Idem, 'The early days of the W.E.A. in Wales', *Cambria* (1930)

Thomas, P. S., 'Adult education in Swansea', *Cambria* (1931)

Turner, C. B., 'Conflicts of faith, religion and labour in Wales, 1890–1914', in D. R. Hopkin and G. S. Kealey (eds.), *Class, Community and the Labour Movement: Wales and Canada, 1850–1930* (Cardiff, 1989)

Watkins, P. E., 'Adult education and the new leisure in Wales', in *Wales and the New Leisure* (Llandysul, 1935)

West, L. R., 'The Tawney legend re-examined', *Studies in Adult Education* (April 1972)

Williams, C. R., 'The religious revival in Wales, 1904–05', *British Journal of Sociology* (1952)

Williams, L. J., 'The new unionism in south Wales', *Welsh History Review*, 1, No. 1 (1963)

Idem, 'The road to Tonypandy', *Llafur*, 1, No. 2 (1973)

Woodhouse, M. G., 'Mines for the nation or mines for the miners? Alternative perspectives on industrial democracy, 1919–21', *Llafur*, 2, No. 3 (1978)

INDEX

Aberaman 117
Aberavon 184n
Abercave 210
Aberdare (Valley, District) 70, 98, 103, 104, 116, 117, 118, 119, 122, 174, 209
Abergwynfi 20n
Abertillery 18, 20n, 93–6, 174
Aberystwyth 43, 147, 148, 149–50, 155, 231
Ablett, Noah xxiv, 26, 62–76 *passim*, 82, 84–92 *passim*, 98, 102, 111, 119, 155–6, 165, 166–7, 174, 175, 244
  governor of Labour College 112, 113
  M.F.G.B. secretaryship 130
  removed as governor 161–2
  as tutor 114, 116
  Easy Outlines of Economics 186–7
Abraham, William 66
adult education *see under* Workers' Educational Association
Adult Education Committee of the Ministry of Reconstruction 147
Afan Valley 176
Allen, (Sir) Thomas W. 4, 10, 18, 93, 94
Amalgamated Society of Railway Servants (A.S.R.S.) 11, 23n, 28, 85
Ammanford 96, 174
anthracite district (and miners) 77–8, 87, 96, 153, 155, 208–9, 210, 218
A Worker Looks at History 117, 167

Badger, A. B. 4, 15
Bangor
  Eisteddfod address 107, 108
  extra-mural classes 147
  Summer School 44
  tutorial classes 43
Barker, Revd George 70, 76, 82, 85, 88, 89, 94, 95, 126, 130n, 217
Barker, R. J. 203
Barry
  Education Society 25–6
  I.L.P. branch 26, 27
  I.W.C.E. classes 97, 118
  Labour College classes 114
  L.R.C. 16
  new theology 45

W.E.A. branch 20n, 23–7, 38, 41, 44, 135, 136, 225
Barry Dock News 24
Barry Herald 24
Beard, Charles 49
Bevan, Aneurin (Nye) 155, 157, 164, 166, 225, 240
Blackwood 174
Blaenavon 70, 78
Blaengarw 97
Blaina 10, 94, 174
Board of Education 43, 108, 149, 179
  Consultative Committee on Continuation Classes 32
  regulations (1924) 146
Bowerman, C. W. 77, 85
Bowie, Dr J. A. 189
Bowman, Guy 96
Bowman, R. 77
Brace, William 15, 18&n, 32, 76, 93, 131
Brewer, Jim 226
Bridgend 135, 197
British Advocates of Industrial Unionism 62
British Steel Smelters' Association 52
Briton Ferry 182, 206
Brockhouse, Henry 129
Brown, W. H. 4, 10, 13
Brynmawr 193
Burrows, Prof. Ronald 4–5, 6–7, 9, 10, 11, 15, 21, 22, 33, 39, 40, 104
Buxton, Charles Sydney 59, 62, 63, 68, 78

Caerau (Maesteg) 20n, 42, 44
Caerphilly 197
Cambria 198–9
Cambrian Combine dispute 80–1, 106
Campbell, Revd R. J. 45, 94, 106
Cardiff
  conference (1916) 115
  Cory Hall conference (1906) 3, 10, 15–16, 17, 23n, 48
  I.L.P. 21
  I.W.C.E. classes 118
  Labour College 176, 184n
  N.C.L.C. day schools 225

Ruskin College correspondence course 49
Splott Settlement 7, 8–9, 15, 40, 22
W.E.A. branch 20, 21–2, 38, 44, 136, 181, 196
Welsh-speakers xxii
Cardiff, University of Wales (and colleges) 5, 8, 42, 107–11, 147–9, 152, 181
AGM (1909) 35–6
extra-mural department/classes 108, 147–8, 152, 178, 181, 215
tutorial classes 43, 108–11, 135, 215
Carmarthenshire 183
Cassell Trust 173, 200
Central Labour College (C.L.C.) (Labour College; Labour College movement) xix, xxiv, 79–100 *passim*
origins of new 'labour' college 48, 53, 68–79 *passim* officially named 112
benefactors 86, 96
classes and subjects 90–1, 98, 109, 114, 121, 157–8, 181, 186–7, 188–9, 222
and the Communist Party (and communists) 156, 158–60, 163, 165, 167, 188, 210–11, 238, 240
correspondence courses 97–8, 119–20
failure and closure 153, 156–67, 207, 211
First World War 102, 103, 110, 111–22, 125–34 *passim*, 140–1 reopens (1919) 152–6 post-war period 152–67 *passim*
funding 85–6, 160–1, 207, 243
I.L.P., conflict with 128–30, 188
influence of 131–3, 166–7, 241–2, 243–4
and the labour movement 84, 88, 89, 122, 127, 128–9, 130, 153, 155–6, 157, 167, 211, 212, 220, 240–1, 243, 244
local colleges and classes 112, 114, 176, 209–10, 212, 230
London premises 86
and the N.C.L.C. 156, 162–3, 165, 183, 184
political links 88–91, 92, 211, 220, 221, 238, 243–4
'Proletcult' 194
and the Spanish civil war 223–4
student unrest 86–9, 112, 156–60
S.W.M.F. (and the miners) 80–6, 87, 89, 90, 97, 98–9, 128, 130, 140, 156, 157, 160–2, 163–6, 174, 240, 241
S.W.M.F. and N.U.R. control of the C.L.C. 85, 87, 90, 111–14
and syndicalism 88
and the trade unions 85–6, 90–1, 111–12, 171, 207–8, 211, 212, 238
tutors and teachers 97–8, 109–10, 111, 126–7, 166, 184, 186–8, 229, 231
victimization of students 163–5
and the W.E.A. 39, 48, 116–17, 134, 144–5, 148, 171, 172
weakness and revival 215
W.E.T.U.C. 183
see also National Council of Labour Colleges
Chalke, Dr R. D. 30
Chapman, Sydney 5–6
Chappell, Edgar L. 40, 41, 106, 132
Chappell, John 4, 10–11
Citrine, Walter 168
C.L.C. League 115
Club and Institute Union 41
Clydach 118
Coaltrimmers' union 11, 22
Coldrick, Will 115, 123, 166n, 241
Coleg Harlech 167, 199, 201–2, 228, 234, 239
Collins, Frank 157
Commission on Industrial Unrest 132, 134, 138, 140, 179, 181
Communist Party (of Great Britain, C.P.G.B.) 156, 158–60, 165, 167, 184, 192, 206, 210–11, 214, 217, 218, 219–20, 240, 241
continuation classes (evening classes) 20–1, 30–2, 34, 35, 36–7, 231
Cook, Arthur J. xxi, 85, 88–9, 91, 114, 115, 119, 121, 155, 163, 194, 240
Co-operative Congress (1900) 48
Co-operative movement/societies xiv, 9–11, 46, 93, 108, 241
Cox, Idris 158, 159, 164n, 184, 240
Craik, W. W. 71, 97–8, 113, 126, 156, 161, 183
'Science of understanding' 187
Cwmavon 20n, 34, 135
Cymmer (Afan Valley) 135

Daggar, George 86, 87, 166n, 175
David, Illtyd 38n, 149, 170–1, 173, 197, 224

Davidson, John 134, 135–6
Davies, David (of Llandinam) 144
Davies, D. H. 202
Davies, D. J. 163–4, 184
Davies family of Llandinam 40, 44, 103, 144, 195
Davies, Gwilym 84
Davies, Henry 36–7, 41
Davies, John 145–6, 148, 151, 169, 172, 180, 194, 196, 197–8, 204
Davies, S. O. 155, 166n
Davison, George 86, 87, 96
Dennithorne, John 193
Dicks, J. 118
Dietzgen, Joseph 125, 187–8
dockers' union 27, 172
Dolling, George 71
Dowlais 49, 118

eastern valleys *see under* Monmouthshire
Ebbw Vale 114, 197
Economic Journal 131
The Economics of Coal 153
Education Act (1902) 12, 15
Education Act (1944) 235
Edwards, Ness 126, 155, 166n, 175, 208, 210, 213, 218, 232
Edwards, Sir Owen M. 42, 107
Edwards, Wil John 38, 57, 61, 62, 98, 116, 117, 119, 126, 127
Edwards, Revd William 231–2
engineering union 25, 27, 176
Evans, Dai Dan 123, 210, 218–19, 220, 221, 223, 238–9
Evans, D. E. 196, 198, 200–1
Evans, D. Emrys 2, 196, 198, 200–1
Evans, Glyn 158, 164
Evans, Gomer 218
Evans, J. Morris 94, 96
Evans, John 65, 71, 115–16
Evans, Ned 157
Evans, Tom 55, 66, 71
Evans, T. T. 94
evening classes *see* continuation classes
extra-mural classes 108, 109, 134, 147–50, 152, 155, 178, 181, 185, 195, 196, 215, 227–8, 235, 242

Fforest Fach 135
Finch, Len 157, 158
Fisher, H. A. L. xviii, 138, 139, 140, 143, 189
Fisher, Samuel 4, 11, 13, 21

Furniss, H. Sanderson 59, 62, 63, 66, 68, 73, 78

Garnant 118
Garw 97
Gas workers' union 173
General and Municipal Workers *see* National Union of General and Municipal Workers
Gibbons, C. L. 88, 89, 97
Gill, Ted 67, 68–9, 71, 75–6, 77, 78, 82, 83, 85, 87, 88, 89, 90, 93, 94, 95, 96, 98, 102, 111, 112–13
Glamorgan xxi, 183, 184
County Council 148, 240
Glamorgan Free Press 29, 34
Glamorgan, Vale of 135
Gorseinon 174, 183
Gower peninsula 205
Green, Ernest 201
Gregory, W. Bill 123
Grenfell, D. R. 226
Grenfell, Mansel 197, 204–5
Griffiths, Tom (later M.P.) 52
Griffiths, James 45, 155, 157, 161–2, 166n, 183, 209, 217, 240
Griffiths, J. (student) 87
Griffiths, Principal of University College 15
Guy, D. T. 206–7
Gwaun-Cae-Gurwen 118
Gwyther, Revd 217

Haldane Commission 108, 109, 121, 132, 147, 149
Haldane, Lord 180
Hall, George 104
Harlech *see* Coleg Harlech
Harris, Oliver 217
Hartshorn, Vernon 82, 89, 93, 132, 232
Hay, W. F. 91, 97
Haywood, T. H. 77
Hewlett, W. A. 182
Hewlett, Will 114, 115, 126
Highway 32
Hird, Dennis 50–1, 59, 60, 65, 66, 69, 70, 72, 73, 75, 76, 77, 82, 86, 90, 93–4, 95, 116
Hodge, John 52, 168
Hodges, Frank xxi, 78, 82, 85, 88, 93, 95, 96, 97, 98, 130, 154, 163, 168, 240
Hookway, E. J. 34, 146n
Hopkins, O. T. 77

Horner, Arthur xxi, 91, 122, 166&n, 210–11, 217, 218
Hughes, Elizabeth Phillips 4, 13–14, 23–4, 25, 26, 27, 42, 105, 139, 145, 170
Hughes, Emrys 128–9
Hyndman, H. M. 129

Independent Labour Party (I.L.P.) xxii–xxiii, 7, 21, 26, 27, 38, 46, 63, 69, 93, 102, 116, 122, 123, 126, 127, 128, 153, 176, 188, 206, 208
Independent Working-Class Education (I.W.C.E.) 48–100
  origins xxiv, 34, 36, 38, 62, 65, 67, 68, 76
  centralized control 174, 211, 213–14
  classes 90–8, 99, 114–22, 124, 177
  demise 239–40
  Haldane Commission 109
  and labour movement 49, 50, 52, 78–9, 80, 104, 120, 211, 215
  miners and union support 76, 78, 79–81, 83, 111, 114–19, 121, 130, 209, 244
  politics and Marxism 124–5, 126–7
  revival (post-1935) 215, 224
  Ruskin College strike 65
  Spanish civil war 223–4
  tutors 97, 115–16, 119–20, 126–7, 128
  and the W.E.A. (and Lleufer Thomas) 110, 134, 179, 203
  see also Central Labour College; Ruskin College
Industrial Workers of the World (I.W.W.) 77
Iron and Steel Trades Confederation (I.S.T.C.) 168–9, 172–3, 183, 236

Jenkins, A. 166n
Jenkins, R. T. 179
Jenkins, W. E. (Eddie) 237
Jenkinson, A. J. 99
Jennings, Hilda 193, 202–3, 217
Jevons, H. S. 22, 33, 106
John, Tom 1, 44
Joint Committee for the Promotion of Educational Facilities 196
Jones, Edgar 38
Jones, Lewis 230, 240
Jones, G. H. 197, 204
Jones, Griffith 1, 2, 13, 108
Jones, Prof. (Sir) Henry xvi–xvii, xviii, 7, 22, 39, 62, 150
Jones, Moses L. 28–9, 30–1, 33, 34, 37

Jones, Russell 40, 44
Jones, Sydney 96, 114–15, 228
Jones, Thomas xviii–xix, 39, 40, 105, 138–9, 145, 170, 181, 195, 199, 234

Kane, J. P. 132–3
Kinsella, – 87

Labour College *see* Central Labour College
Labour College movement *see* Central Labour College
labour movement (organized labour) xiv–xv, xix, xx–xxxi
  and the Communist Party 220
  and education 48, 82, 230, 243–4
  First World War 101–2 post-war period 143, 151, 153, 155, 156, 167–8
  and I.W.C.E. 49, 50, 52, 78–9, 80, 104, 120, 211, 215
  and the N.C.L.C. 211, 222
  Ruskin College 49, 50, 52, 53, 55, 64, 65, 66–7, 68–9, 78, 83
  social service movement 203
  and the W.E.A. 9, 14, 16, 21, 23, 35–6, 38, 39, 43, 44, 45, 46, 48, 68, 105, 106, 140, 143, 171–2, 178, 179–82, 185, 198, 201, 230, 235, 238, 243, 244 *see also* Central Labour College; Labour Party
Labour Party 16, 28, 32, 101, 122, 126, 143, 168, 171, 172, 192, 218, 220, 238
Labour Representation Committees (L.R.C.) 16, 23n
Langland 205
League of Nations Union 224, 231, 241
Lees-Smith, H. B. 53, 57, 59, 60, 62, 65, 68, 71, 73, 77, 78
Left Book Club 205, 221
Lewis, R. C. (Dick) 237
Liberal Party xx, 12, 101, 142–3
Lib-Labs/Lib-Labism xix, 10, 17, 80, 82, 130, 143
Llais Llafur 146
Llanelli 44
Llantwit Major 20n, 135
local authority classes 20–1, 22, 120, 182, 183, 242
Lush, Archie 184, 225

Mackenzie, Prof. John Stuart xviii, 5, 6,

7–8, 9, 10, 12, 13, 35, 37, 38, 39, 40, 46, 103, 105

Mackenzie, Millicent 25

Macpherson, J. T. 52

Mactavish, J. M. xxiii, 136, 137, 169–70, 180

Maerdy 91

Maesteg (District, Valley) 82, 85, 176, 184n, 197, 230, 232

Maes-yr-Haf settlement, Trealaw 192- 3, 215

Mainwaring, Will H. 80, 115, 119, 121, 157, 162–3, 166n, 174–5, 218

Mansbridge, Albert xviii, 6, 9–10, 16, 34, 35, 36, 41, 46, 48, 60, 61, 151

Mardy 229–30

Mardy Jones, T. I. 26, 51, 53–4, 55–6, 57, 65, 71, 72–4, 75, 76–7, 130n, 139, 163

Marxism and Marxists (Marxians) xviii, xix–xx, 62–3, 64–5, 89–90, 92, 95, 98, 117, 120, 121, 125, 126, 127, 128–9, 140, 142, 158–9, 165, 182–3, 185, 186–90, 206, 210–11, 217, 238, 239– 40, 241

Merthyr 20n, 34, 49, 128, 193, 196, 209

Millar, Christine 212, 213

Millar, J. P. M. 156, 162, 163, 174, 175, 183, 184, 208, 211–14, 219–20, 229, 238

Miners' Federation of Great Britain (M.F.G.B.) 16, 130, 154, 155, 240

Miners' Federation of south Wales see South Wales Miners' Federation

miners and miners' union see South Wales Miners' Federation; see also Miners' Federation of Great Britain; South Wales Miners' Industrial Union

The Miners' Next Step 80, 99

Molesworth, B. H. 134

Monmouthshire xxii, 9, 209
    eastern valley 70, 78, 85, 118
    western valley 70, 75–6, 78, 83, 85, 87, 93–4, 118, 161

Morel, E. D. 129

Morgan, Revd Herbert 46, 150

Morgan, W. H. 71

Mountain Ash 117

National Council of Labour Colleges (N.C.L.C.) xiv, 173–8, 207–33 passim, 238–40, 243
    established (1921) 173–4

classes and subjects 177–8, 188- 9, 214– 15, 220–1, 226–8
    and the C.L.C. 156, 162–3, 165
    and communists 211, 214, 219–20, 232, 238, 240
    day and weekend schools 222–3, 225
    decline in attendances 194
    and fascism and war 222–33 passim
    and I.L.P. branch 208
    and the I.W.C.E. 174, 211–12, 213–14, 238–9
    local authority classes 183
    and Marxism 211, 238, 239–40
    postal courses 211–12
    and the S.W.M.F. 173–7, 184, 207–10, 214, 218–19, 220, 227
    trade unions 173, 177, 178–9, 207, 211– 12, 214, 238, 239–40, 241
    tutors/teachers 183–4, 231
    and the W.E.A. (W.E.T.U.C.) 173, 177–8, 184, 226–8
    absorbed into T.U.C. (1964) 240

National Council of Social Service (N.C.S.S.) 193, 195, 197

National Union of General and Municipal Workers (N.U.G.M.W.) 172

National Union of Mineworkers (N.U.M.) 237, 238, 239, 240

National Union of Railwaymen (N.U.R.) 27, 28, 34, 84, 85, 87, 90, 97, 111–12, 115, 118, 121, 156, 160, 176

Neath 208

Neath/Dulais 197

New Era Union 94–6, 114

Newport 10, 135, 136–7

'new theology' 45, 151

Nicholas, Nun 97, 176–7, 182–3, 184, 187, 188, 209, 210, 230, 241

Noble, William and Emma 192–3, 215

Ogmore Vale (Valley) 176, 184n, 224

Onions, Alfred 4, 12, 93

Owen, D. R. 86, 96, 118, 126, 174, 209

Owen, W. J. (Will) 175, 184, 208, 241

Oxford, University of (and colleges) xxiii–xxiv, 50, 62, 64, 69, 72, 75, 83; see also Ruskin College

Oxford report (Oxford and Working-Class Education) xxiii–xxiv, 35–6, 43, 65, 148

Paynter, Will 184, 223

Penarth 38, 136, 138, 176

Phillips, Gwyn 231–2

Phillips, Morgan 165
Phippen, Frank 163
Pioneer (Merthyr) 38, 116, 117, 119, 122, 128
Plaid Cymru 144
Plebs League xxiv, 41, 65, 66–7, 69, 70, 71, 72, 75, 77, 88, 91, 99, 104, 111, 115, 120, 159, 211, 212, 244
Plebs magazine 67, 68, 87, 92, 98, 104, 111, 115, 118, 119, 122, 149, 158, 208, 214, 223
  becomes house journal of N.C.L.C. 211
Pontardawe 97, 183
Pontypool 206, 226
Pontypridd
  District 85
  N.C.L.C. 209
  W.E.A. branch 20n, 28–34, 197
Poor Law 26–7
Porth 20n, 30, 34, 72
Port Talbot 135, 224, 236–7
Pugh, Arthur 168–9

Quakers 192, 194

Raffan, P. Wilson 4, 12, 18&n, 19, 35
railwaymen's union *see* National Union of Railwaymen
Rees, J. L. 51, 118
Rees, Noah 55, 65, 71, 80, 98
religion and religious denominations xx–xxi, 44–6, 93, 94, 95–6, 106–7, 122–3, 148, 150–1, 203, 231–2
Reynolds, J. 88, 113
Rhondda
  C.L.C. 122, 126
  conflict in coalfield 80
  Evening Classes Committee 53, 57
  I.W.C.E. classes 119
  Labour College 114, 115, 209
  local class groups 91–3, 97
  N.C.L.C. 176, 178, 194, 209, 212, 215
  No. 1 District of the S.W.M.F. 54, 55, 60, 65–6, 71, 72, 74, 85, 115, 174–5, 188–9
  Plebs 69, 70, 95
  religion 203
  settlements 192
  unemployment 215–16
  W.E.A. 197, 215
Rhymney Valley 97–8, 118, 209

Richards, Tom (Thomas) 93, 113, 139, 194
Roberts, Bryn 155, 157, 166n, 241
Roberts, R. D. 42–3, 107
Roberts, Silyn 40, 46, 151
Royal Commission on the Poor Law 26
Royal Commission on University Education in Wales (*see* Haldane Commission) 108
Ruskin College, Oxford 49–59, 85, 86 I.S.T.C. 169
  and the labour movement 49, 50, 52, 53, 64, 65, 68–9, 83
  reformed 83–4
  'strike' (1909) 59–79, 88
  union-sponsored scholarships 50, 51–6, 85

Saddler, W. J. 166n, 175
Sankey Commission 154
School of Social Service (Welsh) 107, 150
Scotland 20n
Scottish Labour College 213
settlements xvii, xviii, 1, 5, 6, 7, 8–9, 40, 192–3, 196, 197, 203, 206, 214, 217
Shackleton, David 32
Sims, George 87–8, 161
Sirhowy Valley 114
slate quarrymen's union 43
Socialist Labour Party (S.L.P.) 120, 126
social services response (agencies) 145, 152, 192–6, 198, 202–3, 206, 214, 217, 233, 234
South Wales Daily News xix, 3, 12, 22, 23, 36, 46
South Wales Gazette 12
South Wales Miners' Federation (S.W.M.F.) xix
  centralization campaign 80, 86
  classes (Aberdare District) 117
  C.L.C. (Labour College) 84, 87, 97–8, 128, 130, 140, 160–7 *passim*, 174, 188, 240, 241 scholarships 156n, 157 takes co-control (1914) 85, 90, 111–14
  and the communists 192, 210, 217–18
  extra-mural classes 178
  First World War (and the miners) 101, 123–4, 131–2, 138 and post-war politics 142–3
  and the I.L.P. xxiii, 128

I.W.C.E., and its impact on the miners 79–100 *passim*, 114, 115, 153–67 *passim*, 177
'labour' college campaign 66, 69, 70
and the labour movement 16, 17, 28
lock-out (1921) 143, 154, 174
lock-out (1926) 143, 167–8
Marxism and the miners 121, 124, 125, 189–90
membership problems 191–2, 207
miners' militancy 79–81, 131–3, 141, 189–90, 244
N.C.L.C. scheme (and affiliation) 173–6, 184, 207–10, 214, 218–19, 220, 227, 229
and workers' education 82–3
Ruskin College, miners at 62, 65 scholarships 51, 52–6
strike (1915) 124, 131
submission to Unrest Commission 138
tutors 184, 229
and the W.E.A. 16, 44, 139, 178, 227, 228
W.E.A. committee 11–12
W.E.A./W.E.T.U.C. 173
see also anthracite district; Monmouthshire; Rhondda; unemployment
South Wales Miners' Industrial Union 216
South Wales and Monmouthshire Council of Social Service 197
South Wales News 180
Spanish civil war 217, 223, 225–6
Special Areas Act 197
Standing Industrial Councils 133
Stanton, Charles Butt 82, 101, 122
Starr, Mark xvi, 104, 115, 116–17, 119–20, 121, 125, 126, 128, 130, 156, 167, 176, 184, 212, 243
Stead, Charlie 219, 220, 221, 224, 226, 227, 231
Steel Smelters' union 52, 168
Stevenson, W. H. 53, 57–8, 61
Stonelake, Edmund 56, 57, 122
Sunday Worker 159
Swansea
day schools 225
I.S.T.C. and the W.E.A./W.E.T.U.C. 170, 172–3
Labour College 184n, 223
N.C.L.C. 225
Ruskin College correspondence course 49

university college 149, 171, 185, 205
W.E.A. 135, 196–7, 204–6, 225
W.E.T.U.C. 183, 197
Swansea Valley 97
I.L.P. 129–30
Swansea Valley Trades and Labour Council 176–7
syndicalism/syndicalists 59, 60, 62–3, 68, 69, 77, 80, 81, 88, 125–6, 131

Taff Vale Railway Company 23, 28
Tawney, R. H. xviii, xxiii, 139, 170
Taylor, James 4, 11
Thomas, Ben Bowen 2, 7, 199–200
Thomas, Daniel Lleufer 1–2, 40–1, 105–11, 121, 143–4, 145, 147, 150, 151, 152, 179, 185
chair of Commission for Wales 132, 134, 138, 140
Thomas, David 146n
Thomas, D. H. 201–2
Thomas, E. 4, 13, 21
Thomas, E. George 160&n, 165, 212–13
Thomas, J. H. 112
Thomas, John 37–8, 41, 43, 44, 46, 102, 103–5, 116, 129–30, 145, 152–5, 165, 170, 182, 204
Thomas, P. S. (Phil) 2–3, 13, 104–5
Thomas, Rosser 230–1
Tondu 97
Tonypandy 91, 106
Tonypandy/Llwynypia 79, 80
Trades Union Congress (1911) 85
Trades Union Council (T.U.C.) 83–4, 85, 162, 178–9, 240
trade unions (trade unionists) xv, xix, 244–5
and the C.L.C. 41, 80–1, 82, 159–60, 207, 229
First World War 122–3
I.W.C.E. movement 67, 115
'labour' college 69, 78
members victimized 56–7, 144, 155, 163, 164–5, 176
militancy 79–80, 106
and the N.C.L.C. 207, 211–12, 214, 238, 239
and religion 45–6, 122–3
and Ruskin College 51–6, 65–7, 75–6, 78–9
support for workers' education 7, 82, 168–9, 229, 230
and syndicalists 60–1, 77

and the W.E.A. 3, 11–12, 27, 31, 41, 45, 103, 106, 145, 169–70, 236, 237
Transport and General Workers Union (T.G.W.U.) 172, 176, 236, 243
Trealaw, Community House 203
  see also Maes-yr-Haf settlement
Tredegar 20n, 174
Tredegar Valley District 85

unemployment xxii, 142, 144, 154, 155, 163–4, 168, 190
  as 'the new leisure' 191–233 passim
Unemployment Act (1934) 216, 221
universities (university colleges) xv, xxiii, 5, 42–3, 64, 67, 68, 134, 179, 180, 200–1
  extension lectures 5, 6, 8
  extra-mural teaching 108, 109, 134, 147–50, 235, 242
  tutorial classes (and the W.E.A.) 35–6, 42–3, 107, 108–11, 135, 147, 185, 200, 227
  see also Cardiff, University of Wales
University of Wales see Cardiff
Unofficial Reform Committee 80, 119, 127, 211
Unrest Commission see Commission for Industrial Unrest

Vrooman, Walter 49

Watkins, Percy 40, 139, 145, 170, 194–5
Watkins, Stanley 139
Watts Morgan, D. 71–2, 84, 101
Webb, Lewis 136
Welsh Council of Social Service 106, 194
Welsh language xxi-xxii, 41
Welsh Outlook 40, 104, 122, 128, 131, 137, 138, 139, 144, 151, 185, 194, 198
Welsh School of Social Service 107, 150
Western District of Miners 84
Western Mail 60, 180, 182, 185
Western Valleys District see under Monmouthshire
western valleys see under Monmouthshire
West Wales Labour College 219
Williams, D. J. 157, 158, 175, 209
Williams, Len 198n, 208, 214, 219
Williams, Ted (E. J.) 118, 128, 155, 161, 163, 166n
Williams, W. H. 158, 164
Williams, W. J. 181, 196
Willis, A. C. 17–19, 32, 33, 94, 95
Wilson, Bertram 51, 73, 74, 77

Winstone, James 70, 82, 85, 89, 101, 122
Winterstoke, Lord 73
women
  attending classes 41–2
  in Barry 23–4
  'social service' missionaries 192
Workers' Democratic Education League (W.D.E.L.) 114, 115
Workers' Educational Association (W.E.A.) xiv, xviii–xix, xxiii–xxiv, 1–47, 143–52, 178–86 passim, 195–207 passim, 224–8, 234–8, 242–3
  origins 1–17 first officials 18–19
  adult education 146, 148, 150, 152, 197, 199, 234–5
  branch/continuation classes 19–35, 36–7, 44, 116
  Cardiff conference (1917) 139
  and the churches 150–1, 204
  class attendances/subjects 177–8, 185–7, 188, 224–5, 226–7
  and the C.L.C. (Labour College) 39, 48, 116–17, 134, 144–5, 148, 171, 172
  committee membership 4, 9–14
  co-operative societies 10, 93
  Cory Hall, foundation conference (1906) 1, 3–4, 7, 10, 14, 15–16, 17, 18, 48
  educational reform (1917) 138–40
  day and weekend schools 225, 237
  district level (and Cardiff–Barry coterie) 38–41, 46, 198, 229
  and extra-mural classes 134, 147–50, 152, 178, 181, 185, 195, 196, 215, 227–8, 235, 242
  fascism 222
  First World War 102–11, 121, 134–41 passim and post-war difficulties 143–52
  full-time (district) secretary (1911) 37–8, 44
  funding and benefactors 39, 44, 103, 144–5, 173, 196–8
  influence of 242–3, 244
  and the I.S.T.C. 169–70
  and the I.W.C.E. 120, 183, 228
  journals see Cambria; Welsh Outlook
  and the labour movement 9, 14, 16, 21, 23, 35–6, 38, 39, 43, 44, 45, 46, 48, 68, 105, 106, 140, 143, 171–2, 178–82, 185, 198, 201, 230, 235, 238, 243, 244

local branches (classes) 18, 19–36, 135, 136–7, 145, 197, 204–6, 215, *see also* Barry; Cardiff; Pontypridd; Swansea

Marxism and Marxists 129, 182–5

and the N.C.L.C. 177–8, 226–8

and religion 44–6

Ruskin College's council members 60

Second World War, wartime education 234–5

'social service' response to unemployment, and the joint committee 145, 152, 195–8, 203, 233, 234

and the Spanish civil war 225–6

and the state, relationship with 146, 178–86, 198

state grants 146, 172, 178, 198

students to Coleg Harlech 167

S.W.M.F. and the miners 78, 139, 178, 226, 227, 228

trade union membership and support 22, 27, 28, 31, 33, 37, 41, 103, 145, 169–70, 173, 179, 236–8, 243

tutorial classes and the university) 35–6, 42–3, 107, 108–11, 135, 140, 147, 185, 200, 215, 227

tutors and teachers 109–10, 111, 137–8, 150–1, 170–1, 182, 183–4, 204, 231–2

Welsh District redivision (1925) 151

W.E.T.U.C. 169–70, 172–3, 177, 180, 182–3, 236–8

womens' classes 41–2

Workers' Educational Trade Union Committee (W.E.T.U.C.) 149, 169–70, 171, 172, 173, 176, 180, 182–3, 197, 204, 207, 224, 236

working men's clubs 41, 46, 103

Wright, Peter 13

Ynys-hir 92

Ynysybwl 20n Ruskin College correspondence course 49

Yorkshire 19–20, 46, 160

Zimmern, Alfred xxiii, 148–9